Islam and Democracy in Iran

Islam and Democracy in Iran

Eshkevari and the Quest for Reform

ZIBA MIR-HOSSEINI
AND
RICHARD TAPPER

I.B. TAURIS
LONDON · NEW YORK

Published in 2006 by I.B.Tauris & Co Ltd
6 Salem Road, London W2 4BU
175 Fifth Avenue, New York NY 10010
www.ibtauris.com

In the United States of America and Canada distributed by Palgrave Macmillan a
division of St. Martin's Press
175 Fifth Avenue, New York NY 10010

Library of Modern Middle East Studies 54

HB: ISBN 1 84511 133 8
        EAN 978 1 84511 133 5

PB: ISBN 1 84511 134 6
        EAN 978 1 84511 134 2

A full CIP record for this book is available from the British Library
A full CIP record is available from the Library of Congress

Library of Congress Catalog Card Number: available

Printed and bound in Great Britain by TJ International Ltd, Padstow, Cornwall
Camera-ready copy edited and supplied by the authors

Contents

Note on transliteration, translation and style

We have used standard English spellings, where they exist, for names and Islamic terms: fatwa, hajj, hijab, Imam, Koran, Majlis, Sayyid, Sharia, Shia, Shiism, Sunna, ulama; Khomeini, Mecca, Medina.

We have transliterated Persian terms and names for ease of reading, and so as to use the full range of English vowels and avoid the need for diacritics: we have retained *'ayn* and *hamzeh* except initially. With some terms of Arabic origin (e.g. *fiqh, fuqaha, ijtihad, mujtahid*) we have retained standard Arabic transliteration, but without the diacritics.

We have translated *hokumat* as 'government' and *dowlat* as 'state'. Unfortunately, contemporary writers in Iran tend to use these terms imprecisely and sometimes interchangeably. Often, *hokumat* has a broader connotation and includes *dowlat*; some have chosen to translate it as 'governance'; in recent years, reformists have come to refer to Khatami's government as *dowlat*, while using *hokumat* for 'the regime' (also referred to as *nezam*, 'the system'), i.e. the dominant clerical conservatives. In Chapter 3, written before Khatami's 1997 election, Eshkevari provides precise definitions for each term – relying on an encyclopaedia entry – but his own usage is often inconsistent.

The term *hakemiyat* is used in different ways; sometimes, more technically, as 'sovereignty', as in *hakemiyat allah*; at other times, as more or less equivalent to *hokumat*, government, rulership, governance, or mode of government; the translation tries to take the context into account. The term *hokm* (pl. *ahkam*) is usually translated as (religious) 'ruling' or 'law', sometimes as 'rule'; again, context explains.

We have translated *din, shar', mazhab* all as 'religion'. For the most part they are used in Persian as synonyms, but occasionally they are distinguished: *din*, religion, *shar'*, religious law, *mazhab*, sect or school of law.

Maktab means 'school'; Eshkevari uses it as it is used by Islamic ideologues, for a school of religious thought or law, as well as doctrines and dogmas. We translate it as 'doctrine', though this cannot be a precise equivalent.

When contrasted to *shar'i*, we translate *'orfi* as 'secular' – allowing the intended meanings of this complex term to emerge from the context. Otherwise, we translate it as 'non-religious', 'customary'. Eshkevari sometimes also has *la'ik* and *sekular*, which we translate directly as laic and secular.

There is no grammatical gender in Persian, so Eshkevari's language is gender-free; we have tried to retain this as much as possible in rendering it into English. For example, *ensan, adam* and *bashar*, often translated as 'man' or 'mankind', are all genderless; Eshkevari intends them to 'include woman'; we translate them all, however awkwardly, as 'human being' and *ensaniyat* as 'humanity'.

Persian literary style includes two features that require attention:
    - the pairing of two words with (virtually) the same meaning; usually we have translated with a single word.
    - the pairing of two words with different meanings but alliterative sounds; usually impossible to translate with the appropriate alliteration, the result is often clumsy. For example, *'aqli va naqli*, rational and textual.

Both spoken and literary Persian contain many words of Arabic derivation, a contentious political-cultural issue during the twentieth century; like most clerics (who are familiar with Arabic, particularly with religious treatises written in Arabic) Eshkevari makes extensive use of Arabic vocabulary, including Arabic phrases without translation; sometimes he uses words in senses that are more likely to be found in Arabic than in Persian dictionaries. In all these cases we have sought a compromise translation, giving priority to clarity over literalism.

Eshkevari (and others quoted in the book) use a variety of honorific titles that are conventional in clerical Persian; for example he commonly refers to Ayatollah Khomeini as 'the Imam', and to deceased figures as 'the late', or 'martyr'. We have omitted these, for ease of reading, and used only the names (sometimes with standard titles such as Dr or Ayatollah) for the individuals concerned.

When mentioning Persian or Arabic books by name, except for a few that are well known by their original titles, we give the English translation of the title in the text, the author and date in a footnote, and the full reference (with original title and English translation) in the Bibliography.

Acknowledgements

The idea for this book began in summer 2002, when Ziba Mir-Hosseini was asked by Kari Vogt, Professor of History of Religion at Oslo University, to select and translate some of Hasan Yousefi Eshkevari's work into English, for later translation into Norwegian. We are grateful to Professor Vogt for the idea and to Institusjonen Fritt Ord in Norway for supporting the translation.

We completed a first draft of the book in London in September 2004, and the final draft during the following winter while Ziba Mir-Hosseini was a Fellow at the Wissenschaftskolleg zu Berlin: we are both grateful to WiKo for providing the perfect environment.

We presented a paper summarizing the argument of the book at both the Biennial Conference of the International Society for Iranian Studies in Bethesda, Maryland, in May 2004, and the Annual Conference of the British Society for Middle Eastern Studies at SOAS, London, in June 2004. On both occasions the topic attracted sizeable audiences, and we received robust and encouraging comments, for which we are grateful.

We are indebted to the following: Ruard Absaroka helped with editing the first drafts of the translations; Farideh Farhi, Nader Hashemi and Kim Longinotto, from their different perspectives, offered valuable comments and suggestions on all or part of the first draft of the book; Abdolkarim Soroush (a fellow-Fellow at Wiko), generously read and commented on part of the manuscript, responded to numerous questions, and helped to clarify some theological points and historical puzzles. Finally, we are grateful to Iradj Bagherzade and three anonymous reviewers, whose helpful comments prompted us to clarify certain passages in the book. Remaining errors and infelicities are our own.

As narrated in the Appendix, during 2004-5 we were in contact with Eshkevari and his son Ruhollah, both of whom resolved problems with the translations and corrected matters of record. We are delighted that, in the very week that we completed the final draft of the book, Hasan Yousefi Eshkevari was released from prison.

London and Berlin, 2005

Prologue

In December 2000, Hasan Yousefi Eshkevari, a mid-ranking Iranian cleric, was condemned to death for 'apostasy' and 'war against Islam'. The charges arose from his speeches at the Berlin Conference of April that year, which followed the reformist victory in the Iranian parliamentary elections in February.

The sentence was later commuted to five years in prison – but what was so threatening in Eshkevari's speeches that led to the initial death sentence? Where do he and his ideas fit into the political landscape of Iran, and the wider intellectual debates on the democratization of Islam?

Eshkevari is an outspoken and influential critic of the current Iranian version of theocracy. In this book we introduce a selection of his writings on the relation between Islam and democracy, as a way of telling the story of the rise of the reformist movement in Iran in the 1990s.

* * * * *

Throughout the last quarter of the twentieth century, the world – both Muslim and non-Muslim – watched events in Iran with close interest, as an experiment whose results were likely to have a global impact. What people saw going on, however, differed. For some, the revolution of 1978-79 was the triumph of a modern, political Islam, the beginning of a new dawn, when God's law (the Sharia) would bring to Muslims the justice and prosperity that secular nation-states had failed to deliver. Others, including many of those who had originally participated in the revolution, saw religious fanatics attempting to roll back time by creating a despotic theocracy.

Whatever its nature, and however the rest of the world perceived it, the Iranian Revolution changed the landscape of the Muslim world. It inspired the Muslim masses and reinvigorated intellectual debates on the nature and possibilities of an Islamic state.

What was novel about the new 'Islamic Republic of Iran' was the way in which it combined not just religion and the state, but theocracy and democracy. On the assumptions, first, that given free choice people will choose 'Islam', and secondly, that what makes a state Islamic is adherence to and implementation of the Sharia, the framers of the constitution included both democratic and 'Islamic' principles and institutions. Some institutions, including the parliament and presidency, are elected by direct popular suffrage, but they are subordinate to clerical oversight and veto.

It was not long before the heirs of the revolution were engaged in a protracted struggle over its legacy, which continues into the twenty-first century. The main issues have been the proper role of religion in government, the scope of the Sharia in defining social norms and regulating political and personal relations, and the uneasy balance between republican and Islamic elements in the state. By the early 1990s, a number of dissident thinkers, both lay and clerical, were developing a critique of the Islamic state from within an Islamic framework: they sought a rights-based political order that could open Muslim polities to dissent, tolerance, pluralism, women's rights and civil liberties. Their ideas and writings – which came to be known as 'New Religious Thinking' – were the mainstay of the popular reformist movement that emerged after the unexpected victory of Mohammad Khatami in the 1997 presidential elections.

Khatami's two four-year terms as president have seen extraordinary events both in neighbouring countries and inside Iran. US-led invasions of Afghanistan and Iraq led to the downfall of the extreme Islamist Taliban in the former and the secular dictator Saddam Hussein in the latter. In Iran, the reformists passed through a cycle of hope, frustration and despair. They achieved no significant change in the structures of power, and succumbed to the undemocratic forces of theocratic control – yet they have left a permanent legacy in the form of a radically altered political culture. They have demystified Iranian religious politics, the power games conducted in a religious language and the instrumental use of the Sharia to justify autocratic rule. Clerical leadership has lost its popular legitimacy, and there is a growing popular demand for the separation of religion from government.

During the reformist years, political and intellectual debates in Iran became increasingly polarized, between the 'reformists' who promoted the democratic institutions and the 'conservatives' who supported the clerical theocracy. At the same time, several of the 'New Religious Thinkers' have produced compromise formulations of 'Islamic democracy'.

The issue of the compatibility of 'Islam' with 'democracy' is both of crucial political importance for the future of the world, and (at the time of writing) of intense topical interest in relation to Iran's neighbours, Iraq and Afghanistan. Yet – like many crucial issues – general discussion of Islam and democracy has been worn so thin by repetition and polemic that the topic has become banal and has ceased to have any intellectual interest. For many years, but particularly since the events of 11 September 2001, academics and policy makers have participated in a seemingly endless series of lectures, panels and conferences on the theme. A cursory Internet search reveals 'Islam' and 'democracy' together in the titles of literally hundreds of current books in English, to say nothing of myriad academic and press articles, let alone publications in other languages. Most contributions are patently ideological, in that the conclusion (as to whether the two are compatible or not) is pre-determined by a particular political stance, and a particular understanding of the two terms at issue.

The positions taken are broadly of three kinds, two extreme and one moderate. The extremists (diametrically opposed but sharing the same conclusion, though for different reasons) are either those (including well-known academics as well as politicians and journalists) for whom Islam is inherently violent and despotic and demonstrably alien to the democratic values of Western civilizations; or those 'Islamists' for whom 'democracy' is irredeemably 'Western' and 'colonial' in its origin and character, and therefore to be rejected as alien to Islam. The middle ground is occupied by a broad range of Muslims and non-Muslims for whom the basic democratic values of equality, justice and human dignity are central to Islam.

To a great extent, our comments on the state of the debate over Islam and democracy[1] also apply to post-revolutionary Iranian politics. Here we find again a voluminous literature (titles including the words 'Iran' and 'politics' are even more numerous), much of which has a more or less overt polemical agenda hidden in the trappings of scholarship.

In both cases, we feel, general theoretical arguments are now so hackneyed, and the ideological positions so set, that there seems little point in further debate unless, first, the complexity of the issue is recognized and the rhetorical nature of many arguments exposed, and

---

[1] Among useful recent studies are Esposito and Voll (1996), Abou El Fadl (2004), Hefner (2005), Aslan (2005).

secondly, the discussion is firmly located in actual situations and lived experiences – to be blunt, in ethnography.

With this in mind, in this book we tell the story of the struggle for democracy in post-revolutionary Iran through the writings and experiences of one of its clerical advocates, Hasan Yousefi Eshkevari. We attempt a kind of textual ethnography, in the sense that we put a selection of Eshkevari's writings into their personal, social, cultural and political context with relevant background information, and show how they reveal his intellectual and political trajectory. The texts we translate and contextualize are chiefly those that contain his argument for 'Islamic democratic government', and were originally produced between 1995 and 2000 – the years when the reform movement was still both unformed and full of hope and expectation. We do not take a position ourselves, but rather seek to demonstrate, through this ethnographic approach, how one reformist cleric comes to adopt and defend a particular position on the relation between religion and government.

The reform movement and the 'New Religious Thinkers' have received much attention abroad from both scholars and the media, and are closely followed in the Muslim world. Several recent studies have discussed and evaluated the work of major figures such as Abdolkarim Soroush, Mohsen Kadivar and Mohammad Mojtahed-Shabestari.[2] Their actual writings, however, remain largely unknown outside Iran, with the exception of some of those of Soroush, a religious but non-clerical philosopher.[3] The available studies, moreover, either paraphrase the work of the subjects without providing the reader with direct access to their writings, or, while making a text available in whole or in part, do not examine the specific debate to which it was directed, thus ignoring the context and process of production.

We see such contextualization as essential, for two reasons. First, the important writings of most of the contributors to intellectual debate in Iran have a strong oral component to them. They originate as lectures, speeches, interviews and live debates, which are then transcribed and published as newspaper or journal articles or as book chapters, but they remain oral and spontaneous in style, given that they are

---

[2] See, for example, Abrahamian (2001), Arjomand (2002), Boroujerdi (1996), Cooper (1998), Dahlen (2003), Jahanbakhsh (2001), Matin-Asgari (1997), Sadri (2001) and other articles in Ashraf and Banuazizi (2001a), Vahdat (2000, 2002).

[3] Soroush (2000a).

addressed to, and react to, an audience. Secondly, they are in dialogue with other texts, and often one must read between the lines: the silences, the allusions are as important as what is explicit. It is only by knowing something of the context that the reader can appreciate the dynamic of the debate and make sense of what may seem, to the uninitiated, palpable contradictions. This, we believe, is largely missing from the existing literature on reformist thinkers in Iran. Here, as our protagonist is a cleric, we are concerned to show the importance of context to the understanding of clerical texts, as well as the importance of clerical texts to the understanding of contemporary politics. We aim to give an idea of how reformist clerics like Eshkevari argue, the intellectual dilemmas they are grappling with, how they are trying both to reread the 'Islamic' and 'secular' sources and to create an argument for 'an Islamic democracy'.

We begin each chapter with an introductory section in which we provide background information on the text – when and where it was first produced, what other texts it responds to, and the debates that provide the context. We show how each piece was a response to a political event or to specific issues and debates raised by other reformists or political personalities.

* * * * *

The book comprises five chapters and an Epilogue. Chapter 1 – intended for non-specialists – traces the historical background to the Islam-democracy debate in Iran with reference to the interaction and eruptions of two key tensions: between religiosity and secularism, and between despotism and democracy. We outline the political and intellectual trends in the Islamic Republic, and locate the main events and characters referred to in the chapters that follow. The chapter is not intended as a comprehensive intellectual history – a task that is beyond the scope of this book and has been undertaken already by others.[4]

Chapter 2 introduces Hasan Yousefi Eshkevari as both public figure and private person, through the translations of three texts. The first is Eshkevari's 'Autobiography', published on the Internet while he was in prison. He relates his life story, how he became a cleric, his

---

[4] For example, in addition to works cited in note 2 above, see also Chehabi (1990), Dabashi (1993), Gheissari (1998), Mirsepassi (2000).

politicization, his involvement in the revolution and then in the political life of the Islamic Republic, and his vision and hope for the future. The second is an account of Eshkevari's life by his wife, Mohtaram Golbaba'i, told as a conversation between her and Lily Farhadpoor, a journalist who is trying to understand what drove Eshkevari and his generation to make the revolution. The chapter concludes with Eshkevari's Preface to a collection of his articles, *Reason at the Feast of Religion*. Here he sets out his version of the project of 'religious intellectualism', which is to bring faith and reason together.

The main body of the book, Chapters 3 to 5, consists of a selection of Eshkevari's key writings. Chapter 3, 'Islamic Democratic Government', originated as a lecture given in 1995. Containing the essence of his political theory and his arguments for the compatibility of Islam and democracy, it forms part of a debate about the democratization of religious discourse that took place on the eve of the emergence of the reformist movement. Eshkevari contends that Islam as a religion does not prescribe any specific political system, that the 'political' is always 'secular', and that the Prophet's government in Medina, so often referred to by Islamist political theorists as the prototype of an Islamic state, was in fact secular in nature.

Chapter 4 is the transcript of a discussion with Mohammad Quchani, a young journalist who writes some of the most interesting political commentaries in the reformist press. It is taken from Quchani's 2000 book *Religious State, State Religion*, a compilation of interviews with various political thinkers and activists, but was originally published in spring 1999, in the heyday of the period of press liberalization. The discussion revolves around the consequences of the merger of the clerical establishment with political power in the Islamic Republic, and brings out the dilemmas the Shia clerical establishment faced when it became identified with the state. It also encapsulates the debate between Eshkevari's generation, which made the revolution, and Quchani's generation, which inherited it. Together they revisit the early years of the revolution, when the Islamic Republic was still in formation, and explore how and why it became a 'Clerical Republic'.

Chapter 5 contains Eshkevari's three contributions to the Berlin Conference of April 2000, when the period of press liberalization and public discussion had reached its peak. There is an atmosphere of excitement and optimism that the reforms can go ahead, now that both the executive and the legislative powers are in the hands of the reformist government. These three texts represent Eshkevari's most open expression of his views on key issues. The first, 'Iran after the elections' contains his assessment of the challenges that the reformists face and his predictions of the future of democracy in Iran; it is prophetic in that many of his concerns have proved valid. The second, 'Reformist Islam and modern society', constitutes his manifesto for a democratic Islam. In the third text, 'Women's rights and the women's movement', Eshkevari rejects the notion that compulsory hijab is Islamic and defends Muslim women's right to choose what to wear.

The Epilogue traces relevant developments in Iranian politics after the Berlin Conference: the clampdown on the reformist press and imprisonment of reformist thinkers and activists, the elimination of reformist candidates in subsequent elections, popular disappointment with the failure of reform – but the legacy of a changed and more transparent political culture in Iran, where the rhetoric of religious despotism has lost its power and the struggle for democratic freedoms is stronger than ever.

1

Islam and the Struggle for Democracy in Iran

Iran has been a focus of world attention since the 1978-79 revolution, both because of its continued strategic importance in regional and world politics and because of the impact of the revolution on other Muslim countries. Moreover, the revolution was the latest eruption of two universal tensions: between religiosity and secularism, and between despotism and democracy. Arguably, no country in recent times has escaped these tensions, which are probably inevitable concomitants of 'modernization', and there is every indication that they will continue to be important factors in local and world politics during the twenty-first century. How and when they erupt in conflict results from a combination of local historical processes and social and cultural conditions, as well as global forces.

In Iran, as elsewhere, these tensions have deep roots. In the course of the twentieth century, they gave rise to two revolutions. The Islamic state that resulted from the second revolution aimed to resolve the tension between religiosity and secularism for good; but, a quarter-century later, this solution is widely considered, both inside and outside Iran, to have been a failure, not least because it did not resolve the second tension, having replaced one form of despotism with another. Both tensions have, if anything, intensified, and the debates over alternative solutions in today's Iran are as alive – and acrimonious – as at the time of the first revolution. Indeed, in the early twenty-first century, many Iranians are reflecting with increased interest on similarities between current debates and those that accompanied the Constitutional Revolution a century before.

This chapter provides a brief historical context for the latest outbreak of these tensions, which came to the surface in the elections of 1997 that brought President Khatami to office. It outlines major political and intellectual trends in the Islamic Republic in order to locate the events and characters referred to in the chapters that follow.

Shiism and government in Iran before the 1979 revolution

The only country in the Muslim world where the state religion is Twelver Shiism is Iran, where it was established in 1501 by Shah Isma'il, founder of the Safavid dynasty. Distinguishing features of Twelver Shiism[1] (as referred to in this book) are the imamate, Occultation, and *marja'iyat/taqlid*. All of these concern religious authority and its relation to political power, which is a major source of dispute and difference among the Shia.

According to the Shia, after the Prophet Muhammad, leadership of the Muslims passed not to the (elected) Caliphs, but to his descendants, the Imams. Each Imam was designated by the previous one, starting with the Prophet's cousin and son-in-law Ali and ending with the twelfth Imam, Muhammad Mahdi, the 'Imam of Time', who went into Occultation (*gheybat*). His return will mark the end of time, but, in his absence, the ulama (religious scholars) assume the guidance of the Shia Muslim community.

Among the Shia, senior ulama are known as *mujtahid*, indicating that they are able to exercise *ijtihad*, authoritative judgment in interpreting the law from the sources. According to the Shia theory of *taqlid*, any man or woman who has not reached the stage of *ijtihad* is a *muqallid* (follower) and must choose a *mujtahid* to be their own spiritual guide (*marja' al-taqlid*, 'model for/source of emulation'), whose opinions in matters of religious law are binding on those who follow him.[2]

In the nineteenth century, the institution of *marja'iyat* emerged separately from the state, and came to encapsulate the notion of supreme religious authority. A *marja'* (pl. *maraji'*) becomes recognized after a long process of acquiring respect for his teaching and scholarship, especially by writing a legal treatise or manual (*risaleh*) for those who have chosen to follow him in religious matters. One class of treatises is *towzih al-masa'il* (explanations of problems), a compendium of legal opinions, in a fixed format, starting with rulings about ritual acts such as prayers and fasting, and proceeding to chapters about contracts, such as marriage and divorce.

---

[1] Throughout this book 'Shia' refers to the Twelvers (Ithna 'Ashariya), the largest branch. Other major branches are the Isma'ilis ('Seveners') and the Zeydis. *Taqiyeh* (dissimulation of belief), often identified as a Shia distinguishing feature, plays no part in this book.

[2] This is one aspect in which Shiism has been liked to Sufism, with its core spiritual relationship of teacher-disciple (*pir-morid*); see Chapter 4 below for a discussion.

In addition to *zakat* (annual alms for the poor and needy, mandatory for all Muslims), the Shia owe another religious tax: *khoms*, one-fifth of residual income, payable to the *marja'*. Half of the *khoms* goes to Sayyids, descendants of the Prophet; the other half is *sahm-e emam*, the 'Imam's share', considered to be the Imams' inheritance from the Prophet, and a *marja'* receives it in his capacity as representative of the 'Imam of Time'; he is free to spend it as he deems suitable. The *sahm-e emam* is thus a major source of independent wealth and power for the religious leaders.

The *maraji'* live and teach in seminaries, known collectively as *howzeh* ('circle', short for *howzeh-ye 'elmiyeh*, 'circle of religious learning'). The two most important *howzeh* are in Najaf in Iraq and Qom in Iran; each city has a number of theological colleges, and both have become widely known as centres of not only religious learning but also political Islam.

The Shia do not accept the legitimacy of the rule of the Sunni caliphate. For them, in the absence of the Imams, no worldly power is legitimate. The Safavid shahs had spiritual authority as sheykhs of the Safavi Sufi order to bolster their political power, but since the seventeenth century the relation between the shahs and the Shia ulama has been complex and difficult.[3] In practice, most leading ulama have been quietist, keeping themselves apart from the world of politics and government, advising the ruler but refraining from action, at least so long as he was felt to be preserving Islam. Others, especially since the nineteenth century, have played an active political role, taking different positions on crucial issues such as the scope of *ijtihad* and *marja'iyat*, how injustice and oppression should be opposed, and, in the context of the constitutional movement, whether the Shia faith can accommodate human-made laws.

The Constitutional Revolution

The birth of 'modern' Iran is often dated to the early nineteenth century. After two disastrous wars with Russia, Iran was exposed to a wide range of new ideas, thanks to the increasing presence of European diplomats, merchants and military advisors, the despatch of elite young men to be educated in France, and not least the publication of translations of European literary and political texts. At the same time, Iran found itself the object of imperial rivalry between Russia and

[3] See Lambton (1964), Algar (1969), Akhavi (1980), Keddie (1983), Momen (1985), Arjomand (1988), Bayat (1991).

Britain. The Qajar rulers, especially Naseroddin Shah (1848-96) and his son Mozaffaroddin Shah (1896-1907) came under severe pressures, and their policies compromised the country's integrity. In constant debt, they sought to raise money from foreigners by selling them industrial and commercial concessions; this was widely interpreted, especially by the religious classes, as selling the country and Islam. The Tobacco Concession of 1891 led to a massive and successful popular protest, orchestrated by the leading *mujtahid* Mirza-ye Shirazi. This was the start of the movement that culminated in the Constitutional Revolution of 1905-11.

The constitutional movement (like the revolutionary movement of the 1970s) brought together a wide range of different elements: merchants and clerics, Muslim reformist intellectuals, secular liberals and nationalists. The common aim, if on differing grounds, was to limit the despotism of the shah through a constitution, an elected legislature and an independent judiciary. Many supporters of the movement did not appreciate its implications, in particular how the replacement of despotic by democratic institutions also implied the promotion of secular over religious power. Not surprisingly, the leading Shia clerics were ambivalent, and took different positions. Mirza Mohammad Hoseyn Na'ini (1860-1936), the highest-ranking cleric to support the movement, provided religious arguments for the rejection of despotism and a defence of constitutionalism in his book, *Tanbih al-Ummah wa Tanzih al-Millah* (*Admonition of the Public and Refinement of the People*), published in 1909. The main clerical opponent of the constitution was Sheykh Fazlollah Nuri. He argued that ideas of democracy and freedom, the establishment of a parliament to enact legislation and the reforms advocated by the constitutionalists were in contradiction with Islam; that men and women, and Muslims and non-Muslims, have different status and rights under the Sharia, and cannot be treated on an equal basis. He opposed the establishment of parliament on the grounds that any man-made law would necessarily clash with religious law. The ulama must control the process of law making, as well as the judiciary.

The constitutionalists forced Mozaffaroddin Shah to grant a parliament (*Majles-e Shura-ye Melli*, National Consultative Assembly), and at the end of December 1906, shortly before his death, he signed the first 'Fundamental Law'. This document was largely secular, with a stress on popular sovereignty. The ulama objected, and the 'Supplementary Fundamental Law' included more references to Islam and to the necessity for the ulama to approve all laws.[4] The new shah, Mohammad Ali, signed the new law in October 1907; but the following year, with Russian help, he staged a successful coup against the constitutionalists. In 1909 constitutionalist forces advanced on Tehran, deposed the shah and executed Sheykh Fazlollah. Parliament was restored, and the Fundamental Laws formed the basis of the Iranian constitution until the formation of the Islamic Republic in 1979. The foundations of a secular democracy had been laid, but the religious elements were still strong, and the potential for despotism remained.

The Pahlavis: secular modernity and the return of despotism

For a decade (1911-21) Iran experienced foreign occupation and interference, and disorder and insurgency in many provinces. Though there was not yet an independent judiciary, the new parliament survived, and there was at times a lively independent press. The early 1920s saw the rise of Reza Khan, the end of the Qajars and a return to despotism. Reza Shah Pahlavi, a westernizing secular nationalist, formed a strong military and a centralized bureaucracy, and established both the secular judiciary and the greatly expanded secular educational system that the constitutionalists had wanted. In these and other ways he deprived the clerics of former monopolies and resources, though he did not go as far as his neighbour and model, Kemal Atatürk. Many of his reforms were popular, but the constitution was ignored and dissent was ruthlessly suppressed. The clerics, labelled as fanatical reactionaries in this modernizing milieu, were furious but reduced to silence.

With the start of World War Two, Reza Shah sought to maintain Iran's independence, though he clearly favoured Germany. In 1941, British and Soviet forces occupied Iran and the shah was forced to abdicate in favour of his son Mohammad Reza. Over the next decade, there was renewed political debate and activity, dominated by the communist Tudeh party and Mosaddeq's secular National Front, and culminating in Mosaddeq's nationalist government of 1951-53. Following the CIA-engineered coup. Mohammad Reza Shah resumed his reign as a US-supported autocrat, suppressing further dissent and indeed parliamentary activity.

In 1946, Ayatollah Borujerdi became sole *marja'* (spiritual guide) of the Shia. Though he opposed the Tudeh and Mosaddeq, he was a political quietist and remained in the seminaries, which he is credited

---

[4] See Chapter 3 below, Editors' introduction.

with reorganizing. Meanwhile, other clergy were planning to resume a more active political role in opposition to the shah's policies. This escalated rapidly when Borujerdi's death in 1961 precipitated a crisis in the *marja'iyat*, there being no single scholar prominent enough to succeed him in this capacity.

The shah alienated much of the country by allowing a massive increase of US influence after 1953. In 1962, in an effort to gain popular support, he instituted his 'White Revolution' or 'Revolution of the Shah and People', including land reform and votes for women. Soon after, Ayatollah Khomeini came to prominence, publicly denouncing the shah for undermining Islam with his reforms, his attacks on the clergy and his increasing dependence on foreigners. On 15 Khordad (5 June 1963), Khomeini was arrested. Large protest demonstrations in Tehran, Qom and other cities were violently put down, with many casualties. Khomeini was released in April 1964, but re-arrested in October after a fiery sermon against the shah. This time he was exiled to Turkey; in October 1965 he was allowed to change his place of exile to Najaf, where he stayed until 1978.[5]

The events of the early 1960s marked the start of the revolutionary movement. Opposition to the shah came from many directions. Among leftist groups, the Tudeh had gone underground after 1953, discredited by their links to the USSR. Guerrilla activities against the regime by the Marxist Fedayan-e Khalq and the Islamic-socialist Mojahedin-e Khalq escalated in the early 1970s as the extravagance, corruption and oppression of the shah's regime further alienated the intellectuals and the people.

Among the religious opposition, Ayatollahs Mahmud Taleqani, Morteza Motahhari and Allameh Tabataba'i contributed greatly to the creation of new Islamic discourses, along with lay figures like Mehdi Bazargan and Ali Shariati.[6] A number of Islamic associations of professionals, students and intellectuals became fora for modernist ideas, and sought to counter secular or non-Muslim groups. One of the most important was the Islamic Association of Engineers (*Anjoman-e Eslami-ye Mohandesin*).[7] The founders (in 1957) were religious intellec-

---

[5] See Martin (2000: 62-64).

[6] For the views and writings of all these, see for example Dabashi (1993), Boroujerdi (1996), Jahanbakhsh (2001).

[7] Not to be confused with The Islamic Society of Engineers (*Jame'eh Eslami-ye Mohandesan*), founded in 1989 by the engineers close to the Rightist faction. Conservative groups with almost identical names, but usually termed *jame'eh*

tuals and activists who had had a modern technological education – engineering was then, as now, a highly respected field of study in Iran. The most distinguished among them was Mehdi Bazargan, who also (with Yadollah Sahabi and Ayatollah Taleqani) in 1961 founded the Liberation Movement (*Nehzat-e Azadi*). Also important were the Islamic Association of Students (*Anjoman-e Daneshjuyan-e Eslami*, which became active after 1953), and the Islamic Association of Physicians (*Anjoman-e Eslami-ye Pezeshkan*, founded in 1958).[8] From 1966 until it was closed in 1972, the *Hoseyniyeh Ershad* (a religious meeting-place in north Tehran) was the main forum for new Islamic discourses, and most important Muslim intellectuals lectured there, including Ali Shariati, the most influential and popular Islamic ideologue of the revolution.[9]

The revolutionary forces – nationalist, leftist, religious – that combined to overthrow the Pahlavis were multiple and varied, but united in their main aim: to reject the autocratic, unjust and unaccountable Pahlavi monarchy, the inequalities in society, and the overwhelming influence of the USA. But the alternatives they sought were as varied (and often contradictory) as they were themselves: a popular democracy; a classless society; a socialist state; national autonomy; an Islamic government, with rulers guided by the ulama and the Sharia.

The Islamic Republic, phase one: establishment
The first decade after the revolution was a period of establishment for the Islamic Republic, marked by the war with Iraq (1980-88) and by bitter struggles, first between the different elements that had contributed to the revolution, and then between the proponents of liberal-democratic and of theocratic Islam, whose values were jointly enshrined in the constitution.

On 16 January 1979 the shah left Iran for good. On 1 February Ayatollah Khomeini returned in triumph, and immediately appointed a provisional government headed by Mehdi Bazargan, composed mainly of National Front and Liberation Movement members, moderate non-clerical Islamists and nationalists, who all wanted a secular democratic republic. Khomeini's clerical followers had different ideas;

(society) were founded to counter the *anjomans*, which all shared liberal-leftist leanings. *Anjoman* was the term for the revolutionary associations of the constitutional movement.

[8] For these associations and institutions, and particularly for Bazargan, see Chehabi (1990).

[9] For Shariati's life and work, see Rahnema (1998).

inspired by Ayatollah Motahhari, soon they formed the Islamic Republican Party (IRP), led by Ayatollah Mohammad Beheshti together with Akbar Hashemi Rafsanjani and Ali Khamene'i, both of whom were later to be president. These were populist Islamic radicals, intent on establishing an Islamic state governed by Islamic law. They were opposed by quietists in the seminaries who wanted the clerics to abstain from government, represented by Ayatollah Kazem Shariat-madari, whose supporters formed the Islamic People's Republican Party. Also contending for power and popular support were the Islamic-socialist Mojahedin-e Khalq (MK), and leftist groups such as the Marxist Tudeh and the Fedayan, who wanted a socialist state (and some autonomy for ethnic minorities).

The early months of 1979 were marked by the first Reign of Terror, as religious extremists implemented hard-line interpretations of Islamic law. Members of the previous regime (military officers, members of the shah's court, capitalists) were summarily executed for *moharebeh* (waging war against God), and prostitutes, adulterers and homosexuals for *efsad fi'l-arz* (corruption on earth). In May, Ayatollah Motahhari, a leading moderate political cleric close to Khomeini, was assassinated.[10] Ayatollah Taleqani, another influential moderate, died in September.

On 4 November, radical student 'Followers of the Imam's Line' (*Peyravan-e Khatt-e Emam*) occupied the US Embassy and took hostages; Bazargan resigned in protest, and the religious hardliners took control of government. They had already begun their offensive against democrats, liberals, secularists and leftists, as well as regional insurgents from ethnic minorities (Kurds, Khuzistan Arabs, Turkmen, Baluch) – most them Sunni. Members of Bazargan's Liberation Movement were removed from the structures of power, though they remained the only tolerated opposition party; they were dismissed as 'liberals', implying they were not Islamic enough; in the 1990s they became known as the Nationalist-Religious Alliance (*Jaryan-e Melli-Mazhabi*).

In January 1980, Abol-Hasan Bani-Sadr, an Islamic modernist who had been among Khomeini's advisors in Paris but was opposed to clerical rule, was elected president; but in March, elections to the new parliament brought the radical IRP to power. The struggle intensified between the main Islamist factions (IRP and the Followers of the Imam's Line), Bani-Sadr's followers, and the MK, the most prominent

---

[10] For his ideas and contribution to the discourse of the revolution, see Dabashi (1993: 147-215)

and popular Islamic leftist organization. Meanwhile, in September 1980, Iraqi forces invaded, starting a war that was to last eight years. In June 1981 parliament impeached Bani-Sadr and, with Khomeini's agreement, he was dismissed. The MK were banned, and clashes with them grew more violent. On 28 June (7 Tir 1360), a powerful bomb exploded at the IRP headquarters while a meeting of party leaders was in progress. The death toll included Ayatollah Beheshti (who had held a number of posts, including chief justice), four cabinet ministers, twenty-seven Majlis deputies, and several other government officials. The MK were blamed for these and other political assassinations, notably, in August, those of newly elected president Ali Reja'i and Prime Minister Mohammad Javad Bahonar. In July both former president Bani-Sadr and MK leader Massoud Rajavi fled to France. Between June 1981 and May 1982, in a second Reign of Terror, most of the MK were executed or imprisoned; those who survived went into exile.[11] The Islamic state and clerical government were secured. In a violent return swing of the pendulum, religious despotism had ousted both secularism and democracy.

The new constitution: a theocratic democracy?

Amid this violence, the new order took shape. On 30 March 1979 a referendum overwhelmingly approved the formation of an Islamic Republic. Many of the early leaders such as Bazargan wanted it to be called 'Democratic Islamic Republic'; but at Khomeini's insistence the version put to the referendum did not include the term 'democratic'. During the spring Bazargan's government and the Revolutionary Council prepared a draft constitution, which was approved by Khomeini; at this stage, there was no mention of clerical rule. In August, an assembly of experts – dominated by the IRP – began to produce a final draft that included the notion of *velayat-e faqih* (guardianship of the jurist, or expert in *fiqh*, jurisprudence). A further referendum approved this constitution on 2 December.

The unresolved tensions that brought about the revolution were in effect written into the constitution of the new order, a compromise document with an uneven fusion of democratic and theocratic principles and institutions.[12] On the one hand, it recognizes the people's right to choose who will govern them, establishing democratic and legislative institutions such as the parliament (*majles-e shura-ye melli*) and

---

[11] For the Mojahedin-e Khalq, see Abrahamian (1989).
[12] See Arjomand (1992), Schirazi (1998).

the presidency, both elected by direct popular vote. On the other, it subordinates the people's will to that of the clerical establishment through the institutions of *velayat-e faqih* or Leadership (*rahbari*) of the Revolution[13] and the Guardian Council (*shura-ye negahban*), composed of twelve members, six of whom are *fuqaha* (pl. of *faqih*) appointed by the Leader, the other six being laymen nominated by the head of the judiciary and approved by parliament, with a tenure of six years.[14] It grants the Leader a wide mandate and a final say in running the state, and charges the Guardian Council, acting as an 'Upper House' with veto powers, with deciding whether laws passed by parliament conform to the Sharia and the constitution – in effect they are the official interpreters of the constitution and Sharia.

The constitution names Khomeini as Leader for life, and creates an Assembly of Experts (*majles-e khebregan-e rahbari*) to choose his eventual successor and supervise his activities, to ensure that he complies with his religious and constitutional duties. The 86 members of this assembly are elected every eight years; only *mujtahids* (senior clerics) are eligible to stand, and from the outset conservative clerics have dominated the assembly. Since it was inaugurated in 1983, the assembly has been headed by Ayatollah Ali Meshkini, a powerful conservative who often acts as Friday Prayer Leader in Qom. In practice so far, the Assembly has merely endorsed the actions of the Leader. The constitution allows the Guardian Council to supervise all elections, which they have interpreted as the right to vet candidates' eligibility to stand. This means that, in effect, the Assembly of Experts and the Guardian Council form a closed system that allows the Leader unlimited power. Through his appointees to the Guardian Council, he can control both the legislative and the executive powers.[15]

Authority and legitimacy: velayat *vs.* marja'iyat

In the aftermath of the revolution, the inherent tension between theocratic and democratic elements in the state, the two competing notions of sovereignty embodied in the concepts of *eslamiyat* and *jomhuriyat*

---

[13] Article 110 of the constitution. These two institutions are the same: *rahbar*, short for *rahbar-e enqelab* (Leader of the Revolution), is the term commonly used, both in the constitution and in everyday political discourse in Iran, for the leading *faqih*.

[14] Articles 91 to 99 set out the role, composition, and scope of activity of this council.

[15] For the power structure of the Islamic Republic, see Buchta (2000).

(roughly, 'Islamism' and 'republicanism'), had been the main site of confrontation among the Islamist, nationalist and leftist forces whose alliance had led to the revolution's success. With secularists and 'liberal' Islamists like Bani-Sadr and the MK, Bazargan and the Liberation Movement defeated and excluded from the structures of power, argument was confined to religious terms and focused on the issue of the religious legitimacy of political authority.[16]

As long as Ayatollah Khomeini was alive, the basic tension was managed and did not confront the Islamic Republic with a crisis of legitimacy. There were several reasons for this. First, apart from Khomeini's personal charisma as Leader, his style of leadership helped to bridge the gap between the two sides. Not only was he mindful of – and responsive to – the popular will, he managed to rise above factional politics and to avoid being claimed by any faction. Perhaps the most important reasons were the freshness of the revolutionary momentum, and the fact that the politics of the period were preoccupied with the Iran-Iraq war, a unifying force that provided the mechanisms for suppressing dissent.

But the issue of legitimate authority remained crucial. On the eve of the revolution, there were six *maraji'* in the Shia world. Ayatollah Khomeini was one of them.[17] They were equal in rank and religious authority; each had his followers and supporters among ordinary Shia all over the world and among clerics and students in various seminaries; none was recognized as sole *marja'*, and none had a modern state apparatus at his disposal. The revolution changed the balance. As its Leader, Ayatollah Khomeini now combined supreme temporal and religious authority. None of the other *maraji'* shared Ayatollah Khomeini's vision of an Islamic state, built on his concept of *velayat-e faqih*.

As the Islamic Republic consolidated itself, a structural contradiction between the two notions of supreme authority – the *marja'iyat* and the *velayat-e faqih* – became increasingly evident. The first has no overt political claims, having evolved through a tacit consensus

---

[16] As Eshkevari puts it in Chapter 3, 'as in the constitutional era, the disagreement is not between believers and non-believers, but rather it is among those who are highly religious and are followers of religious law, over the approach to religion and government.'

[17] Ayatollah Khoi'i (d. 1992) lived in Najaf, the rest in Iran: Ayatollahs Shariatmadari (d. 1982), Mar'ashi-Najafi (d. 1992) and Golpaygani (d. 1993) in Qom, and Khonsari (d. 1985) in Tehran; see Momen (1985: 249), Fischer (1980: 88).

between Shia masses and clerics; it is democratic in nature, in that a *marja'* derives his position from personal recognition by individual followers. The second exerts power over and demands allegiance from all the Shia and relies on the apparatus of state; it not only establishes the authority of one single *faqih* over all others but also breaks away from orthodox Shia political theory, which denies legitimacy to any form of government in the absence of the twelfth Imam. It invests the Leader with the kind of powers and mandate that Shia theology recognizes only for the Prophet and the twelve Infallible Imams,[18] yet it is closer to the Sunni political theory of caliphate than to the Shia theory of imamate.[19]

No one could challenge or oppose either Khomeini or his concept, which was legitimated by popular will, enshrined in the constitution of the Islamic Republic, and ratified in the referendum of December 1979. From now on, those who raised objections were harshly dealt with, and compromised their place in the clerical establishment. Ayatollah Kazem Shariat-madari, who had a large following, particularly in his home province of Azarbaijan, was the only *marja'* to speak openly against *velayat-e faqih*. In 1982, he was stripped of his credentials and confined to his house until his death in 1986.[20]

By 1988, the tension between the two notions of authority intensified and brought about a constitutional crisis. There was conflict not only between the clerical supporters and opponents of *velayat-e faqih*, but also between the factions within the ruling elite, who held differing views of authority and the way the country should be run. In March 1989, Khomeini's dismissal of his designated successor, Grand Ayatollah Hoseyn Ali Montazeri, added a new edge to the tension. Montazeri was the most senior clerical supporter of the theory of *velayat-e faqih*, and also the only one whose own *marja'iyat* was recognized. He had impeccable revolutionary credentials: he had spent years in the previous regime's prisons, played an instrumental role in inserting the *velayat-e faqih* into the constitution, and published discussions on the subject from both theoretical and theological angles.[21]

---

[18] See Arjomand (1988), Sachedina (1988), Akhavi (1996).

[19] See Zubaida (1993).

[20] Bakhash (1984: 223).

[21] Montazeri (1988-90). Published in four volumes in Arabic, this work is the text of Montazeri's lectures in Qom on *velayat-e faqih* and governmental jurisprudence, transcribed and redacted by his students. It was chosen as book of the year in 1988.

But he was also a vocal critic of government policies and practices, and was not willing to keep silent in the face of what saw to be contrary to his religious beliefs. His dismissal, the outcome of an acrimonious struggle for the succession, was in effect a proof of the impossibility of combining the old and new notions of authority.

The crisis was resolved when Ayatollah Khomeini himself gave his blessing to the separation of *velayat* and *marja'iyat*, and authorized a committee to revise the constitution. Following his death in June 1989, the Assembly of Experts chose President Ali Khamene'i as the new Leader of the Revolution. As a middle-ranking cleric, Khamene'i had no possible claim to *marja'iyat*, and he lacked Khomeini's religious authority and charisma. The concept of *velayat-e faqih*, and the legitimacy of its mandate, had to be revised. The committee duly produced a revised constitution, which no longer specifies *marja'iyat* as a necessary attribute of the Leader, who must merely be able to issue fatwas in all fields of Islamic law.[22]

The Islamic Republic, phase two: reconstruction

In July 1989, Majlis speaker Ali Akbar Hashemi Rafsanjani was elected president and a popular referendum ratified the amended constitution. With Khamene'i as the new Leader and Rafsanjani as president, the Islamic Republic entered a second phase, named 'Reconstruction' by its supporters, 'Mercantile Bourgeois Republic' by others.[23] Rafsanjani's priorities and his pragmatic approach reversed some of the earlier policies, notably in the areas of economy and foreign affairs. The welfare policies of the wartime government were replaced by measures that encouraged the growth of the mercantile bourgeoisie and state-connected entrepreneurs.[24]

The new phase saw important changes, notably some tactical ideological shifts that accompanied the breakdown of the delicate balance of power and the working relationship that had developed between the two ruling 'factions', the so-called 'Rightists' and 'Leftists'. Although often spoken of as polarized factions, these terms are relative, the Rightists being more conservative and theocratic, the Leftists more progressive and democratic; they were all, of course, Islamists and

---

[22] For a succinct discussion see Arjomand (1992).
[23] Ehteshami (1995), Ansari (2000).
[24] For the impact of these policies, see Ansari (2000: 52-81).

supporters of Khomeini.[25] Indeed, differences among them are best seen as positions around which people gathered in relation to specific issues, many in the centre shifting position according to the issue.[26]

The Leftists, who had dominated the state under Khomeini and enjoyed his implicit sanction, were now gradually ousted from the structures of power. Their 'radical' elements – including those who had engineered the seizure of the US Embassy in 1979 – were purged from key positions. A new configuration of 'Islamic republicanism' was forged, facilitated by the revised constitution and the consolidation of the Rightist faction.

The constitutional amendments may have settled the crisis over legitimate authority, but they led to a renewed tension between the two competing notions of sovereignty, which dominated Rafsanjani's presidency and forced a redefinition of the relationship between religious authority and the state. To resolve the institutional conflict between *velayat* and *marja'iyat*, to defuse the discord between the Guardian Council and the parliament, to ensure a more pragmatic approach to the application of Islamic law, and to compensate for the loss of the Khomeini's charisma, the revised 1989 constitution extended the mandate of the Leader. This extension drew sanction from a letter by Khomeini in 1988 in response to a question by President Khamene'i, who wanted his consent to oppose the parliament and government policies dominated by the Leftists. Khomeini had written that the Leader's mandate is absolute, that he can even order the suspension of the primary rules of Islam (for example regarding prayer or pilgrimage) if the interests of the Islamic state demand it.[27]

This letter, revealing the tension between the application of the Sharia and the demands of running a state, was welcomed by the Leftists at the time, as they saw the empowerment of the state as one way of defusing legalistic objections and obstacles coming from the seminaries. It was also evidence that, when Khomeini had to choose between the Sharia and the survival of the state, he chose the latter. Now the Rightists, with Khomeini dead and one of their number as Leader, argued – in an ideological U-turn – for further expansion of the Leader's power.[28]

---

[25] And the Leftists should not be confused with earlier leftist groups such as Tudeh, Fedayan, Mojahedin.

[26] For factionalism, see Moslem (2002).

[27] For this crisis and the amendments, see Arjomand (1992: 156-8).

[28] See Moslem (2002: 74)

The revised constitution gave the Leader not only the power to determine the general policies of the state and to oversee their implementation, but also the control of more institutions, notably Television and Radio (IRIB).[29] A new body, the *Majma'-e Tashkhis-e Maslehat-e Nezam* (Assembly to Discern the Interest of the System, known as the Expediency Council), created by Khomeini in February 1988, was now constitutionally sanctioned.[30] The Leader appoints the thirty-one members of this council from various ideological factions loyal to the regime. Its mandate is to vet laws passed by parliament (now renamed *Majles-e Shura-ye Eslami*) but found by the Guardian Council to be in contradiction with the Sharia; in other words, to mediate conflict between popular sovereignty (as represented in parliament) and clerical sovereignty (as represented by the Council of Guardians). The Expediency Council also has the task of advising the Leader on important issues of national concern.[31]

The 1989 constitution increased the power of the non-elected institutions at the expense of the elected ones, and thus came to reflect the views of those who reject the restrictions imposed on *velayat-e faqih* by the 1980 constitution.[32] Emptied of the aura of sanctity that is traditionally associated with the person of the *marja'* in the eyes of believing Shia, with its revolutionary base eroded and its democratic credentials seriously dented, the Leadership now had to rely more and more on the consensus of the clerical establishment and to serve the interests of the Rightist faction. This, in practice, made Khamene'i, the new Leader, a hostage to the seminary politics in which the most traditional Rightist elements – those connected to the bazaar – had the upper hand. Rightists gradually began to dominate all those institutions that represented the theocratic side of power in the Islamic Republic, notably the judiciary, whose head is appointed by the Leader, and the Guardian Council. During the first phase of the Islamic Republic, this council had included both Leftists and Rightists; it had used its constitutional mandate of supervision (*nezarat*) of all elections in the Islamic Republic to allow only insiders ('our people', *khodi*) to run for elected office, excluding secularists, religious liberals,

---

[29] Compare the revised version of Article 110 with the original one.

[30] Articles 110 & 112; for a discussion of this Council and the background to its emergence, see Schirazi (1998: 233-47).

[31] See Buchta (2000: 61-63).

[32] For the argument of the exponents of this view at the time of drafting the constitution, see Schirazi (1998: 52-55).

the 'uncommitted', and outsiders (*gheyr-e khodi*) generally. In the second phase, the council contained solely Rightists, and during the 1992 parliamentary elections it started to use its power – now reinterpreted as a duty of 'approbatory supervision' (*nezarat-e estesvabi*) – to disqualify candidates from the Left so as effectively to ensure that the Right had a majority in the new Majlis.[33]

By the mid-1990s, the Leftist faction also lost all their influence in the judiciary, and while they kept their middle-rank officials in government, they no longer had ministers. One of the last was Mohammad Khatami, Minister of Culture and Islamic Guidance; he resigned in 1992 under pressure from the Rightist faction, who saw his liberal policies as allowing a form of 'cultural invasion'. But the honeymoon between Rafsanjani's government and the traditional Right was soon over; and by the time of the fifth parliamentary elections in 1996, a modernist Rightist group, known as Servants of Construction, emerged under Rafsanjani's patronage.[34]

Ironically, the Leftists were marginalized by the same undemocratic methods they had themselves used to eliminate their main political rivals, Bani-Sadr, Bazargan's Liberation Movement and other secular and liberal forces; they lost power in the 1990s as a result of the very process they had themselves advocated in the 1980s, that is, an instrumental approach to elite politics in the Islamic Republic. Set aside from decision-making bodies, some of the senior Leftist clerics retired from politics and returned to the seminaries,[35] others formed political groups and bodies in the seminaries,[36] or set up research and study groups in Tehran and devoted themselves to 'cultural activities'.[37] They entered a period of political retreat and reflection, during which some of them broke away from theocratic and absolutist ideo-

[33] See Menashri (1992), Baktiari (1996).
[34] For these developments, see Ansari (2000: 82-109), Moslem (2002: 180-251).
[35] For instance Ayatollah Yusef Sane'i, head of the Guardian Council until 1984, and Ayatollah Musavi Ardabili, head of the judiciary until 1987. Both returned to Qom and their seminary activities, but have continued to speak out in favour of reform.
[36] For instance, *Majma'-e Modarresin va Mohaqqeqin-e Howzeh-ye 'Elmiyeh* (Assembly of Teachers and Researchers of Qom Seminaries) was founded as an alternative reformist body to the conservative-dominated *Jame'eh Modarresin-e Howzeh-ye 'Elmiyeh* (Society of Teachers of Qom Seminaries). This assembly has been among the strong advocates of a reformist and democratic Islam.
[37] For the different circles of religious intellectuals and their link with the reformist movement, see Jalaeipour (2003).

logy and started to argue for democratic principles and the rule of law.[38] In so doing, they joined the increasing numbers of ordinary citizens disillusioned by the increasing rift between the ideals of the revolution they had supported and the realities of the Islamic state. Meanwhile, Iranian society was becoming younger, more educated and more urban, and felt increasingly oppressed by restrictions imposed on personal freedoms by a leadership regarded as old and imprisoned by a legalistic notion of Islam. More than any other sector, women had reasons to be disaffected. They felt the harsh reality of subjection to a patriarchal interpretation of Islamic law when applied by the legal machinery of a modern state. They kept their suffrage rights, but most of the pre-revolutionary legal reforms were abolished. Men regained their rights to unilateral divorce and polygamy, while women's rights to divorce and child custody were limited and they were forbidden to study mining and agriculture, to serve as judges, and to appear in public without hijab. Many Islamist women, who had genuinely, if naively, believed that women's position would automatically improve under an Islamic state, had now become increasingly disillusioned. They included some early activists,[39] who had played instrumental roles in discrediting secular feminists and destroying the pre-revolutionary women's press and organizations, as well as many ordinary women for whom Islam meant justice and fairness.

Debates about gender issues, harshly suppressed after the revolution, started to resurface. By the early 1990s, there were clear signs of the emergence of an 'Islamic feminism': a new gender consciousness and a critique of the gender biases in Islamic law. It is certainly true that the Islamic Republic's rhetoric and policies in the 1980s marginalized and excluded so-called 'Westernized' women, but it is equally true that they empowered many other women, who came to see themselves as citizens entitled to equal rights. It was becoming more and more apparent to them that they could not become full citizens unless a modern, democratic reading of Islamic law was accepted.[40]

This reading was what a group of Muslim intellectuals, advocates of what came to be known as 'New Religious Thinking' (now-andishi-ye dini), were trying to achieve. The adverse impact of the implement-

[38] For an overview of the intellectual and socio-political roots of this transformation, see Ashraf and Banuazizi (2001b).
[39] Such as Zahra Rahnavard, Azam Taleqani and Monir Gorji. See Mir-Hosseini (2001).
[40] For clerical debates on gender rights, see Mir-Hosseini (1999).

ation of Islamic law, as defined in classical texts of traditional jurisprudence (*fiqh-e sonnati*), had already produced a kind of rethinking and reworking among the clerics. A new school of 'Dynamic Jurisprudence' (*fiqh-e puya*), tried to arrive at a new interpretation of Islamic law by taking into account the factors of time and place. This school emerged in the late 1980s, following two rulings by Ayatollah Khomeini making chess games and music halal. It has supporters among the younger generation of clerics, and its senior advocates, such as Ayatollahs Ebrahim Janati, Musavi-Bojnurdi and Yusef Sane'i, have issued a number of progressive fatwas with regard to women's rights and other social issues. So far, however, this new school has failed to produce a coherent basis for rethinking the basis of *ijtihad* or the assumptions behind the *fiqh* theories that inform the classical interpretations of Islamic law. As we shall see, those who attempt such rethinking face persecution by conservative clerics.

The New Religious Thinkers included laymen and women as well as clerics, all of whom now saw a widening gap between the ideals of the revolution and the realities and policies of the Islamic state in which they lived. Representing various strands of modernist Shia thought that had remained dormant during the war with Iraq, they offered new interpretations of Islam and began to articulate a theoretical critique of the Islamic state from an Islamic perspective.[41]

This critique can be dated to the late 1980s, and traced to developments in the Kayhan Publishing Institute, which had come under the control of the Islamists shortly after the revolution. In the early 1980s, Kayhan became one of the main centres of activity of Muslim intellectuals, mostly those close to the Leftist faction. Two of its publications, the quarterly *Keyhan-e Farhangi* (*Cultural Kayhan*) and the weekly *Zan-e Ruz* (*Woman of Today*), contained state-of-the-art Islamist thinking on political thought and gender issues. By the mid-1980s, some of the writers in both journals were increasingly critical of state policies, and started to distance themselves from the official discourse of the regime. Most prominent among them was Abdolkarim Soroush, who published a series of controversial articles in *Keyhan-e Farhangi* between 1988 and 1990 on the historicity and relativity of religious knowledge, later developed as 'The Theoretical Contraction and Expansion of Sharia'. Separating religion from religious knowledge, Soroush argued in these articles that, while the first was sacred and immutable, the

---

[41] For the range of views and arguments, see Sadri (2001), Jahanbakhsh (2001).

second was human and evolved over time as a result of forces external to religion itself.[42]

The clerical establishment saw Soroush's approach as a direct challenge to their religious authority. A heated debate followed, which led to the closure of *Keyhan-e Farhangi* in June 1990. As the Kayhan Institute came under the control of the Rightist faction, several Muslim contributors sympathetic to Soroush's ideas departed to form a new intellectual circle. Two key figures among them were Mashallah Shamsolvaezin (who after Khatami's election was to edit the most influential and popular daily papers *Jame'eh*, *Tus*, *Neshat* and *Asr-e Azadegan*) and Shahla Sherkat (who had played a role in the Islamization of the women's press: from 1982 she edited *Zan-e Ruz*, the most popular and outspoken women's magazine in the pre-revolutionary era). Both now became editors of new monthly journals: Shamsolvaezin of *Kiyan* (Foundation), launched in October 1991, and Sherkat of *Zanan* (Women), launched in February 1992.

Kiyan and *Zanan* were prominent platforms for the Islamic dissent that began to be voiced among 'insiders' after over a decade of the experience of Islam in power, and became a magnet for intellectuals whose ideas and writings now formed the backbone of the New Religious Thinking. Whereas in the 1980s these men and women saw their role as the islamization of culture and society, in the 1990s, armed with Soroush's theory of the relativity of religious knowledge, they wanted to create a worldview reconciling Islam and modernity, and argued for a demarcation between state and religion. They argued that the human understanding of Islam is flexible, that Islam's tenets can be interpreted to encourage both pluralism and democracy, and to allow change according to time, place and experience. For them the question was no longer who should rule, but how they should rule, and what mechanisms there should be to curb the excesses of power. In this way, they began to cross the red lines that had previously circumscribed any critical discussion of the political dogma of *velayat-e faqih*.

Those who wrote for *Kiyan* and *Zanan* showed a genuine willingness to reassess old positions, and sought a dialogue with secular thinkers, whose views were reflected in new journals such as *Iran-e Farda*, *Jame'eh Salem*, *Goftogu*, *Adineh* and *Towse'eh*, as well as with the liberal Islamists of the Nationalist-Religious Alliance.

---

[42] For English translations of some of his writings, see Kurzman (1998), Soroush (2000a)

In the Iran of the early 1990s, journals like *Kiyan* and *Zanan* played a role similar to that of the *Hoseyniyeh Ershad* two decades earlier. Like Shariati in his lectures at the *Hoseyniyeh Ershad*, Soroush in *Kiyan* tried to redefine and rework Islamic concepts and succeeded in producing discourses that were to become highly attractive to youth and women. At the same time, both were immensely popular while being criticized and disdained by secular intellectuals. But there are fundamental differences in their visions and conceptions of Islam, which were undoubtedly shaped by the politics of their own times. Shariati turned Islam into an ideology to challenge the Pahlavi monarchy. For Soroush, Islam is 'richer than ideology', and all his thinking and writing are aimed at separating the two.[43] But he has himself become the ideologue of a reformist, democratic Islam, by his critique of '*fiqh*-based Islam', widely read as an attack on *velayat-e faqih*.

The New Religious Thinking has revived classical debates on the nature of the divine law, which in turn reactivated two crucial distinctions that the early wave of Islamic activists distorted and obscured. The first is the distinction between the Sharia and the science of *fiqh*, which lies at the root of the emergence of the various 'orthodox' schools of Islamic law.[44] Sharia literally means 'the way', and in Muslim belief it is the totality of God's law as revealed to the Prophet Muhammad. *Fiqh*, 'understanding', is this process of human endeavour to discern and extract legal rules from the sacred sources of Islam: the Koran and the Sunna (the practice of the Prophet). In other words, while the Sharia is sacred, universal and eternal, *fiqh*, like any other system of jurisprudence, is local, multiple and subject to change in its doctrines and premises. In contrast to many contemporary Islamist activists, classical Muslim *fuqaha* have always admitted that their understanding of the revealed law – the Sharia – is contingent.[45]

The second distinction is one made in all schools of Islamic law between the two main categories of legal rulings: *'ibadat* (ritual/spiritual acts) and *mu'amilat* (social/private contracts). Rulings of the first category, *'ibadat*, regulate relations between God and the believer, and

---

[43] See Cooper (1998), Kurzman (2001), Ghamari-Tabrizi (2004)
[44] For this distinction, see Kamali (1989: 216). For an argument not employing the distinction, see An-Na'im (2000: 33-4).
[45] In classical texts one often comes across phrases such as 'this is what I understood', or 'and God knows best', phrases by which the *fuqaha* qualified the laws that they discerned and separated them from 'God's law'. See Abou El Fadl (1997).

there is limited scope for rationalization and explanation, as they contain divine mysteries. But this is not the case with rulings of the second category, *mu'amilat*; they regulate relations among humans, and remain open, almost without restriction, to rational considerations. In other words, it is argued, while the Sharia sets specific rulings on relations with the divine, in the realm of human relations it seeks only to establish basic principles and guidance so as to ensure propriety and fair play.

The Islamic Republic, phase three: reform

In the 1997 presidential elections, a last-minute political alliance between Rafsanjani's pragmatic modernist right and the Islamic left put forward former culture minister Mohammad Khatami to oppose Akbar Nateq-Nuri, the candidate of the traditionalist right. The people voted en masse for Khatami, who stood for 'democracy' and 'rule of law', and whose ideas and language were drawn largely from Soroush and his co-thinkers. Once again the popular will began to assert itself, expressing resentment of the injustices brought by the application of pre-modern interpretations of the Sharia, and of the undemocratic nature of the current Leadership. The reformist movement that emerged in the aftermath of this election was the logical and inevitable outcome of the spread of the New Religious Thinking at both popular and political levels.[46]

Almost overnight, new political alliances were forged and cleavages shifted. Those who had campaigned for Nateq-Nuri, mainly of the traditionalist right, were labelled 'conservatives'. Those who voted for Khatami and supported his vision called themselves 'reformists', but came to be known as the 'Second Khordad Front' (after the date of Khatami's election). The reformists were a loose coalition with a wide range of views and little consensus on aims and directions of reform. They included 'insiders' in government who still supported an Islamic state, headed by a ruling *faqih*; secularists who wanted not only democracy and civil society but the separation of religion from government; and the Nationalist-Religious Alliance. The last was now a loose association of different groups: the 'tolerated' opposition Liberation Movement (headed by Ebrahim Yazdi after Bazargan's death in 1995); the *Iran-e Farda* group formed around Ezzatollah Sahabi; Azam Taleq-

---

[46] For analysis that puts the focus on elite factionalism, see Wells (1999), Moslem (2002).

ani (publisher of *Payam-e Hajer*), who followed her father Ayatollah Taleqani's line; and those faithful to Shariati's vision.

One general demand, espoused by Khatami, was for transparency in government, and this was soon manifested in the emergence of a varied, lively, outspoken and critical press (newspapers, journals, books) – all the more important now, given the continuing conservative control of the broadcast media. Before the election, the only daily newspaper that offered a critical perspective towards government was *Salam*. Now, most notable and most widely read of a score of national and many more provincial reformist dailies were *Jame'eh*, *Tus*, *Neshat* and *Asr-e Azadegan*, published in succession between January 1998 and summer 2000: the same team of journalists (headed by Mashallah Shamsolvaezin, editor of *Kiyan*) produced all four dailies, each opened immediately after the forced closure of the previous one.

The newly expanded public sphere, comprising not only this vocal and dynamic press but also the universities, the seminaries and parliament, now debated with increasing candour the ambiguities and contradictions in the original idea of the Islamic state and its translation into the constitution.[47] Views that were previously confined to the elite, and aired only in specialist journals (or low-circulation opposition intellectual publications), started to reach the public and were discussed in the daily press.

For the conservatives, the dogma of *velayat-e faqih* was the foundation of their power. They now condemned direct and indirect criticisms of this dogm as attacks on the 'system' (*nezam*), on 'Islam', and on 'religious sanctities'. From early 1998, they embarked on an apparently coordinated, three-pronged assault on reform and dissent: through their control of parliament and of the processes of election to other bodies; through the judiciary and prosecution of key reformists; and through violence by both official state agents and vigilante thugs.

With their majority in the current parliament, the conservatives were able to impede the reformist government's programme of legislation. In August, deputies approved the list of ministers Khatami presented to them, perhaps because he included, as Ministers of Intelligence and Defence, two conservatives close to the Leader; but from then on matters grew more difficult. For example, parliament had been active in promoting women's rights; now they reversed direction, introducing and passing two regressive bills. The first, 'Adaptation of medical services to religious law', extended the code of gender segreg-

---

[47] See Arjomand (2000).

ation to medicine, a realm that had been left more or less untouched until then. The second, 'Banning the exploitation of women's images and the creation of conflicts between men and women by propagating women's rights outside the legal and Islamic framework', sought to put an end to the lively press debate on women's rights. Both bills were not only regressive, they were impossible to implement; but, as we shall see, they were used to put pressure on Khatami's new government and to prepare the ground for the impeachment of some of his ministers.

The next elections, in October 1998, were for the Assembly of Experts, a body of clerics tasked with ensuring that the Leader keeps within Islamic and constitutional bounds. As these elections were an opportunity for reassessing theocratic rule, reformist criticism focused on the closed system that gave absolute power to the Leader. The reformists argued for free elections and also for the inclusion of non-clerics as candidates, in order to ensure that the assembly represented the people rather than the clerical establishment. In the event, the Guardian Council once again eliminated many reformist candidates as insufficiently qualified; this questioning of clerics' *ijtihad* was of course highly offensive. Most reformist groups boycotted the elections and the traditional right retained its control.

In February 1999, for the first time since 1980, the government held elections to town and village councils. In preparation for them, Khatami's supporters formed the Mosharekat (Participation) Party. The Guardian Council was unable to disqualify candidates, since these elections were entirely in the hands of the Interior Ministry. There was a huge turnout and reformists won most of the seats, almost sweeping the board in Tehran and other large cities.[48]

The conservatives' second strategy was to use the their control of the judiciary – and Khatami's slogan of 'rule of law' – to clamp down on press freedom and to prosecute key reformist figures on blatantly artificial charges, in order to eliminate them from the political scene. The Press Court closed outspoken papers on spurious charges, only to find that the Ministry of Culture allowed the same journalists to open a new one under a different name (as in the case of *Jame'eh* and its successors). Eventually, in its last months, the outgoing parliament passed a more repressive Press Law. Meanwhile, the Revolutionary Courts prosecuted reformist intellectuals, journalists and even government officials. The task of containing clerical proponents of reform was assumed by the non-constitutional Special Clergy Court,

---

[48] For the town and village council elections, see Tajbakhsh (2000).

which since 1997 has acted as an inquisition.[49] The most prominent clerical target was Khatami's controversial Minister of the Interior, Abdollah Nuri. In June 1998, after a long witch-hunt by conservative parliamentary deputies, a vote of no confidence forced Nuri to resign as minister. Khatami responded by appointing him a vice-president, and Nuri began publishing the popular newspaper *Khordad*. In the February 1999 council elections he topped the poll in Tehran, but in October the Special Clergy Court tried him and sentenced him to five years in prison (see Chapter 5).

The charges brought against clerical targets included apostasy (*ertedad*), waging war against God (*moharebeh*), disturbing the public mind, propaganda against the regime, challenging Khomeini's perspectives, insulting the authorities, insulting religious sanctities. These all reflect the conservatives' anxiety to keep discussion of controversial issues in the seminaries and out of public attention.

Violence, the third conservative strategy, carried out by elements of official bodies such as the *Pasdaran* (Revolutionary Guards) or the *Basij* paramilitaries, or by bands of vigilante thugs such as the *Ansar-e Hezbollah*,[50] has long been the standard method of suppressing opposition to the Leader, both publicly and in secret. The aim has been both to eliminate and intimidate opposition, and to provoke a violent reaction among reformists and students that can be even more violently and easily suppressed.

---

[49] The Special Clergy Court (*dadgah-e vizheh-e rowhaniyat*) was formed at Ayatollah Khomeini's order in the aftermath of the revolution in order to try clerics associated with the previous regime. It was revived in 1987 to convict Mehdi Hashemi, a close associate of Ayatollah Montazeri. Its formation then was disputed as unconstitutional; and in 1988, in a letter to parliament, Khomeini suggested that the court should be aligned with the mandates of the constitution, but only after the Iraq war ended. After Khomeini's death (and the end of the war) the court continued to function, coming under the control of the conservatives. According to some reports, the court has secretly executed many hundreds of clerics, and beaten, fined and imprisoned thousands (see for example, ICG 2002: 9-10). For the history and the illegality of this court, see Baqi (2001), and for its role in silencing clerical dissent, see Buchta (2000: 97-8).

[50] On the *Basij* volunteer militia, see Buchta (2000: 65-7). The *Ansar-e Hezbollah* emerged in 1995, attacking Soroush and university students, and burning bookshops. They were said to enjoy the patronage of high-ranking clerics; Farshad Amir-Ebrahimi, a renegade member, revealed in 1998 how the group was ordered to disrupt rallies.

From spring 1998, anti-reformist violence became more open, and the press did their best to expose it. In April, Rahim Safavi, commander of the *Pasdaran*, threatened to 'break the pens and cut out the tongues' of those who wrote or spoke against the sanctities of the regime. Threats to reformist intellectuals (such as Soroush) and in particular to members of the Nationalist-Religious Alliance (such as Ezzatollah Sahabi) increased. The following winter the public were alarmed by what became known as the 'serial killings' (*qatl-ha-ye zanjiri*). On 22 November, two well-known secular nationalist dissidents, Daryush Foruhar (who had been Minister of Labour in Bazargan's goverment), and his wife, Parvaneh Eskandari, were stabbed to death in their house. Shortly after, three prominent writers (all secular) were found dead after their families reported them missing under suspicious circumstances. These murders created an atmosphere of fear among both secular and religious dissident intellectuals and there were rumours of the existence of a 'hit-list'. The reformist press demanded transparency and an explanation, and President Khatami set up a committee to investigate the issue. In January 1999, after complex behind-the-scenes negotiations, the Ministry of Intelligence and Information admitted that the killings had been carried out by 'rogue elements' in the ministry, masterminded by Sa'id Emami, who headed the Internal Security division. In February, Emami and his gang were arrested. Dorri-Najafabadi, the minister, resigned, and was replaced by Ali Yunesi, a non-partisan rightist.

Reformist journalists such as Akbar Ganji pursued the matter, and wrote articles implicating some of the highest-ranking authorities, including former president Rafsanjani (who now headed the Expediency Council) and his Minister of Intelligence, Fallahian, as well as other high-ranking clerics, close to the Leader, who had issued fatwas authorizing the killings.[51]

Ganji had emerged as one of the most outspoken reformists; a former revolutionary guard, he was influenced by Soroush, wrote for *Kiyan* and headed the Serat Institute, which disseminated Soroush's lectures (on audiotape) and published volumes of his articles. After Khatami's election, Ganji was one of the first reformists to run foul of the courts. In a talk at Shiraz University in June 1997 on the twentieth anniversary of Shariati's death, he spoke of a fascist reading of religion and gave as examples the *Ansar-e Hezbollah* and their publications, as well as rightist newspapers such as *Keyhan* (close to the Leader). In

[51] See Ganji's collection of articles (1999b).

December he was arrested by the Revolutionary Court and charged with 'insulting the Leader of the Revolution' and 'disturbing the public mind'. In March 1998, he was convicted on the second charge and given a suspended sentence. He then brought out a weekly *Rah-e Now* (New Way), but this was closed down after twenty issues.

While in prison, Ganji kept writing letters of protest, and his defence was published in *Kiyan*; his writings were extremely popular with the students and he was soon known as the most radical voice among the reformists for civil society and democracy (see Chapter 5).

In June 1999, in the run-up to the trial of the 'serial killers', it was suddenly announced that Sa'id Emami – the leading suspect – had committed suicide in prison.[52] On 7 July, while parliament was passing a new restrictive Press Bill, the newspaper *Salam* took the risk of publishing a secret memo by Emami advising a tightening of the Press Law. The judiciary promptly ordered the closure of *Salam*, and the Special Clergy Court summoned its managing director. Tehran students held a peaceful protest against both the closure and the Press Bill. That night, vigilantes attacked the student dormitories while the security forces watched. The result was five days of student demonstrations, larger than any since the revolution, which were ended by a show of force summoned by the Leader. Radical elements among the conservatives are said to have wanted to provoke a showdown, in order to deal with Khatami. Law enforcement agents and vigilante thugs acted with brutality, killing or maiming large numbers of students, arresting hundreds. Following this, a number of *Pasdaran* commanders wrote to Khatami threatening a coup if he did not deal with such demonstrations. While a number of reformist leaders went to talk to the students, trying to find a peaceful resolution, Khatami was preoccupied with behind-the-scenes negotiations. His failure to come out in support of the students, as well as the harsh sentences many of them received and the immunity given to those who had attacked them, marked the beginning of his loss of credibility.

Despite such failures to protect dissident voices, Khatami's government had some important tangible effects, notably the energizing of the public sphere. Neither the prosecution of outspoken reformists nor the closure of their publications succeeded in silencing the democracy debate. Conservative attempts to censor the public sphere further highlighted the urgency of the debate and the necessity for preserving

---

[52] The rest of his gang were tried and convicted in January 2001, but repercussions of the case continued for some time.

such a sphere. Indeed, attempts to narrow the scope of the debate, and to confine it to 'Islam and the constitution', polarized the opposition between conservatives and reformists and sharpened the contrast between their visions of Islam and readings of the constitution.

For the conservatives, *fiqh* has answers to all the problems of society; their vision of Islam, premised on notions of 'duty' and 'obedience', is legalistic and absolutist, tolerates no dissent and makes little concession to the people's will and contemporary realities. Their reading of the constitution is theocratic; the Leader derives his mandate from God and his powers are not to be limited by human laws; the Assembly of Experts and other elected bodies, including parliament and the presidency, are at his disposal.

To the reformists, not only does such a reading of the constitution negate its clear and definite *jomhuriyat* (republicanism), it is a travesty of the ideals and achievements of the 1979 revolution, by those who want to reproduce despotic relations in an Islamic format. The reformists' vision of Islam is pluralistic and tolerant, based on human rights and democratic values. Their reading of the constitution is democratic; *velayat-e faqih* is a religio-political theory; the Leader derives his mandate from the people, who elect him indirectly through the Assembly of Experts and can depose him if he fails to fulfil his constitutional duties and abuses his constitutional prerogatives.

When Khatami was first elected, there was no public criticism of *velayat-e faqih*. Barely three months after he took office, however, on 14 November 1997, Grand Ayatollah Montazeri – one of the main architects of the institution of *velayat-e faqih* in the constitution – gave a public sermon in Qom in which he not merely laid the theoretical foundation for the democratization of *velayat-e faqih* and the separation of the clerical establishment from the state, but he openly questioned the legitimacy of the rule of the current Leader.[53] He encouraged Khatami to use the mandate given him by 22 million voters to reform the system.

The conservative reaction to Montazeri's sermon was harsh and immediate. His house was attacked, his classes were closed and he was put under house arrest, and any discussion of the sermon was banned. But the genie was out of the bottle. One of his prominent students, Mohsen Kadivar, now started to speak out. In early 1999, in Nuri's newspaper, *Khordad*, he compared the current practice of *velayat* (clerical rule) to *saltanat* (monarchy) and referred to the 'serial killings',

[53] Montazeri's previous discussions of all this were confined to the seminaries.

declaring them to be against Islam. As a result, in February Kadivar was arrested and jailed on the orders of the Special Clergy Court (for his trial, see Chapter 4).

Kadivar's and Nuri's trials made public the deep rift among the clerics, and laid bare the crisis of the theocratic state. In the February 2000 elections for the sixth Majlis, despite the elimination of their key personalities by the judiciary, and the Guardian Council's disqualification of others, the reformists won a landslide victory on a large turnout. In the absence of political parties, the reformist press produced lists of candidates for people to vote for; almost all those named on their lists won seats. The people showed that they supported a more liberal and democratic Islamic Republic.

Having already lost the presidency, and with the reformists due to take control of parliament (at the inauguration in June), the conservatives revealed that they could not retain a monopoly of power in an open and democratic society. Alarmed by their heavy losses in the elections, they accelerated their offensive. Their main priority, as before, was to silence the reformists and to eliminate key figures from the political scene. In early March an attempt was made to assassinate Sa'id Hajjarian, the chief strategist of reform, adviser to President Khatami and editor of the paper *Sobh-e Emruz*. In April, following a speech by the Leader, the judiciary ordered the closure of twenty reformist papers: an excuse was found in the Berlin Conference.

The Berlin Conference

On 6-9 April 2000 the Heinrich Böll Foundation, a German organization associated with the Green Party, sponsored a three-day conference on 'Iran after the Elections, and the Dynamics of Reform in the Islamic Republic', hosted by the House of World Cultures in Berlin. The conference had two aims. The publicized aim was both to introduce the different strands of thought among the reformists around Khatami and to provide a forum for discussion of the social and political situation in Iran after the February parliamentary elections. In this 'Tehran spring' atmosphere, conferences on such themes were taking place all over Europe and America.

The conference's un-stated aim was to help repair German-Iranian relations and to rehabilitate Iran in German public opinion. The Green Party had played a role when in opposition in bringing about the much-publicized 'Mykonos trial', which implicated the Iranian government (and Intelligence Minister Fallahian) in the assassination of four leading opposition Kurds in September 1992 in the Mykonos Restaurant in Berlin. The trial took place between August 1996 and April 1997, and brought a rupture in political relations between Iran and Germany. Shortly before the conference, Joschka Fischer, Foreign Minister (and Green Party leader in the Coalition Government) made a trip to Iran, and a visit to Germany by President Khatami was due to take place afterwards.

A number of prominent Iranian reformists – both secular and religious – were invited to the conference to debate the future of the reforms. Among them, and the only cleric, was Hasan Yousefi Eshkevari. Other speakers from Iran included Akbar Ganji, Ezzatollah Sahabi (director of *Iran-e Farda* and prominent member of the Nationalist-Religious Alliance), Reza Afshari (representing the students), Mehrangiz Kar (secular feminist lawyer), Shahla Sherkat (editor of *Zanan* and close to the reformist camp), Shahla Lahiji (publisher and women's rights activist), and Sayyid Kazem Kardavani, Changiz Pahlevan and Mahmud Dowlatabadi (secular dissident intellectuals and writers).

The conference became notorious in Iran for two things: disruptions by 'naked' men and women, and the outspokenness of some of the panellists from Iran. Both were filmed by well-primed crews from (conservative-dominated) Iranian Television (IRIB).

Not represented among the speakers were the conservatives in Iran and the exiled Iranian opposition abroad, both of which saw the conference as a threat to their own agendas. There seems to be evidence of collusion between extremist elements from both groups in organizing the disruptions.[54] Not all opposition groups participated in disrupting the conference, but two were very active: the Workers' Communist Party and the Berlin Exiled Women of Iran Against Fundamentalism. Among the others, the Fedayan Majority and the Tudeh Party were in favour of the conference, while the Mojahedin-e Khalq did not make their presence known.

On 18 April, IRIB broadcast film of the Berlin Conference on television, carefully edited so as to discredit the reformists. On 20 April the Leader, Ayatollah Khamene'i, in a speech to a large gathering of *Pasdaran* and *Basij* militia, accused the reformist press of treachery, of misleading people and taking orders from foreign powers. On 23 April, the judiciary ordered the closure of fourteen reformist papers, the first

---

[54] See Riyahi (2000: 34), quoting a report in the reformist newspaper *Sobh-e Emruz*, 4.2.79/22 April 2000.

of many press closures.[55] This began what the reformists have called a 'creeping coup d'état'. Many of the participants in the conference were arrested on their return to Iran, charged with acting against national security by taking part in propaganda against the Islamic Republic.

Hasan Yousefi Eshkevari, the only clerical participant in the Berlin Conference, remained in Europe for three months after the conference for a lecture tour that had been planned in advance. When he returned to Iran on 4 August, family and friends met him at the airport, but the following day he was arrested, as widely anticipated. In October 2000, he appeared before the Special Clergy Court and was charged with apostasy, waging war against God, and other offences resulting from his participation in the conference.

[55] For the events leading to the press closures, see Khiabani and Sreberny (2001).

2

Hasan Yousefi Eshkevari
Public and Private

Editors' introduction

In this chapter we introduce Eshkevari by means of three texts, all written in summer 2000, before his arrest. Together, they tell how the 1979 revolution transformed the lives of young idealist clerics like Eshkevari and how by the mid-1980s their enthusiasm and optimism turned to disillusion and disappointment.[1]

Eshkevari's main pre-occupation after the revolution was the relation between Islam and democracy, which had not been of much concern to militant Islamists like him in the 1970s. Ali Shariati, Eshkevari's enduring inspiration, died in 1977; his vision of Islam was revolutionary rather than democratic. He reworked Islamic concepts to provide Muslims with an ideology for political action, to enable them to use their faith and reclaim their identity, to challenge religious traditionalism, secular authoritarianism and the legacy of colonialism. To achieve this, to realize the justice of Islam, they had to gain power. In this project, democracy was not a priority. Shariati had reservations about democracy in countries where religion and tradition rule supreme. Given the choice, he argued, the masses will simply vote for those who think like them, and thus government will remain in the hands of these who want to preserve traditional ways. For such societies, Shariati advocated *démocratie engagé*, where government is in the hands of an enlightened elite committed to a progressive ideology and following a revolutionary agenda.[2] Eshkevari continues to believe in

---

[1] To our knowledge, the only previous extended discussions of Eshkevari's work in English are Shadid (2001: 187-91) and Dahlén (2003: 159-63).

[2] For a clear and concise discussion of Shariati's views of democracy, see Jahanbakhsh (2001: 119-126). For a more comprehensive account, see Rahnema (1998).

Shariati's 'political Islam', which he now calls 'social Islam', seeking to redeem it through democratizing it.

Eshkevari intended the first text, 'Autobiography', for a proposed biographical dictionary of Iranian scholars. After his imprisonment, his son Ruhollah updated it and posted it on the website of the Nationalist-Religious Alliance, the political tendency with which Eshkevari is identified. Writing in a rather detached style, Eshkevari traces his intellectual and political trajectory chronologically: how he became a cleric, his move to Qom and his political awakening and activities before and during the revolution, his enduring devotion to Shariati and his ideas, his decision in the early 1980s to distance himself from governmental politics to focus on what he calls 'cultural activities' – a euphemism for a different kind of politics that puts the emphasis on critical thinking about both traditional Islamic ideas and the new revolutionary ideology. He lists his numerous books and articles, and ends his account with a statement of his political vision, which is his project of 'religious intellectualism'.

The second piece, 'The calm of this house remains', is a chapter from Lili Farhadpoor's *The Women of Berlin: a Different Narrative*, published in summer 2000, soon after the Berlin Conference. Farhadpoor, a journalist who came of age under the Islamic Republic, writes for a number of reformist newspapers. She has interviewed the women participants in the conference as well as others close to some of the male participants. Her book is a good example of a genre known as *Dovvom-e Khordadi* (the label for the reform movement inaugurated by President Khatami's first election, on 2 Khordad 1376/23 May 1997). These books, written by journalists, or collections of material from reformist journals, were intended as 'instant history' of key events or crises that had affected or derailed the reforms, such as the serial political killings, the student dormitory attacks, the attempted assassination of Hajjarian.

The main character in 'The calm' is Eshkevari's wife, Mohtaram Golbaba'i. Lili and Mohtaram together, in an accessible, informal and chatty narrative, tell the story of Eshkevari's life and how the Berlin Conference affected his family. Mohtaram's account complements that given by her husband in 'Autobiography'. It is an imaginatively written piece that opens an intimate window onto the home and family life of clerics like Eshkevari. Farhadpoor gives an insight into Eshkevari as a husband and father with 'modern' ideas, and a good idea of how their life changed after the revolution and of the encounter between traditional and modern religious codes and practices. Such accounts are rare: very little is publicly known about the private and family life of clerics, or how their world was transformed by the revolution. These two texts are in many ways complementary. Farhadpoor's narrative starts where Eshkevari's account of his own life ends – after the Berlin Conference that led to his arrest. Both were written for an Iranian readership familiar with the history of the revolution and the subsequent two decades. Aware of the constraints that still limited what could be said and published in the Iran of 2000, both texts avoid overt criticism of Islamic ideology or reference to the politics that resulted in the exclusion of Islamic liberal and secular forces from the structures of power. In Chapter 1 we have outlined the events they refer to; here we use footnotes to draw the reader's attention to what remains unsaid, implicit or hinted at in both accounts.

The chapter concludes with the Preface that Eshkevari wrote in July 2000 (while still in Europe after the conference) to *Reason at the Feast of Religion*, which came out the following winter when he was in prison. The book is the edited version of some of the lectures Eshkevari delivered between 1996 and 1997 in the library of the Al-Ghadir mosque in Tehran for the Islamic Association of Physicians (see Chapter 1). The topics covered by the lectures – Religion and Government, Religion and Democracy, Religion and Ideology, Religion and Development, Religion and Science, Religion and Religious Institutions, Religion and Religious Revival, Religion and Symbols, Religion and Ijtihad, and Religion and the Last of Prophets – indicate the range of issues that are central to Eshkevari's version of the project of 'religious intellectualism'. In the Preface, Eshkevari outlines this project and his vision of 'social Islam', a reworking of Shariati's concept of 'political Islam'.

'Autobiography'[3]
I was born in 1949 in Eshkevar (in the Rudsar district of Gilan province).[4] My father was a farmer and my mother a housewife, both of

---

[3] The original, in Eshkevari's handwriting, was accessed on 15 September 2003 at *http://www.mellimazhabi.org/biography/eshkevari/eshkevari.htm*, the website of the Nationalist-Religious Alliance Also available on the site were a typewritten transcript (with minor differences from the original) and an English summary. To make the account more accessible to a general reader, we have slightly edited and shortened it.

[4] Round brackets indicate Eshkevari's insertions; square brackets and all footnotes are additions (or elisions) by the current editors.

them being unable to read or write. In my childhood years, there was no school in the area (which is still reckoned to be one of the most deprived in the country). So, as soon as a Koranic school was set up in one of the villages, some families would send their children there to learn the Koran, or at least to read and write.

In 1957 a Koranic school was set up in one of the villages near us; and my father sent me there as the oldest child of the family. These Koranic schools were in operation only for three summer months. Between 1957 and 1961 I went to several of these schools, learned the Koran and reading and writing, and studied schoolbooks (those taught at modern primary schools).

In 1961 my father sent me to Rudsar seminary to become a religious student. At that time I was 12 years old and had no say in choosing this field of study. My father's [paternal] uncle was a notable local cleric (who had studied in Najaf). I think it was out of deep respect for him that my father wanted his son too to undertake religious studies and become a cleric like [my uncle]. From 1961 to 1965 I stayed in Rudsar and took preliminary courses in syntax, grammar, logic and literature.[5] At the same time I also took the sixth grade primary school exams and passed. But because of my pre-occupation with seminary courses, I was not interested in continuing with modern studies [i.e. going to high school]. But I developed a passionate interest in reading (newspapers, magazines, novels and modern scientific publications, especially in natural sciences) and began to read, without direction.

In 1965 I went to Qom to continue my studies. I was deeply affected by my entry to the Qom seminaries and by the rapidly changing conditions of the city in those years – I had entered a totally new world. I was enthralled by the presence of different scholars, religious leaders and teachers, the numerous libraries and various journals and publications, diverse and conflicting ideas, and above all the political ferment. While continuing my formal studies, I used the unlimited resources of the two libraries of the Hazrat-e Ma'sumeh shrine and the Qom grand mosque for my further reading. I would spend part of the day in these two libraries. I would also read maga-

---

[5] There are three levels at which seminary students study: *moqaddamat* (preliminary), *sotuh* (texts, i.e. intermediate), and *dars-e kharej* (external study, i.e. advanced). For the system of seminary education, subjects taken and books studied at each level, see Fischer (1980), Momen (1985: 200-03), Mottahedeh (1985: 69-109),

zines such as *Zan-e Ruz* – which I think started publication in 1965[6] – and I would rent or buy or borrow novels. Whatever I could get hold of, I would read eagerly – as though reading were an end in itself. Sometimes I would read throughout the night until the time for Morning Prayer. Gradually I became interested in writing, and from 1968 onwards I started writing on social issues, and occasionally I wrote short stories; of course, they were derivative imitations of what I had read. In those years I found most attractive and readable the writings of Javad Fazel, and in particular Mohammad Hejazi.[7]

Politics had its own special allure for me. My entry to Rudsar seminary (1961) had coincided with the death of Ayatollah Borujerdi, the emergence of the crisis of *marja'iyat*, a relative opening up of the political climate and the resumption of the activities of political parties. Then the regime announced a programme of social, political, economic and cultural reforms, later called 'The White Revolution' or 'The Revolution of the Shah and People', to be implemented under the direct leadership of the shah. The opposition of most national and religious political parties, and the intense opposition of the ulama to these reforms, ended in the arrest of a number of national and religious leaders in 1962 and 1963. Then came the uprising of 15 Khordad 1342 (5 June 1963) and the exile of Ayatollah Khomeini – the militant leader of the clergy – to Turkey until 1964. It was in such a climate that, as a teenager, my eyes were opened to politics and society. In 1962, I became a follower of Ayatollah Khomeini[8] and one of his most passionate advocates. In Qom, as this tendency [militant Shiism] grew stronger, intellectual and political activities naturally intensified.

Between 1965 and 1971, nevertheless, I was largely occupied with my seminary studies, and with reading other things. The writings of Mehdi Bazargan, Dr Sahabi, Ayatollah Taleqani, Ayatollah Motahhari and Allameh Tabataba'i were widely read;[9] and I think that there is not a single book or article that they published in those

---

[6] In pre-revolutionary Iran, *Zan-e Ruz* (*Woman of Today*) was the most popular women's magazine and had a modernist agenda; it ran a campaign to reform Islamic family laws, in particular men's unilateral right to divorce or *talaq*. Ayatollah Motahhari's response to this campaign later became the official gender discourse of the Islamic Republic, see Mir-Hosseini (1999: 23-25).

[7] Authors of popular novels and short stories, often serialized in magazines.

[8] That is, he chose Khomeini as his *marja'-e taqlid*.

[9] All key figures in religious modernism at the time, see Chapter 1.

years that I did not read. I also liked the *Maktab-e Eslam*[10] of Mr Makarem's group and read it regularly [...][11] We used to form study groups to do research and write articles, including one [group] that did studies on other religions.

I was not content with the seminary curriculum and its usual teachings and I was constantly in search of new knowledge. I looked for this knowledge mainly outside the seminary. One of the centres that offered new ideas was the *Hoseyniyeh Ershad* of Tehran, which had begun its activities in 1966. The main speakers there were usually clerics but the lectures often dealt with current intellectual issues and the speakers were well informed. Thus, as far as possible, I tried to attend all the lectures and seminars held in *Ershad*. It was there, in either 1969 or 1970, that I came to know Dr Ali Shariati. I had already read his book *Eslam-shenasi*,[12] published in Mashhad, but I had not met him in person. The first of his lectures that I heard was 'Hejrat va tamaddon' [*Migration and civilization*]. I was captivated by Shariati's personality, thought, mind and language. When Shariati moved to Tehran and began his '*Eslam-shenasi*' lecture series[13] and his regular seminars, *Ershad* became a warm centre of faith, thought and struggle; and my attendance there increased in the years 1970-72. Later (after *Ershad*'s closure in November 1972 and Shariati's imprisonment) I became even more passionate than before about studying his work and began propagating his ideas by distributing his writings and cassettes [of his lectures]. I also organized lectures and educational classes about Shariati for young people, which continued until the revolution.

For me and my generation, Shariati represented a harmonious mixture of 'faith', 'thought' and 'struggle'. In other words, Shariati combined 'reason' and 'passion' in a way that influenced everyone. For him, 'thought' (*andisheh*) was as important as jihad against despotism, colonialism and exploitation. Although Shariati's basic message was that awareness and reason take precedence over passion and struggle, or should come before any kind of political or social revol-

---

[10] This journal (full title *Dars-ha'i az Maktab-e Eslam, Lessons from the Doctrine/School of Islam*) started publication in 1958 under the auspices of the Qom seminaries and the editorship of Naser Makarem Shirazi (by 2005 an influential *marja'*, close to the conservatives). It opposed Shariati and in 1969 published a highly critical review of his *Eslam-shenasi*.

[11] Here Eshkevari lists other journals he used to read.

[12] Shariati (1969).

[13] Shariati (1979) includes translations of some of these lectures.

ution, it was not until some years after the revolution that I came to understand the importance of this – as I will explain later. In 1972, I got married. After our marriage, my propagation activities and my travelling to country towns and villages increased; my wife too, being already a religious person and an activist, began preaching and started holding meetings for women. And it was after 1972 that Iranian society became daily more politicized, the eventual result being the crumbling of the Pahlavi regime and the creation of the Islamic Republic. This politicization had various causes: Shariati's revolutionary teachings, the armed struggle of various Marxist and Islamic groups (the most important being the guerrillas of the Fedayan-e Khalq and the Mojahedin-e Khalq), the spread of the struggles of the clergy, and the close collaboration between young militant students in the seminaries and the universities.

My activities were basically intellectual and cultural but with a strong political aim. In 1970, my first article appeared in *Daneshmand*, a journal published in Tehran [...] [14] In my travels to towns and villages (mostly in the Caspian provinces of East Gilan and West Mazandaran) – largely during the month of Ramadan or the 'Ashura days of Moharram – my main activity consisted of organizing meetings to teach ideological and intellectual issues. Besides the north, the chief arena of intellectual and political activities for my wife and myself was the [central] towns of Arak, Khomeyn, Golpaigan, Garmsar, Semnan and Damghan.

In 1974, I was arrested in Gilan; but I was freed a few months later. Then in 1975 I was seized in Qom and brought to Tehran, where I spent a few months in Komiteh prison.[15] Both times I was released without trial. At the time of the revolution (1977-79) we were on the move. During 1978 our life was especially nomadic, with a baby just a few months old (our son Ruhollah was born in late March 1978), travelling from town to town on our work of propagation. On 11 February [1979], the day of the victory of the revolution and the fall of the Pahlavi regime, we were in Bandar Anzali [a Caspian port, formerly Bandar Pahlavi]. It was one of the most important and unforgettable days of my life. We were in Ramsar on 1 February, the day when the

---

[14] Here Eshkevari lists the journals he contributed to in the 1970s.
[15] Where SAVAK (the Shah's secret police) held political prisoners.

Leader of the Revolution [Khomeini] arrived, another day I count among the sweetest in my life [...][16]

After the victory of the revolution, (along with a friend) I was commissioned by Ayatollah Khomeini's daughter [Zahra Mostafavi] to run Radio Darya ('Sea Radio'), based in Chalus [a coastal town in Mazandaran]. Before the revolution, this station broadcast a special programme for six months of the year (spring and summer) for listeners in Gilan and Mazandaran.[17] We remained there until September, and, in addition to supervising the work of the station, we produced programmes and at times we also acted as presenters.

After this, I returned to the seminary so that I could continue my unfinished studies. Before 1978, of course, I had already completed Intermediate level, and had begun Advanced studies in *fiqh*. But it was not to turn out as I wished. Persuaded by some people and officials of Tonakabon and Ramsar district, I stood for the first Majlis, and I was elected. Thus I stayed in Tehran until 1984 and fulfilled my duties as a member of Majlis. From the outset I was an independent candidate and I kept this independence in the Majlis. I remained neutral during the intense struggles and rivalries between the Islamic Republican Party and the 'Followers of the Imam's Line' on the one hand, and Abol Hasan Bani-Sadr (then president) on the other.[18] A number of us (around 15 deputies) in practice formed a kind of coalition. From a political and factional point of view, we were neutral, but from an intellectual and ideological point of view we were inclined towards 'social democracy'. That is, we believed in freedom and democracy and insisted on upholding them, and at same time we advocated social and economic justice. After 1981, however, freedom and democracy became daily more important to us.

Although I had intended to leave politics and other such activities at the end of the first Majlis and return to Qom, for some reason this did not happen and I stayed in Tehran. However, I did give up politics

---

[16] Here Eshkevari lists the books he published before the revolution: Eshkevari (1974, 1977, 1975, 1978). All of them are out of print, and we have not seen any of them.

[17] Both these Caspian provinces were – and are – destinations for holidaymakers. Before the revolution, the station broadcast pop music and entertainment programmes, and was also popular with locals.

[18] For the dismissal of Bani-Sadr and factionalism in the first Majlis, see for example, Abrahamian (1989: capter 9), Bakhash (1984: 125- 65), Baktiari (1996: 53-98).

and governmental work and I devoted myself to academic, intellectual and cultural activities. This was because after the revolution I came to realize that, as Shariati puts it, 'Any revolution before awareness is a tragedy'; and I saw that the basic problem in the post-revolutionary crisis was theoretical weakness and intellectual immaturity.

After the revolution and during my time in the Majlis, I never abandoned my intellectual and teaching activities. For instance, between autumn 1979 and spring 1980, I published a bi-weekly called *Payam-e Enqelab* [*The Message of the Revolution*], prepared and printed in Qom with the help of some friends, and distributed particularly in northern areas (eastern Gilan and western Mazandaran). In late 1980 and early 1981, I went from Tehran to Semnan to hold sessions for young people – a continuation of my pre-revolutionary activities. I also wrote articles for the Tehran press. My chief press collaboration was with Ms Azam Taleqani [daughter of Ayatollah Taleqani, deputy in the first Majlis, and managing director of the weekly journal *Payam-e Hajer*],[19] for whom I wrote several articles. Among them was a series entitled 'A critique of *Martyr Motahhari: Divulger of Conspiracy*', published as a book.[20] At the same time I attended and lectured at meetings held by Ms Taleqani's Society of Women of the Islamic Revolution (*Jame'eh Zanan-e Enqelab-e Eslami*), and at other cultural centres.

After the end of the first Majlis, on the invitation of Ezzatollah Sahabi, I joined The Publishing Company[21] and worked on cultural matters as editor-in-chief until 1990. The objective was to get closer, through publishing and press activities, to 'the intellectual revolution' in which we believed.

In 1985 I was invited to teach the history of Islam in Allameh Tabataba'i University, which lasted until 1989. After a speech I made at the memorial service for Dr Kazem Sami[22] in November 1988, I was forbidden to teach and left the university.

---

[19] For this journal and its place among the voices of dissent, see Mir-Hosseini (2002a).

[20] Eshkevari (1985). This was a response to an anonymous cleric's compilation of Motahhari's highly critical marginal comments on his copy of Shariati's *Eslam-shenasi*.

[21] *Sherkat-e Sahami-ye Enteshar*, established in 1959 by a group of religious intellectuals close to Bazargan with the aim of making progressive religious books available to the youth and general public.

[22] Kazem Sami, founder of the liberal Islamic JAMA (Liberation Movement of the People of Iran) in 1963, was minister of health in Bazargan's transitional

The same year (1985) I was also invited as a writer to join the Centre for the *Great Encyclopaedia of Islam*, under the directorship of Sayyid Mohammad Kazem Bojnurdi. My work with them continues [...]²³ I have also contributed articles to other encyclopaedias, the *Encyclopaedia of Palestine* and the *Encyclopaedia of Shiism* (of which I was also a member of the editorial board).

Publishing opportunities were limited for people like me in the 1980s, nonetheless I sometimes wrote for dailies like *Keyhan* (when Mr Khatami was director)²⁴ and some other magazines and journals. My most prominent press activity during this era, however, was the publication of a periodical called *Ehya* (Revival), collections of articles that came out in five issues between 1988 and 1990, when the Ministry of Guidance stopped its publication [...]²⁵

In 1992, Sahabi got a licence to publish the journal *Iran-e Farda* (*Iran of Tomorrow*) and I began working with them from the beginning as both a writer and a member of the editorial board, until the journal was closed [in 2000]. I wrote many articles for the journal during these eight years. In the same period, the 1990s, I also sometimes wrote articles for *Kiyan*.

On the whole, during the 1990s my activities increased and diversified, perhaps because of the opening of the cultural and political climate of society and the greater opportunities for activity. Between 1990 and 1996, I held fortnightly meetings at my house attended by a number of young people, for discussions of intellectual and ideological issues. I gave about one hundred talks at those meetings [...]²⁶

During the 1980s and 1990s, the Islamic Association of Engineers (founded in 1957) and the Islamic Association of Physicians (founded in 1958) were the two main venues where I gave numerous lectures. In effect they were two centres for my intellectual and teaching activities.

After 2 Khordad [23 May 1997, Khatami's first election as president], with the new political and cultural conditions and the publication of new newspapers, known as '*Dovvom-e Khordadi* newspapers', my pub-

government; he was then elected to the First Majlis. He was assassinated in 1988, possibly by the security forces.

²³ Here Eshkevari enumerates the articles he wrote for this encyclopedia.

²⁴ *Keyhan* did not then represent the views of hardliners as it does today.

²⁵ Here Eshkevari mentions two translations he did at this time: Eshkevari (1990, 1991).

²⁶ Here Eshkevari lists his books written between 1992 and 1998: Eshkevari (1993, 1997a, 1997b, 1998a, 1998b, 1998c, 2000a, 2000b, 2000c, 2000d).

lishing activity increased too. From the outset (with the launch of *Jame'eh* in winter 1998) to the end of that era (May 2000 and the mass closure of papers), many articles by and interviews with me were printed in these papers (of course mainly in *Jame'eh*, *Tus*, *Neshat* and *'Asr-e Azadegan*).

However, my most significant cultural activity has been the foundation, in 1996, with the help of some friends, of the Dr Ali Shariati Cultural Research Centre. It started operations in 1997, and continues despite many difficulties, financial and otherwise, including the lack of official authorization from the Ministry of Islamic Guidance. I hope that in the future it will be a source of important intellectual and cultural developments.

Since 1996 I have been invited to talk at Iranian cultural centres (Islamic and nationalist) abroad as well as some foreign academic and cultural centres. I have travelled to America, France, Sweden and Germany – most recently for the Berlin Conference, which created a great deal of controversy and led to my arrest and that of several others.

As for my political activities, from 1984 until 1997 these were limited because, on the one hand, political activities generally were restricted, and on the other hand, for me, the expansion of awareness, in other words 'intellectual revolution' and 'cultural development', was a priority. My political activity largely took the form of signing political statements or [open] letters that were issued on certain occasions, signed by independent individuals or those with organizational links with Nationalist-Religious groups. Sometimes I expressed my political views by giving talks or writing critical and social articles. But after 2 Khordad, when the political and cultural climate started to open up, social needs increased and the level of people's demands rose, and like other active personalities of the Nationalist-Religious Alliance, I too intensified my political activities. This I did by speaking or publishing articles in the new newspapers and signing political statements. At the same time, for me, politics has always been secondary to thought and culture. I have chosen [to be involved in] politics for two reasons. First, I feel it is my religious and national duty to the people, and secondly because I believe that, for a thinking person, intellectual development, and even the acquisition of intellectual awareness, do not happen in an ivory tower, in isolation, in the world of the mind or in the world of books and libraries. Rather it is through direct contact with realities, through experience of change, through unmediated appreciation of the needs, pains and demands of society, that an intellectual can understand the problems of his time. It is also in the context of political and social activities that an intellectual can bring the element of 'self-consciousness' to the people, and help others to such consciousness.

On the other hand, the intellectual should not stop at the mere act of thinking but must endeavour to deal with obstacles that impede the path of people's freedom and awareness. He should try to remove such obstacles and if necessary even to assume executive and practical tasks.

Besides, in my thirty-year intellectual-political life my way has been that of trying to 'free' people from all types of bondage through the creation and expansion of 'awareness'. In this course, in my view, 'thought' and 'society', 'politics' and 'ethics' are intertwined; and there is a dialectical relationship between 'theory' and 'practice'. The project of 'religious intellectualism' is the most suitable option for the realization of the weighty ideal of 'freedom' and 'awareness' for the people.

'The calm of this house remains' by Lili Farhadpoor

Journalists who went to Hojjat ol-Eslam Hasan Yousefi Eshkevari's home to get news or interviews – or students and youngsters who were interested in the issues he raised and went to his home, probably for the first time, to ask a question – would be received in a little room filled with well-worn furniture. The first thing that would catch the newcomer's eye in that little reception room was a wooden piano, sitting in a recess between two bookcases full of books. Many of these guests were so amazed by the oddity of a piano in a cleric's house that they probably did not notice Eshkevari's wife, who was busy entertaining them; a petite, middle-aged woman, who at first glance looks like any other mother and housewife. However she is a woman with much in her heart that is untold.

Some people think she is a dreamer, others see her as a mystic. Whatever, many of her relatives and friends believe in her premonitions and even the most cautious of them will admit that her dreams come true. Zahra, Yousefi Eshkevari's only daughter, tells how one day her father was discussing the supernatural with a friend, and during their discussion he referred to her mother, hinting that she could make contact with the supernatural! Perhaps this was the only time that Eshkevari referred to his wife's insights. *His manly pride did not let him say more than this; this pride must be respected!*[27]

* * * * *

[27] Italics in this section are all from the original.

Mohtaram Golbaba'i is 54 years old. Twenty-seven years ago she married a young clerical student and moved to Qom. The young student had a small room, with one *zilu*,[28] one straw mat, one rusty coat-hanger for a wardrobe; a fruit-crate in a corner contained pans and dishes, and next to it stood a small primus stove. The only [luxury] the room boasted was a bookcase made of piles of bricks. *Golbaba'i's daughter becomes a preacher's wife!*

The poverty that filled the room brought Mohtaram a strange joy – joy and love, a pure love, a love of God!

I was born into a traditional family. We were not badly off, a middle-class Tehrani family. When I finished my schooling, the family were proud that their daughter had got a [high school] diploma. When I was twenty I began studying religion. I used to attend Mrs Malek's gatherings on Koranic exegesis and I became one of Mrs Kharrazi's students at the Women's Mahdiyeh.[29] We studied Koranic exegesis and *towzih al-masa'il*.[30] From childhood I had an intense love for God. After I got interested in Sharia matters I chose the chador as hijab. When discussion of marriage came up, I decided to marry a cleric and I was firm about my decision. My family were against it, because at the time most clerics' wives were illiterate; very few educated girls were prepared to marry a cleric, go to Qom and live in poverty. But my mind was made up!

Hasan Yousefi was a young seminary student who came to Tehran from Qom to attend meetings at the *Hoseyniyeh Ershad*. He never missed one of Dr Ali Shariati's lectures. Eshkevari was looking for an educated wife, a woman he could talk to about the books that he was reading and writing. When he was told that there was a girl from Tehran, a high school graduate from a good family who wanted to marry a cleric, he said: 'either she is a very bright girl or she's a dreamer! If she

---

[28] A simple, rough, and cheap flat-woven rug.

[29] The Women's Mahdiyeh (seminary), funded by bazaar merchants, was opened in the late 1960s and gradually became a centre for women religious activists, largely from traditional backgrounds. Mrs Malek's Koranic exegesis classes were particularly popular with young women.

[30] 'Explanation of problems': a class of treatises that a *marja'* produces for his followers.

thinks that marrying a seminary student means having a life similar to that of some clerics who have a lot of worldly things and are honoured and respected, then she is a dreamer. But if she thinks life with a seminary student is a life of the spirit, then she is a very bright girl...'

The girl's maternal uncle introduced them. It was arranged that they should have a meeting for the introduction. When Mohtaram saw her suitor through the window, she hesitated for a moment and remembered her family's ridicule; 'Do I want to walk the streets from now on with this man, with a mullah?' But her hesitation was momentary, and she told herself confidently: 'he will be a bridge for me to reach Him!'

That day, the two talked for two hours, without even looking at each other.[31] The girl had covered her face so that perhaps only a corner of her eye could be seen. Hasan Yousefi had no one in Tehran. Some friends asked in amazement, 'Are you sure you want to marry someone whose face you've never seen?' They even suggested sending a woman acquaintance to look at the bride – what if she were blind or lame! The young student said confidently: 'there is no need, we have talked with each other. That's enough. I liked her!' Mohtaram's two sons and daughter have heard their mother tell the story of that day's talk many times, and can reconstruct it for themselves with the lively imaginations they have inherited from her:

> Bride: I would like to have a very simple life in which there is only love for God.
>
> Groom: I am only a seminary student, and my sole worldly wealth is a cloak and my only capital is a bunch of books. I heard you like reading: what do you read?
>
> Bride: Apart from religious books and the Koran, I also read *Maktab-e Eslam*, which comes from Qom.[32]
>
> Groom: Do you also go to *Hoseyniyeh Ershad*?
>
> Bride: I went once, I didn't like it. A man with no beard and wearing a tie [Shariati] was talking about religion. I found the scene so upsetting that I didn't hear his words; I even fell asleep!
>
> Groom: Is a person's Muslimness in his beard? Is that why you didn't like him?

---

[31] A sign of religiosity: the rules for looking at unrelated persons of the opposite sex are discussed in the above treatises, in the Chapter on Marriage; for a discussion of these rules, see Mir-Hosseini (1999: 26-79).

[32] See note 23 below.

Bride: But you clerics yourselves say from the pulpit that shaving
the beard is a forbidden act. If someone is a believer, he must
follow these instructions.

Groom: Who is your *marja'-e taqlid?*

Bride: Ayatollah Shahrudi.[33] What about you?

Groom: Ayatollah Khomeini! ...

A ring, a watch, a white dress and a black chador ... and the marriage
was arranged. *May it be a bridge to You; Amen!*

* * * * *

Mr Eshkevari[34] and I were walking down an alley. I don't know
where it was. I saw a figure covered head-to-toe in black
approaching him from behind; a hand came out with a dagger
about to strike him ... but another hand appeared and grabbed
the hand holding the dagger ... I asked 'who are you'? He said,
'I am only carrying out orders!' Then a house appeared, full of
black figures, covered up ...

Eshkevari's wife had this nightmare after the serial killings and before
the Information Ministry's announcement and the arrest of Sa'id
Emami's gang.[35] She told her husband confidently that the veil would
soon be removed from this secret, but other veils would remain! *'His
pride would not let him admit that he believes in my dreams!'*

News of the serial killings had sown the seeds of fear everywhere.
The rumour of a long list of future targets – and that Eshkevari's name
was on the list – heightened the Eshkevari family's fear. At this time,
Mohtaram in practice became her husband's full-time bodyguard. She
went everywhere with him. Saying that Ruhollah, their eldest son, had
to attend his classes at the university was only an excuse. All the family
recognized that their mother was the best and most powerful
protector. She believed that her faith would be hers and her family's
guardian: *no power can upset the calm of this house!*

---

[33] A non-political, traditionalist cleric.

[34] In traditional Iranian families, wives commonly refer to their husbands in
this way.

[35] She means the assassinations of political dissidents by security forces in
autumn 1998, see Chapter 1.

Those who knew the Eshkevari family from afar, knew how the lady of this house went out with her basket to the local shops several times a day, to buy necessities; and like all Iranian housewives she worked all day long to make her family happy and comfortable:

> I do everything in the house. I run around all day so that the rest can get to work. I do all this with love. I like to see Mr Eshkevari sitting and working at his desk. Ruhollah is a student and Zahra finished high school this year and is now preparing for university entrance exams. Mahmud is in the second year [of 4] of high school. This piano is a loan. A friend lent it to us and said that whenever we could afford it, we should pay an amount equal to its price, 500,000 tomans [about $600], into a charitable fund.[36] I play it a bit, and now my daughter continues. Our children are free to make their own decisions. They choose whether to do their prayers; neither their father nor I have ever forced them to do anything. Eshkevari is a very principled and moderate person and a real family man. He used to work at home until noon, and then three times a week he would go to the Research Office. This house is so filled with love and calm that wherever the kids and Mr Eshkevari go, they are keen to get home, even to have their meals.

Mohtaram's birthday is 11 February[37] and all the children of this family are in some ways children of the revolution. Ruhollah was born in 1979, and his name is a sign of the same year and of their attachment to Ayatollah [Ruhollah] Khomeini. Zahra was born on 28 June 1981, that is the day of the Islamic Republican Party incident.[38] Mahmud was born in September on the anniversary of Ayatollah [Mahmud] Taleqani's death, which is why he was called Mahmud.

In the years before the revolution – before Ruhollah was born – Mohtaram had lived with the constant fear of her husband's arrest and persecution by the shah's secret police. Twice he was arrested and she had the experience of seeing him behind bars. The poverty and fear of her life in those years were accompanied by the pain of losing the first child of the new family. In 1978-79, in the throes of the revolution, Yousefi Eshkevari travelled to different parts of the country to preach

---

[36] *Sanduq-e qarz ol-hasaneh*, a religious fund that provides interest-free loans.
[37] The day the Revolutionary forces took power in 1979.
[38] 7 Tir, the day the IRP headquarters was bombed, see Chapter 1.

and teach. He suggested to his young wife that on these travels she too should organize meetings and talks for women. *What should I say in these meetings?* The answer was simple: whatever she had learned in her own Koran and Sharia classes. Mohtaram went to these meetings with her baby – Ruhollah – and delivered sermons. This pattern continued until Zahra was born. Yousefi Eshkevari was then a deputy in the First Majlis:

> It was then that the symptoms of diabetes became visible – because he was boiling with agitation. Eshkevari is one of the few diabetics whose illness has psychological, not hereditary causes! Overwork and stress are poison for him. It's now three years since he started to inject insulin. If his food is late, he can get an attack. Every morning at 8.30 he has an insulin injection. He must have lots of milk and fruit. We usually have lunch at 1 pm; if it is a quarter of an hour late, he goes pale and then I know that he might collapse. Each time he goes out, I must put sweet things in his briefcase so that he does not faint on the way. Once because of high blood sugar he bled from the eyes and had to have surgery. Usually he faints from low blood sugar one or two nights a week and he must be quickly attended to and given sugary substances.

Mohtaram has all these worries. After the arrest of some of the participants in the Berlin Conference, when she heard that [Akbar] Ganji and [Shahla] Lahiji[39] got their medicines late in prison, she thought to herself, *What happens if Eshkevari is jailed?* Quite possibly he would die.

* * * * *

Before the Berlin Conference Yousefi Eshkevari had been invited to conferences in America, Sweden and France, and everything had gone well. The Berlin Conference was to be combined with other invitations, a trip of three months. In recent times, too much work – including writing articles for newspapers and various lectures – as well as political anxieties, were the same deadly poison for Eshkevari.

---

[39] Two of the Berlin Conference participants, who had been arrested as soon as they returned to Iran. Eshkevari was still in Europe at the time.

His wife was happy about this trip – *three months of rest and calm, away from crisis!* But she had a dream: *I knew that something was going to happen but I felt sure that it would turn out all right in the end!*

After the second day of the conference, Eshkevari called his family. They remember well what he said: 'they did whatever they wanted!'[40] In order to calm their anxieties he had said that the Iranian women abroad and even the German women had received his talks very well; and Mohtaram had joked in reply, 'lucky me!!'

The day before the broadcast of parts of the Berlin Conference film, one of the morning newspapers had printed something attacking Yousefi Eshkevari and his talk in Berlin. It had even stated that this cleric must be tried and defrocked. They had also announced that the film of the conference would be broadcast. Eshkevari's family sat watching the film with trepidation:

> Broadcasting a film of a cleric's lecture and then showing a dancer dancing! For a second I saw the devil incarnate. I had no doubt that this was devilry. When I saw that scene for a moment I lost my balance; I was stunned, flabbergasted. Then I quickly came to my senses and saw that it was a trick. I had been so upset that I had been taken in by this trick.

In their next telephone call, this time it was the family who expressed their anxiety. Eshkevari was still trying to calm them. He told them about his talk and that what he had said was exactly what he had already said at home in his lectures and articles. His family had to explain that the edited film had raised other problems in Iran, particularly ethical ones. But Eshkevari could not understand what they were talking about, because after the session had been disrupted he had walked out, along with the rest of the panel, and had seen nothing of the dancer dancing or the man undressing!

> After the broadcast of the film, the phone kept ringing – friends, acquaintances, relatives and even strangers, all of them concerned. Some tried to comfort us, others wanted to know what the story was. Some had been taken in by the trickery and were crying; we reassured them and in effect we wiped their tears. Some of our friends told us how their relatives had laughed at

[40] See Chapter 1 for the background to the conference, and Chapter 5 for the disruptions.

them and how they had lost face. My response was: Wait! The truth will out.

But gradually attitudes changed. Mohtaram noticed that people in their neighbourhood, who were mostly from middle or even lower income groups of society, were showing their respect. As soon as they saw her, they prayed for Yousefi Eshkevari. People who had not known their neighbour's full name – since Eshkevari was Yousefi's *shohrat*[41] and not part of his family name – now they all started to greet the little woman with her basket. The grocer put aside cheap rationed items and every day became more and more polite when she bought things from him. Some asked her whether 'Hajji Agha'[42] would come back, or advised that he should not return until things had calmed down.

In response, I always said, of course he'll come back, just as scheduled. Now he is busy. This is his home and he'll never choose anywhere else as his home. He belongs here!

But the situation was rather different at Eshkevari's youngest son's school. The deputy head and his assistant and Mahmud's teachers knew what had happened but advised him not say anything to his classmates so as to avoid trouble and abuse. In fact they kept him well protected. Some time later, Mohtaram understood the reason for this vigilance. The headteacher was sympathetic to those who were opposed to the Berlin Conference participants.

One day I went to Mahmud's school to sort something out to do with his studies. Mahmud is a very gentle and well-behaved boy and the headteacher likes him very much and always talks of him as the best pupil in the school. That day a boy was being questioned in the office for breaking one of the rules; he was defending himself awkwardly and telling lies. The head turned to us and said: 'What times we live in, when these boys can't utter a

---

[41] Many people, especially clerics, have a *shohrat*, a name by which they are popularly known, indicating the place they come from: e.g. Khomeini, Rafsanjani, Khamene'i.
[42] An honorific title, common and fashionable after the revolution, to show respect and religiosity; the person referred to may or may not have made the hajj to Mecca.

single true word, like that mullah who went to Berlin and talked
nonsense and the television showed it!' I wanted to answer him
back but the deputy and the teachers winked at me to say
nothing. I only said: you must be very naïve if you believe that
what's shown on television is all true.

However happy Mohtaram seems with the reactions of her neighbours, friends and acquaintances, she was very much hurt by others:

Before the Berlin Conference the newspapers would not let us
alone. They not only phoned several times a day but most of
Eshkevari's time was taken up by writing the stuff they commissioned. They burdened him with so much work, and no
payment for it! But after this incident – and even before the closure of the newspapers – suddenly all fell silent; they didn't raise
a finger to defend him. It wasn't only him: the papers forgot the
two ladies who were arrested and jailed too – not a word.[43]

Meanwhile Mohtaram recalls a dream that she had twenty-seven years
ago – before she married Eshkevari – a dream that after all these years
may have been embellished by her imaginative mind.

I was flying in the sky. Suddenly I landed in the middle of the
goldsmith's bazaar. Gold and jewellery glittered and shone
everywhere. Everywhere I looked was bathed in light. All the
shopkeepers were standing at the doors of their shops, looking at
me. They were all women! I was shown to the largest goldsmith's
shop. Inside, the women assistants brought me precious silk cloth
and put it on my head. I asked: 'Am I getting married?' They
said: 'Don't ask!' Then they looked at each other and said: 'What
a nice family! How much they love each other and what a
beautiful bridge they will make…'

---

[43] She is referring to Mehrangiz Kar and Shahla Lahiji, the two women at the
Berlin Conference who were in detention then; there is also an implied
criticism of the reformist press for not taking up the cause of those participants
of the conference who were not 'insiders', that is, religious dissidents like
Eshkevari or 'secularists' like Kar and Lahiji. At the time the press was under
pressure and the editors were most concerned with the survival of their
newspapers.

The day I went to see Eshkevari's family, after an hour of conversation the doorbell rang. It was one of the neighbours who came to say that it had just been announced on the News that the Berlin Conference attendees who had been summoned by the court, but had not yet reported, were now considered fugitives. Ruhollah and Zahra were upset by the news. Zahra kept repeating 'Fugitive!? My father is not a fugitive!' and Ruhollah was trying to give a political analysis of the situation. As they were talking about it, Mohtaram was anxiously observing the smallest details of their actions –

No power can disrupt the calm of my house!

She tried to calm the children down. She said with dignity: 'A voice is coming into this house, a voice that says: *we will guard this bridge!*'

'Preface' to *Reason at the Feast of Religion*

For about two centuries Eastern societies, among them the Muslims, have been acquainted with the Western world and new developments and find themselves faced with various problems and dilemmas. It has been widely felt that some of the consequences of modernity and the products of the New World are incompatible with religion and piety, and especially with some of the religious laws of Islam. Muslim thinkers have tried to respond to the developments of the new age, and in effect somehow to resolve the problem of this incompatibility between religion and the fruits of modernity. It can be said that the conflict between Islam and Western modernity has been the most critical and fateful social problem that the Muslim world has faced in the last 150 years. This is so serious that the destiny of Muslim societies now depends on the outcome of the confrontation.

Perhaps the task is not so difficult for some Muslims, notably for those Muslim intellectuals and modernists who have found the solution in a personal Islam, and who try to interpret Islam, like Christianity, in terms of an inner relationship between the 'individual' and 'God'. Either they do not recognize a social role for religion and religious law, or, under the influence of a thoroughly traditional Shiism, they consider the full implementation of religious law to belong to the era of the imamate. In any case, by drawing sharp lines between religious and worldly, sacred and profane, spiritual and legal, ethical and political, rational and social, and so on, on the one hand, they create a real contradiction [between them], and on the other hand, they put the entire society and the social order at the disposal of a non-religious government. Ultimately, by declaring a cease-fire between religion and the world, and by making religiosity personal, they submit to the conventions of the time, for a peaceful and trouble-free existence.

The thinkers of this group may entertain some criticisms of the modern world and express their dissatisfaction with life under modernity, but they have no other option than submission and obedience to the indisputable rule of modernity and modernism in the public sphere. Nevertheless, these thinkers are also faced with some serious and unavoidable questions. For instance, they must explain how and by what magic can a religion like Islam, a book like the Koran, a prophet like Muhammad and an Imam like Ali be simply turned into Christianity, the Bible, Christ and the Pope? In any case, by (temporarily) avoiding the question, these Muslims see no need to provide serious answers to the new issues arising from the conflict between Islam and the West. In so doing, they think they can both preserve the purity of their own religion and see their own world prosper.

But those who have a social approach to religion, and who also recognize a social function for Islam, face more difficulties, and must essentially find answers for more numerous and more serious questions. This is particularly so in a world where, under the impact of Western modernity and the secularism and laicism of the new age, people are trying to break the mould in all fields, and to purge society, politics and government of any ideology, even of religion and belief, so that the 'God-centredness' of religion gives way to the 'Human-centredness' of modernity, and humankind becomes the pole and centre of the universe.

To speak of social religion, and especially to believe in the social and political function of religion and religiosity, poses a huge challenge. After the collapse of the Soviet Union, the declaration of the end of the era of ideology, and the experience of Islamic fundamentalism, such a stance appears to be a grave error, an unacceptable thought, or at the very least dangerous; and defending it is difficult and goes against the discourse of the time.

Whatever the case, those who regard Islam as a modern social movement believe that the essential truth of a religion like Islam cannot but be social, and must encompass both social and personal life. For them, any attempt to Christianize Islam, or to interpret Islam as a personal faith, is to return to the pre-constitutional era in Iran, which is neither possible nor desirable. There are many problems and questions for which relevant and firm answers must be provided. During the last two hundred years, and more specifically the past half-century, in

Iran and the world of Islam, great thinkers and theorists have tried to find answers and left a valuable heritage. Today we owe them much, but the fact is that the current conditions of the world, and in particular the recent developments in Iran, present us with new questions, and have made the defence of Islam as an ideology immensely difficult. For this reason, solving the intellectual and social problems of Muslims (including those in Iran) demands a serious struggle and re-doubled efforts.

In spite of this, and as the pioneers of contemporary Muslim religious and social reform movements have said, we believe that conditions will not change for us Muslims and Iranians unless there is a fundamental transformation in our attitudes and ethics. In other words, we will get nowhere unless we turn from superstition to truth, from irrationality to rationality, from blinkeredness to awareness, from ignorance to knowledge. In one word, we must move from backwardness to progress. From a position of weakness and an attachment to tradition, and from being infatuated or intimidated by modernity and the West, we must find a position of moral courage and the firm resolution to embark on change. Through awareness, 'production' and 'foundation' (two important principles for building the future) we must free ourselves from both traditionalism and the absolute domination of the modern world and the New World Order.

It must be noted that during these two centuries we have neither stayed entirely in the world of tradition (which would have been impossible), nor become completely modern and Western (equally impossible). Nor were we able to design and implement the solution [offered] by Muslim intellectuals (such as Sayyid Jamal [Afghani], Muhammad Iqbal, Shariati), based on a kind of indigenous modernity. Therefore Islamic societies today face both a huge conceptual confusion and social disintegration. On one side they are threatened by fundamentalism and anti-modernism, and on the other, infatuation with the products of modernity brings Muslims nothing but the loss of their historical, national and religious identity.

In any event, we believe that the basic solution to the dead-end of this backwardness is the project of the New [Religious] Thinkers. The successive stages in the realization of this project can be stated as: 1) critique of tradition, 2) critique of modernity, 3) clarification and consolidation of the basic cultural sources of relevant and valid elements of both tradition and modernity, 4) combining these fundamental elements into a modern and efficient intellectual and ideological system, and 5) designing a kind of indigenous (Iranian-Islamic) modernity.

As one of the advocates of this project, and a follower of the path of social Islam, inspired by the New [Religious] Thinking, for two decades I have tried, to the best of my modest scientific and practical abilities, to shed light on this project or at least to clarify certain aspects of it for the youth and for new learners. Some sixteen books and hundreds of articles that I have published are evidence for this claim.

3

'Islamic Democratic Government'

Editors' introduction

Islamic democratic government' (*hokumat-e demokratik-e eslami*) is a
chapter from the book *Religion and Government*, published by the
Islamic Association of Engineers in 1999.[1] The book consists of
edited versions of papers delivered in a seminar series organized by the
association in 1995. Eshkevari was a member of the organizing
committee for the seminar and helped with preparing the proceedings
for publication.

This text contains the gist of Eshkevari's political theory and his
arguments for the compatibility of Islam and democracy. It forms part
of a debate about the democratization of religious discourse that took
place on the eve of the emergence of the reformist movement, but has
its roots in political and intellectual developments several decades
earlier, which we now trace.

The forum

The Islamic Association of Engineers, founded in 1957, is one of a
number of professional bodies that played an important role in shaping
the Islamic ideology of the 1979 revolution.[2] The most distinguished of
the founding members was Mehdi Bazargan, also a founder of the
Liberation Movement (1961), and prime minister of the provisional
government after the revolution.[3] Drawing its inspiration from Islamic
modernism, the association has served as a forum for debating key
issues among religious thinkers and activists. In the pre-revolutionary
era it was a platform for religious activism. Its main concerns were to

[1] Anjoman (1999: 285-311).
[2] See Chapter 1.
[3] For Bazargan's intellectual and political trajectory, see Chehabi (1990: 50-
100), Dabashi (1993: 324-66), Jahanbakhsh (2001: 80-112), Eshkevari (1997a,
2000). In his two-volume study of the life and works of Bazargan, Eshkevari
tells the story of the formation of the association (1997a: 233-37).

find ways to curb the power of the secular Pahlavi state and to provide solutions for the social and political problems that face the believer in modern times. This involved a two-pronged approach: to draw on religious faith and organizations to bring about social and political change, and to offer an Islamic ideology that could offset the attractions of competing ideologies – notably communism.

In 1961, following the death of Ayatollah Borujerdi, who had led the Shia community as the sole *marja'-e taqlid* for 14 years, the association planned a series of meetings to discuss what it considered to be a pressing question: 'the selection of *marja'-e taqlid* and the role of the clergy,' that is, the nature of supreme authority in Shia Islam and its political significance.[4] The papers prepared for the meetings were published as a book. Bazargan was one of the contributors, and the only non-cleric; others included leading modernist clerics such as Allameh Tabataba'i, Morteza Motahhari, Mahmud Taleqani and Mohammad Beheshti. The book,[5] and the debates that it launched, marked a defining moment in rethinking the relation between religious and political authority in the Shia context. Two other important pre-revolutionary books – Motahhari's *The Mutual Service of Islam and Iran* and Mohammad Taqi Ja'fari's *Sources of Islamic Jurisprudence*[6] – had their roots in discussions organized by the association.

In addition to these occasional meetings, the association established annual lectures by Bazargan to celebrate the appointment of Muhammad as Prophet (*jashn-e mab'as*), some of which appeared in print. In each lecture Bazargan took as text a segment of verse 2 of Sura Al-Jum'ah, known as the *be'sat* (appointment) verse. He had begun these annual lectures some years earlier, for the Islamic Association of Students, and he continued them even when he was in prison. One of his important books (*Appointment and Ideology*), which sets out the basis of an Islamic ideology, originated in one of these lectures, prepared in 1964 while he was in prison; after his release he developed it in his 1966 lecture, before turning it into a book.[7]

---

[4] Anjoman (1999: 5). Lambton writes that the seminar did not take place because of 'financial and other difficulties' (1964: 102), but it seems that several sessions were held (Dabashi 1993: 161-2, Eshkevari 1997a: 339-40).

[5] Anjoman (1962).

[6] Motahhari (1960), Ja'fari (1960).

[7] Bazargan (1966). For analysis of this book, see Jahanbakhsh (2001: 99-106), Chehabi (1990: 67-8), Eshkevari (1999a: 414-15).

After the revolution, the association continued its activities and remained a platform for religious modernism, this time in the context of the Islamic state. As the revolutionary fervour subsided, disillusionment with the outcome of the revolution and the policies of the government grew. Ayatollah Khomeini's death, and the failure of the Islamic ideology to deliver, made it urgent to revisit the issue of the relation between political and religious power. Thus, 'after the victory of the revolution, in line with the needs of society', the association held two research sessions on the themes of *'velayat-e faqih'* and 'The history and destiny of the clergy'.[8]

The new debate

The turning point for the association came in January 1992, when Bazargan delivered his annual *jashn-e mab'as* lecture under the title, 'The afterlife and God: the only purpose of the appointment of prophets'. In 1985, having completed his commentary on the *be'sat* verse, he had begun to speak of the 'Unsaid of *be'sat*', exploring the theme of worldly power and government and stating that they are not part of the mission of the prophets.[9] His 1992 lecture took this new theme to its logical conclusion. Now he declared: 'The only purpose of sending prophets is to alert people to the existence of God and prepare them for the hereafter, not to tell them how to conduct their politics and run their affairs in this world.'

This was seen a radical departure from his earlier stance, as questioning the religious legitimacy of the project that members of the association, like many other religious intellectuals and activists, had pursued in the pre-revolutionary era. To debate the issues raised, the following year the association organized a seminar series for a critical evaluation of the lecture. Bazargan welcomed the idea and participated in the eight seminars held between October and December 1993. In the first seven sessions there were sixteen speakers, two supporting Bazargan's position, fourteen opposing it; in the final session he responded to his critics. In 1998, after Bazargan's death, the association printed his original lecture, accompanied by some of the critical responses. His text remained the same as the 1992 lecture, except that

---

[8] Anjoman (1999: 6). The proceedings of these meetings were not published.
[9] Bazargan (1998: 7) – from the Preface.

the word 'only' was omitted from the title – the only change Bazargan made in response to the seminar discussions.[10]

Meanwhile, the theme of Bazargan's lecture was taken up by *Kiyan*, which had become the main forum for airing the views of Dr Abdolkarim Soroush. What Bazargan said in his lecture was in line with the argument that Soroush and his co-thinkers had been developing as a critique of the ideologization of religion and its use as political tool and a legitimizing force.

In summer 1992, a few months after Bazargan's lecture, Soroush too questioned the project of political Islam, and in three lectures delivered in the Imam Sadeq mosque he offered a forceful critical analysis of Ali Shariati's project. He pointed out a central contradiction in Shariati's thought that might explain why events did not turn out as Shariati and those who believed in political Islam intended. On the one hand Shariati wanted society and religion to be ideological, which calls for an official class of interpreters; on the other hand, he was against the clergy and wanted an Islam without clerics. In ideologizing religion Shariati did not intend to foster a closed, obedient and brainwashed society; but, Soroush reminded his audience, at times one must separate the soundness of a political theory from the intentions of its producer. A theory has its own independent life, its own logic, and can have consequences not intended or even anticipated by its makers.[11]

---

[10] Bazargan (1998). The Preface (signed by the association) gives an account of the seminar. In October 1993, Bazargan sent the text of his lectures to Ayatollah Montazeri and asked for his comments; Montazeri responded that he disagreed, insisting that Islam and politics are inseparable. In November 1994, the association invited Montazeri to the seminar (see correspondence in Montazeri 2003: Appendices 60 & 61). Eshkevari's critique (he was one of the speakers) also appears in the book. He has given his own account of the seminar and an assessment of Bazargan's lecture in his biography (2000a, pp. 561-8), and also in a later article (2003a) in a special issue of the journal *Nameh* devoted to the revolution and Bazargan.

[11] These lectures were published as Soroush (1993); see Jahanbakhsh (2001: 151-53). In 1995, in an interview intended for a special publication on the anniversary of Shariati's death, Eshkevari refuted Soroush's critique: religion and ideology cannot be separated; Soroush has taken Shariati's work out of context and his rejection of religion as ideology is itself an ideology. This was eventually published as a chapter ('A clarification of Soroush's *Richer than Ideology*') in Eshkevari (1998b), a collection of papers on Shariati.

Meanwhile *Kiyan* 11 (spring 1993) featured two articles on the project of Islamic modernism and the perils of mixing religion with politics. The first was an editorial interview and discussion with Bazargan, entitled 'The route of contemporary religious thought: a conversation with Mehdi Bazargan'. The second was Soroush's 'Religious democratic government?' which comprises the texts of two lectures given in two different fora. Soroush makes a distinction between two different understandings of religion, which in turn shape two different types of religious society: *fiqh*-based and faith-based. While the first is incompatible with democratic principles and institutions, the second cannot be anything but democratic.

These two articles opened a lively debate on Islam and democracy that continued, notably in *Kiyan* but also in other fora, including the 1995 seminar of the Association of Engineers, where the text of this chapter was first delivered. Since Soroush's article is available in English and his views on the issue have been widely treated,[12] we focus here on the 'Conversation with Bazargan' as background to Eshkevari's article.

Bazargan's critique

The *Kiyan* discussion with Bazargan was prefaced by a short note that reads like an apology to him, seeking amends. It begins with an acknowledgement of his contribution to political thought and life in the past fifty years, and ends with an admission of the error of not having supported his vision of a liberal and democratic Islam and his politics of moderation in the early years of the Islamic Republic.

> Now that the [revolutionary] fervour has subsided and fiery radicalism is over, and also the direction of social developments has become evident, many are now trying to ask for his forgiveness, especially the young generation who [then] attacked his policies.[13]

---

[12] Soroush (2000b). For his notion of 'religious democratic government', see Jahanbakhsh (2001: 153-62), Sadri (2002), Vahdat (2002), Vakili (1996).

[13] *Kiyan* 11, p. 2. Student leaders at the time harshly criticized Bazargan and the policies of his provisional government for not being 'revolutionary' enough; 13 years later, some of them were writing in *Kiyan*, or were close to other reformist groups.

In the course of the interview, Bazargan reiterates the argument of his 1992 lecture, but this time more explicitly. Reflecting on the development of modern Islamic thought in Iran, to which he has been a key contributor, he points out that it confused religion with politics and expected the former to provide solutions for the problems of this world. The hope of bettering this world, he argues, is an idea taken from European thought, with its concern for the progress and improvement of individual and collective life. What is ignored is that, in all monotheist religions,

> the purpose and reason for sending prophets is nothing but introducing humankind to ideas of God and the hereafter; or, in Koranic terms, it was and is nothing but the hereafter and God. Building [this] world and the correct handling of personal and social life are left to us. At the same time, certain limits and regulations are devised for worldly relations and affairs with a view to ensuring eternal happiness [in the other world] and preventing any deviation in the movement towards God. Following them reduces the hardship and dangers of this world, and the pains of oppression and corruption in life. With charity, compassion, love and helping people – which are the essence of divine worship – the doors of abundance and happiness will be opened to human societies.[14]

Mistaking religion for ideology is one of the main reasons for the failure of modern Islamic thought to bring about the needed reforms.

> It you take from religion its divine authenticity and its otherworldly purpose, turn it into a human school of thought and use it for this-worldly purposes, nothing will be left of it. It will be no good for this world and of no use for the other world.[15]

In clear terms, Bazargan denies that Islam has anything to offer to Muslims seeking guidance on how to build a political system:

> one should not turn to religion for bettering life and running the world. The Prophet himself said that there is no need for it; what

---

[14] Bazargan (1993: 8).
[15] Ibid.

causes ruin in [this] world is oppression and injustice: a country survives with heresy but not with oppression.[16]

Basing political legitimacy on religious grounds, he continues, sooner or later will result in oppression, and the lesson of history is that:

> Wherever religion and government (even ideology and state) are merged and put in the hands of one ruler, people are deprived of freedom of opinion and the will to manage their affairs. It is always religion that loses, not government. People's faith and God's religion – in general, the affairs of both this world and the other – fall into the hands of someone who is ready and waiting with money and power.[17]

In his critique of the dangers of using Islam as a political tool, Bazargan does not mince words:

> Until now, people from socially aware and religious classes saw themselves as under attack by foreign cultural and intellectual forces whose impact they saw as the cause of the weakening or destruction of faith. But now there are [kinds of] weakening and destruction that largely stem from the revolution and its internal impact. They have seen such a face of Islam and Muslimness, of those who claim to act in the name of religion and government, as they have been presented to the world, that they have come to doubt their own religious beliefs and knowledge.[18]

Citing a Koranic verse in which the Prophet is assured that, when people see his victories, they will join the religion of God, Bazargan continues with a veiled reference to the institution of *velayat-e faqih*, which conservatives consider to be an article of faith and the continuation of the Prophet's mission:

> Now, with the claim of the continuation of the [Prophet's] mission, we can see how people are leaving religion in their masses. What hatred, what enmity, and what massacre against Islam and Muslims! On the other hand, as it was believed and

[16] *Al-mulk yabqi ma' al-kufr va la yabqi ma' al-zulm* [original footnote]. Ibid. p. 9.
[17] Ibid, pp. 10-11.
[18] Ibid.

claimed that religion could improve life in this world, and the opposite turned out to be the case, many believers have lost their faith and interest in religion.[19]

In the light of these developments, Bazargan sees the task and mission of religious thinkers in post-revolutionary Iran to be that of finding ways to return to the authentic message of Islam. In the first place, there is a need to understand and analyse the reasons why people have been turning away from Islam, and then to revive their faith.

The seminar: Reassessing Islam and government

It was against this background that, in September 1994, the association decided to organize a seminar series to explore the ideas articulated by Bazargan and Soroush. The key issue that 'occupies the minds of religious thinkers and educated Muslims', its organizers stated, is that of 'the relation between religion and government'.[20] By now the critique of religious government, so forcefully articulated by Bazargan in his 1992 lecture, had broadened. The debate generated by Soroush's initial article on the possibilities of cohabitation between Islam and democracy was no longer confined to the *Kiyan* circle. It had been taken up in various fora, opening a new chapter in Islamic political thought in Iran.

In November, the association invited thirty religious 'thinkers and researchers' to prepare talks, asking them to consider five alternative political theories, which represent the complete range of available perspectives on relations between religion and government:

1. Sovereignty (*hakemiyat*) belongs to *fuqaha* elected by the people but the opinion of the *vali-ye faqih* is above that of the people and the law (absolute *velayat-e faqih*)
2. Sovereignty belongs to *fuqaha* elected by the people, but their powers are limited by the constitution as ratified by the people ([constitutional] *velayat-e faqih*)
3. Sovereignty belongs to the people provided that laws are not in contradiction with religious [Sharia] criteria (Na'ini's theory of secular government).
4. Sovereignty of religious values by means of sovereignty of the people (religious democratic government).

---

[19] Ibid, p. 11.
[20] Anjoman (1999: 6).

5. Separation of religion from government (liberalism and secularism).[21]

Before the seminar could begin its work, Bazargan's death on 18 January 1995 became the occasion for another appraisal of the project of political Islam.[22] In a memorial gathering for Bazargan in the *Hoseyniyeh Ershad* – the very place where he and Shariati and other religious modernists used to speak before the revolution and one of the fora where the notion of political Islam was propagated – Soroush forcefully denounced that very project and defined the mission of religious intellectuals to be that of freeing religion from politics, as:

> [a] society in which religion becomes the tool of oppression and humans are crushed and deprived is more sinister than a society without religion, where the oppressor does not commit his criminal acts in the name of God and does not attribute them to religion.

Soroush argued that Bazargan too reached this conclusion towards the end of his life, as evident in his 1992 lecture. His death, he stated rhetorically, marked the passing of the era of infatuation with religious ideology:

> Our religious intellectualism, which has so far been trying to use religion to better the world or to make it fit for the world, must now free it from the clutches of the world and its concerns … Bazargan was once infatuated with religious ideology, but his death has put an end to that idea. His death is a symbol of the death of that idea. But unlike other politicians or religion-mongers, he did not want to benefit from religion for himself, but assumed that religion was for this world; as soon as he realized that this is not the case, he abandoned that idea.

---

[21] Anjoman (1999: 7).
[22] Ten days earlier, though very ill, Bazargan gave his last annual *be'sat* lecture, on '*Be'sat* and freedom'. He died on his way to hospital in Switzerland.

The text of Soroush's speech in the *Hoseyniyeh Ershad* appears in *Kiyan* 23 (winter 1995), under a title that puns on *bazargan*, which in Persian means 'trader': 'He who was a trader [only] by name'.[23]

Eshkevari's contributions to the seminar

The seminar opened in April 1995 with two speakers. The first was Mostafa Katira'i, a member of the association, who gave an overview of the seminar's objectives, then surveyed the evolution of the Islamic theory of the state from the Occultation of the twelfth Imam to the Islamic Republic, remarking on the conflict between traditional *fiqh* and democratic ideals that surfaced during the Constitutional Revolution and remained unresolved. Quoting Soroush, Katira'i sarcastically declares that Fazlollah Nuri was right to declare constitutionalism to be opposed to Sharia; he understood the project of modernity and rejected it. Na'ini, on the other hand, did not really understood the project and tried to make a match that was in line neither with *fiqh* nor with modern ideas. The second speaker was Eshkevari, who gave a more detailed critical analysis of Na'ini's argument for the compatibility of the Sharia and modern government.[24]

The seminar continued for another 16 sessions, for three hours each Thursday evening (ending on 13 September).[25] On 4 July Eshkevari delivered his paper on 'Islamic democratic government'. Here, while denying that Islam prescribes any specific form of government, he made a strong case for the fourth political theory. He engaged with Bazargan's rejection of Islamic ideology. Another target was Soroush's critique of Shariati's ideological Islam, and his vision of faith-based Islam primarily concerned with the individual. While sharing their assessment of the experience of Islamic government in Iran, Eshkevari objected to their attempts to distance religion from politics and tried to redeem the project of political Islam.[26]

---

[23] Soroush (1995). Many rejected Soroush's reading of Bazargan's 1992 lecture; for example, in the same issue of *Kiyan*, Gholam Abbas Tavassoli, a university professor close to Bazargan, denied the existence of any chasm between his earlier and later perspectives on the relation between religion and politics (Tavassoli 1995).

[24] Katira'i (1999), Eshkevari (1999).

[25] Other speakers included prominent Islamic intellectuals such as Soroush, Mohammad Mojtahed-Shabestari, Ezzatollah Sahabi, Mohsen Kadivar, Ebrahim Yazdi and Habibollah Peyman.

[26] Some of Eshkevari's arguments in this chapter are to be found in his other writings, notably in 'The paradox of Islam and democracy?' (1994), written in

'Islamic democratic government'

Background and significance of the religion and government debate

In Islam and in the history of Muslims, the problem of government and the relationship between government and religion have had a special importance and role from the outset. The reason is that the Prophet himself, as the founder of the religion and the messenger of Islam, ruled for ten years in Medina, and like other statesmen was engaged in running the daily affairs of the people, matters of war and peace, economics and society. After his death, the first thing the Muslims had to do was to elect a ruler for themselves, which they did in accordance with the traditions of the Qureysh,[27] and inspired by the Prophet's life and the Koranic principles of allegiance and consultation[28] – though of course, according to our Shia beliefs, appeal to these two principles was not justified, in view of the event at Ghadir.[29] The title later became Caliph of the Muslims or Commander of the Faithful. Since the Prophet had the positions of both prophethood and command, the caliphate retained the fusion of religion with politics and government.

This situation continues, more or less, despite the varied developments in the Muslim world and the disparate rulers who have ruled

response to Omid Paydar's dismissal of Soroush's theoretical attempt at reconciling Islam and democracy (1994). Paydar argued that this was impossible without the complete secularization of Islam, invoking Koranic verses and *fiqh* rules that contradict democratic principles. Eshkevari responds to Paydar's specific objections point by point. This was part of the debate started by Soroush (2000b). See also Eshkevari's *Reason at the Feast of Religion* (2000c), and Chapter 2 above.

[27] Qureysh was the leading Meccan tribe, into which the Prophet was born.

[28] *Bey'at*, literally clasping of hands, is the oath of allegiance to the Caliph by his electors. *Shura*, consultation, is the Koranic term adopted in modern times for councils and parliaments.

[29] According to the Shia, during his return from his last pilgrimage to Mecca the Prophet appointed Ali, his son-in-law and nephew, as his successor. This appointment took place at a place called the Ghadir (pool) of Khumm on the eighteenth day of the month of Dhu'l-hajjah of the year 632 (11 years after his migration to Medina and the establishment of an Islamic state). The most popular version of the Prophet's declaration goes as follows: 'He for whom I was the master, should hence have Ali as his master.' This declaration of the Prophet is also reported in Sunni sources, but it is interpreted differently. For differences between the Shia and Sunni theories of leadership, see Enayat (1982: 4).

under different titles. Even local governments, with their own ethnic and nationalist sentiments, which arose from the mid-Abbasid period onwards[30] in various parts of the Islamic world (including Iran), to a certain extent retained this fusion of religion and government. This was so because the [rulers] considered themselves the representatives and executives of the Caliph of Baghdad, and claimed legitimacy on this basis. No other way of ruling over Muslims seemed possible. This tradition continued, to a lesser extent, after the break-up of the Baghdad Caliphate in the mid-thirteenth century. All ruling dynasties retained this fusion [of religion and government]. This was the case with the Egyptian Mamluks, the Ottoman Caliphate, and later in Egypt and Iran. Because of the merging of religion and government in the first era of Islam, and the congruence of prophethood and leadership in the person of Muhammad, the most important issue with respect to political thought for Muslim rulers – from the very beginning until recently – has been a 'crisis of legitimacy'.

In the past half-century, however, after the break-up and abolition of the Ottoman Caliphate in 1924, these questions were raised: Are religion and politics necessarily the same and inextricable from each other? Must government be religious? Has a particular form of government been recommended in Islam and are Muslims obliged to follow that form forever? What about a secular government, and concepts such as liberty, democracy, human rights, etc.? What is their place in an Islamic religious system? Some have reached the conclusion that from the start the caliphate was not a religious matter, but emerged out of the social needs and conditions of the time; therefore it is neither necessary nor obligatory to follow that historical form of caliphate. Others opposed this view and accepted the principle of caliphate but, by ignoring the Ottoman Caliphate, considered the creation of a new form of Islamic caliphate that would, of course, be compatible with current conditions and modern concepts (democracy, etc.).[31]

Among the former is Ali Abd al-Raziq, the Egyptian author of *Islam and the Principles of Rule*;[32] and among the latter is Sayyid [Rashid]

---

[30] The Abbasid dynasty replaced the Umayyads in the mid-eighth century and flourished until the Mongol destruction of Baghdad in 1258. The provinces became independent between 861 and 945.

[31] Eshkevari elaborates this in Chapters 4 and 5 below.

[32] Abd al-Raziq (1925); for discussions of this work, see Enayat (1982: 62-8) and Hourani (1962: 183-9). A Persian translation (from a French edition by

Rida, author of *The Caliphate or the Supreme Imamate*.[33] There were others among the Muslim thinkers who rejected the system of caliphate and religious government (at least in its traditional sense), seeing government to be civil in nature; they said that the source of power and government is civil not religious. Sheykh Muhammad Abduh[34] was among them.

Anyway, at present the following three theories still have their supporters in the Muslim world:

1. Supporters of a religious government of the caliphate type (such as most Islamic fundamentalist movements).

2. In complete contrast, another group completely separates the realms of religion and government, and in practice supports a laic and secular government (non-religious, of course, but not necessarily anti-religious).

3. Another group have chosen a third way: Islamic government – provided it is democratic.

In reality the main differences between [supporters of] the last and the other two are thus: the first group sees religion and democracy as in contradiction, abandons democracy in the interest of religion, and believes that in a religious system there is no room for democracy. On the whole, they consider democracy as 'permissiveness', giving free reign to human desires and lust.

The second group also sees an inherent contradiction between religion and democracy, but they forsake religion in the interest of democracy to give government a free hand in legislative and executive matters; ultimately they defend the theory of 'liberal democracy' in its Western form.

But the defenders of the third theory believe that there is no contradiction between religion and democracy that would compel us to forsake one for the sake of the other: [they hold] that Islamic government cannot be undemocratic.

Abdou Filali) was reviewed by Eshkevari in 2002 (*Aftab* 14 (1381), pp. 40-43). While accepting the thrust of Abd al-Raziq's argument, Eshkevari disagreed with him in one respect: the Prophet's rule in Medina was also temporal and the legitimacy of his rule came from people who chose him as their leader, not from his status as Prophet.

[33] Rida (1923). For a discussion of this book, see Enayat (1982: 69-83).

[34] The Egyptian thinker, one of the founders of Islamic modernism, see Haddad (1994).

Defenders of each theory, of course, offer arguments and evidence for their theory, recorded in their written works. It should be mentioned that each of the above theories contains sub-theories that are important and worthy of investigation.

In Iran, too, since the advent of modern Western thought, and later at the height of the constitutional movement, we can see the impact of these three theories. The caliphate, however, in its Sunni ideological-historical conception, has had no place among the Shia and the Iranians. So the demise of the Ottoman Caliphate did not have much impact on Iranians and the Shia; and today no one advocates and defends the caliphate. Nevertheless, Sheykh Fazlollah [Nuri]'s theory at the time of the Constitutional Revolution, and the theory of absolute *velayat-e faqih* in the contemporary era, can be regarded as analogous to Rashid Rida's theory of the caliphate (on this, see Hamid Enayat's book on *Modern Islamic Political Thought*).[35] At least, according to such theories, legitimacy comes from religion and consent from the people. That is to say, the ruler is generally appointed by God in accordance with Sharia from among certain people who are religiously qualified; and the essential and exclusive right to govern on behalf of God belongs to this group; the people, by choosing one among them, make government possible; in effect they indicate which one – among this group – they consider the best and most eligible, and in this way others are excluded from government.

The theory of liberal democracy too has some supporters among the religious people, but most of its supporters are non-religious. However, in the present condition of society, of course, its supporters do not have the opportunity to air and promote their views openly.[36]

But the third theory, that is, the idea of religious democratic government, is mainly supported by Muslim intellectuals, some of whom defend it. Before the victory of the Islamic Revolution in Iran, the [idea of an] Islamic state (which later became the Islamic Republic) was promoted with the qualification 'democratic'. The Leader of the Revolution, Ayatollah Khomeini, several times in Paris and Tehran declared that the democracy of the Islamic system has a strength and credibility that is unique among the democratic systems of the world. It was even said that Islamic democracy is more advanced than Western

---

[35] Enayat (1982). Eshkevari is referring to the Persian translation.
[36] Eshkevari is alluding to the silencing of secular voices after the revolution.

democracy (*Sahifeh-ye Nur* 13/3).[37] 'Democratic Islamic Republic' was the name used by the Revolutionary Council (Mehdi Bazargan, *Iranian Revolution in Two Movements*, p. 92),[38] and later, Dr Beheshti supported this stipulation [democratic]. At that time, Bazargan too preferred the name 'Democratic Islamic Republic'. But eventually Khomeini's proposal for an 'Islamic Republic' was accepted and put to a referendum.[39] In recent years, once again, the issue of the relationship between religion and government, or, at another level, that of religion and democracy, has emerged more intensely and with greater force; and it is being debated in the media and in [political] gatherings. Yet there are some who explicitly consider democracy as contrary to Islam – or even as its enemy; while there are others who consider the two compatible – or even concomitant.

So we see that, in the Muslim world and also for us in Iran, the issue of religion and government has the utmost importance; and the resolution of many of our ideological, political and social problems is hostage to it. We must thus undertake great efforts and intellectual struggle in order to get closer to finding a way. Today, as in the constitutional era, the disagreement is not one between believers and non-believers, but rather among those who are highly religious and are followers of religious law, over the approach to religion and government. It should even be said that there is no complete consensus among supporters of Islamic government. I defend the theory of 'Islamic democratic government'. That is, I believe in Islamic government, but I believe that, basically, in today's world, without following a democratic system, Islamic government is neither possible nor desirable.

Some important questions about religion and government

A correct and comprehensive depiction and interpretation of 'government' (*hokumat*) and 'state' (*dowlat*) as well as a precise definition of their relationship with the 'religion of Islam', require that [we] address some important questions. Otherwise, merely declaring that 'I accept Islamic government' or 'I reject an Islamic state' does not solve any problem.

---

[37] Khomeini (1983-90). *Sahifeh-ye Nur* (*Book of Light*) is a compilation of Khomeini's speeches, declarations and writings, running to 21 volumes and also available on CD-ROM.

[38] In this book (published in 1984) Bazargan provides a critical history of the revolution.

[39] For these events, see Schirazi (1998); see also Chapter 4 below.

Obviously, if we advocate Islamic government, or more generally religious government, besides a series of general and preliminary questions, we will be faced with some specific questions that need answering. If we reject all interpretations of religious government, we still face other questions that must be addressed.

Generally, these questions are of two kinds:

First, questions that arise before any answer can be given about the relation (positive or negative) between religion and government.

Second, questions that emerge after stating our position on the kind of relation (positive or negative) between religion and government. These important questions (some of which must be dealt with before and some after [stating our position]) include:

1.   What is the philosophy of religion? How far do its scope, role and mission extend? In other words, 'what should be expected of religion?' Here, we must specifically consider Islam, and ascertain its role and scope in the light of the Koran and Sunna.

2.   What sort of book is the Koran? What is its place in religious knowledge and sciences? And what problem is the Koran expected to solve for Muslims?

3.   Why is Islam the last of the revealed religions, and what does it mean when we say that Islam is a 'complete religion'? What is the completeness of religion?

4.   What is our definition of 'human being'? How do we define his relationship with God and religion, and especially do we see them as constrained or free?

5.   Did the prophets (and in particular the Prophet of Islam) intend to establish a 'special society'?

6.   Was the rule of the Prophet of Islam (and other prophets who were rulers) inherent to his mission and part of his prophethood?

7.   Who is the legislator? God? Human beings? Or both?

8.   Do we have fixed and changeable laws in Islam? If so, which ones are the fixed and which are the changeable?

9.   What is the place of *fiqh* and its application (*feqahat*)[40] and *ijtihad* in Islam? And what is the scope of authority of the *fuqaha*?

10.   What were the role and mission of the Shia Imams? Did they consider government to be their exclusive right?

11.   Has God delegated political authority and the right to govern to special individuals, forever, essentially and exclusively?

---

[40] For a discussion of these terms and their usage in Iran, see Sa'idzadeh (2002).

12. How do we define the role and duties of government and state (given their emerging philosophy)?
13. What picture do we have of 'democracy'? Do we consider it (leaving religion aside) to be desirable, useful and humane?
14. Is government a concern of religion or religious laws?

I attempt to ascertain the nature of the relationship between 'religion' and 'government', and to define the political system I believe in, which can be called by the term 'Islamic democratic government'. Given the lack of time, I cannot answer all the questions raised, but in order to illustrate my theory, I shall address some of them in the course of my talk.

What, then, is the relationship between 'religion' and 'government'? Can we have a religious government? Since I advocate the theory of 'Islamic Democratic Government', I must first define three terms: religion, government and democracy.

The definition of religion, government and democracy
It is evident that definitions of terms and concepts are basically neither comprehensive nor exclusive. This is so because, first, in any ideological and philosophical system, terms and concepts acquire definitions suitable to that system; and secondly, because these same concepts are influenced by time and place and are subject to change.

On the other hand, in order to express one's point, to debate, to engage in dialogue and to come to an understanding, we have no choice but to define concepts, or at least to draw conclusions only after establishing relatively agreed definitions. One problem I have noticed in these discussion sessions is that the speaker often does not give a clear definition of the concepts used, so it is difficult to come to an understanding on the conclusions drawn.

In view of this, then, for the present discussion I try to give clear definitions and interpretations of the key concepts, and then ascertain their relationship, and in effect how they interconnect.

Religion: many different definitions of religion have been offered, many of which can complement each other. In my view, in one sense it can be said that in terms of a doctrinal system, religion comprises world-view (*jahanbini*), value or ideological rulings (*ahkam-e arzeshi*), and practical rulings (*ahkam-e 'amali*).

World-view is derived from inner belief, and personal experience [of religion]; its function is to give people an outlook so that they can understand the world and mankind in a certain way. That is to say, believers, above anything else, possesses the belief and experience that enable them to see, understand and interpret the world and existence (nature, humanity, history and society) in a different way, a perspective that others lack.

Value rulings that are the same as the ideological 'musts' and 'must-nots' are shaped on the basis of worldview and the philosophical understanding of the world and humankind. They are general guides to action on all aspects of life, and principled 'pointers' to conduct and behaviour.

Practical rulings, which are based on ideals, principles and ideological values, concern the [appropriate] religious conduct for attaining the ideals. For example, 'daily prayer' is a practical ruling of religion that stems from the ideological ruling and general principle of worship; and worship in turn is derived from the monotheistic (*towhidi*)[41] worldview and interpretation of God and human beings and regulation of the kind of human-God relationship.

All these three categories (world-view, ideology, and practical rulings) are embedded in the content and notion of religion. One can offer a shorter definition and say that religion consists of 'guidance' and 'justice'. Guidance, meaning 'serve Allah and shun the Idol' (Koran, Nahl, 36), is mentioned in the Koran many times by different prophets. Its purpose is the moral purification and spiritual elevation of humankind. And 'justice' is the pre-condition for moral elevation and becoming human. Of course, justice is meant in its broad sense: justice in the field of ethics, economics, law, and in fact as a basis and criterion for regulating social and personal relations among human beings. Freedom is thus an aspect of justice. In relation to the prophet's invitation to religion and its philosophy, both guidance and justice are frequently invoked in the Koran. Koranic verses invoking guidance are

[41] In Islamic theology, *towhid* is the doctrine of the Unity of God; Shariati reworks it as a 'worldview', which is how Eshkevari intends it. In Shariati's words, 'Tawhid as a world-view in the sense I intend in my theory means the whole universe as a unity, instead of dividing it into this world and the hereafter, the natural and the supernatural, substance and meanings, spirit and body. It means regarding the whole existence as a single form, a single living and conscious organism, possessing will, intelligence, feeling and purpose. There are many people who believe in tawhid, but only as a religious-philosophical theory, meaning nothing but "God is one, not more than one". But I take tawhid in the sense of a world-view, and I am convinced that Islam also intends it in this sense' (Shariati 1979: 82); see also Enayat (1982: 155-6). Others interpret Shariati's *towhidi* worldview as implying a classless society.

numerous, and there is no need to refer to them here; but with respect to justice, I refer to two verses:

'... and justice is next to piety' (Al-Ma'idah, 8)

And the famous verse:

'We sent aforetime our messengers with Clear Signs and sent down with them the Book and the Balance (of Right and Wrong), that men may stand forth in justice' (Al-Hadid, 25)

(See also Ma'idah, 8 & 43; An'am, 152; A'raf, 29; Yunis, 47; Hood, 85).

State and government: Government and state are idioms that have acquired essentially new and different definitions in the contemporary world as compared to the past; and, of course, this change stems from the important changes in the phenomena of government and political power – so that today government, state, and political power are quite different. When reality changes fundamentally, its definition and interpretations will also change essentially. That is why, with earlier perceptions of ruler, sovereignty and government, we cannot speak of [relations between] religion and democracy or religion and government, or the like. There are, however, disagreements and obvious differences in present-day definitions of such categories. Here, to ground our discussion, we refer to a definition on which, I think, there is a general consensus:

> In the wider sense of the word, a state consists of: a society in which political power is determined and defined according to 'basic laws'. In the narrower sense, a state is the power that controls the destiny of the said society. As a general concept, a state means a collection of executive organizations that is granted the power to run society. But government is a collection of social organizations that came into existence to safeguard social relations and maintain order in society.[42]

---

[42] *Farhang-e 'Olum-e Siyasi* [*Dictionary of Political Sciences*], Gholam-Reza Baba'i and Bahman Aqa'i, Volume I [original footnote].

Democracy: Democracy too is one of the most controversial concepts. But it appears that – irrespective of various definitions – two features are inseparable from the spirit and essence of democracy:

1 – The worldly and popular origin of state, government and power.
2 – Pluralism and the widest possible distribution of political power among people.

Democratic methods, therefore, are ways and means for the distribution of power and the execution of the popular right of sovereignty and the fulfilment of the duties of the government chosen by the people – just as socialism too has this aim. According to this definition, democracy is a method, based, of course, on a specific kind of philosophy, world-view, anthropology and ideas. Therefore, without considering and practising these ideas and ideals, democracy will be meaningless and unattainable. For instance, democracy is compatible with the belief in freedom and human free will, not with determinism.

The connection between religion and government

We must now see what connection and relationship exists between religion and government. If our definitions of religion and government are correct and acceptable, we can say that the essence and spirit of religion is guidance, worship, moral purification, human elevation and perfection. In other words, human attention to the centre of the universe and the worship and service of God has no connection with government and state, neither in theory nor in practice. This is so because these objectives and concepts transcend history and society, and admit no limitation of any kind; they must be attainable and followed by believers in any conditions of time and place, in any social and political situation. The government and political powers – even if they call themselves religious and claim to implement Islam – are unable in practice to intervene in matters of faith, belief and service of God; if they should intervene, not only do they overstep their mandate but in the end they will not succeed. That is, a religious state is unable to force people to perform a certain act or to prevent them from doing it. Why? Because there can be no compulsion in religion.

But the other objective [of religion], that is justice, has a direct connection with government. In religious and Koranic culture, we said that the purpose of sending prophets is justice, and its scope is wide, encompassing all dimensions of human life. Moreover, the philosophy and impetus behind the rise of state and government is justice: 'Justice is the basis of rule.'[43]

Clearly, religious justice, or the justice intended by religion, is impossible without established political power, state and executive power. It is here that religion and state meet, and in effect intersect at a crossroads. In other words, justice is the hinge that joins religion to government. In my view, although the Prophet's government in Medina was not an aspect of his prophetic mission – and thus, if the Prophet had not governed, he would still be a prophet – probably the great man established a state, or at least agreed to govern, so that he could dispense justice and realize the society of *towhidi* justice. Likewise, despite all his piety and his disdain of the world, the Commander of the Faithful Ali considered it his right to succeed the Prophet, and often said that he agreed to govern in order to revive the truth and eliminate falsehood. It is for this reason that we say that, in Islam and in a religious world-view, religion and state are intertwined; at least, without an Islamic state and correct and religious governance, the moral values and justice intended by the Divine Legislator are not possible.[44] This has certainly been one of the factors in the blending of religion and state in the history of Islam – a phenomenon that until recent times has never been questioned.

It may well be asked: Can justice not be attained by a government without religion? In other words, is it only religion that invites justice and equity? Justice, certainly, is an extra-religious ideal and a deep human need, and theologians have also said that the virtues of justice and the defects of injustice are questions of reason, not religion, and [justice] has nothing to do with Islam or [any other] religion. Therefore, logically and in practice, a kind of justice can be attained without establishing a religious government. But we are talking about the connection between religion and government, and the question is: how to attain the justice to which the religion invites us; and how to establish the kind of equity in relations among the believers that is inherent in the religion and philosophy of the prophetic mission? Is it possible to carry out justice without government and the acquisition of political power by believers?

---

[43] *Al-'adl asas al-hukm*, a Saying of Imam Ali [footnote in original].

[44] This is the heart of Eshkevari's argument: that without establishing a state, the justice of Islam cannot be realized. It is also the basic dogma of the so-called fundamentalists. But by the time of the Berlin Conference, as we shall see in Chapter 5, Eshkevari modifies this argument substantially.

The Koran says, God sent the prophets to rouse the people to administer justice; it appears that this justice is not achievable unless in the shade of a powerful, just and popular government and state. It can be said that in an Islamic society and system, the government and the state are the administrators of justice. Besides, in different or opposing schools of thought, justice acquires different and opposing definitions. Religious justice will be a special [type of] justice, part of which, in principle, being innate or stemming from shared human experience, will be the same as religion, or, at least, will be compatible with religion; though another part will for sure be incompatible with other interpretations of justice or other ways of administering justice.

For instance, in defining justice and injustice it is said that justice is putting an object in its [proper] place, and so naturally injustice is removing an object from its place. In different world-views and schools of ideological thought, this very etymological[45] definition of justice becomes different, and at times opposite. For instance, if, like Aristotle, we believed that God created some to be slaves and others to be masters, then we would consider a social order just and correct when each person is put in his/her place; and as a result a master must always have slaves and slaves must remain slaves and never disobey or rebel. In this case, a slave rebellion, or even their mere protest at the system of slavery, is unjust and contrary to justice. But in a religious and *towhidi* world-view, where all human beings are servants of God and all are created equal, and where they acquire superiority to others only by [virtue of] humanity and piety, dealing in slavery is oppression, and it is a religious duty and commitment to seek its abolition. This is what all *towhidi* prophets did, including the Prophet of Islam. Why do exploitation and social justice and equality acquire such importance in the Marxist school? The reason lies in the special way in which the founders of this school (especially Marx and Engels) viewed the world and humanity, in which justice acquires a special definition and a special method is devised to realize justice and to abolish exploitation. On the basis of a *towhidi* and Koranic worldview, justice in Islam acquires a special meaning, and naturally this justice and equity are not compatible with every means for their realization. In Islam justice cannot be administered in an unjust way – we shall deal with this later.

---

[45] *'Adl*, justice, in its verb form means to straighten out – to regulate, set right, put something in its place.

The connection between religion and democracy

Now that we have clarified the connection between government and religion and the nature of relations between them, we shall explain the nature of the relation between religion and democracy. As I said, just as religious guidance and worship have nothing to do with government, so also this dimension of religion has no connection with democracy. This is so because guidance and devotion are matters that give direction and motivation to [individual] ethical and spiritual perfection, but democracy is a method of running society, a type of social conduct and a way of collective living; and these two are not dealing with the same subject matter.

But as for the justice dimension, it has direct and important links with a specific form and content of government and governors – that is, with democracy. The problem is: how and in what type of administration is Islamic justice (by any definition of justice that we might have) attainable? Or, at least, can it be sought in the most correct and desirable form? In other words, if we accept that government is necessary for Muslims, and that social justice on the basis of Islam necessitates a specific kind of Muslim government, the question is: what kind of government is more desirable within the framework of religious philosophy, anthropology and political thought?

In our view, in the present state of the world, the democratic method is the most religious and the most correct way of social administration for Muslims. If we consider the ideal of religion – in social and actual terms – to be justice, and the ideal and essence of democracy to be the establishment of political power and the implementation of truth and justice based on [people's] will, and [their] conscious and free choice based on pluralism, then without doubt religious justice is not attainable without using democratic methods – or, at least, democracy is the most suitable means for implementing justice. This is because the simplest meaning of justice is giving everybody their rights, putting everybody in their rightful place, preventing discrimination and injustice, and finally establishing a reasonable balance in society; and the most natural, the most humane, and the most useful way to create balance in human society is the establishment of a state and the creation of political and governmental power, by people exercising their conscious free will, with the maximum participation of all different opinions and ideological persuasions.

This claimed logical and practical link between justice and democracy is not only derived from the core of religion and religious anthropology but is also the product of human experience throughout history. In Koranic anthropology, humans are created with free will, and according to numerous undeniable rational and textual (*'aqli va naqli*) proofs, every human is responsible for their own thoughts, actions and behaviour, and for choosing religion or any other [system of law] as an act of free will (not because it is given or predestined); therefore any kind of compulsion and force is essentially in contradiction with religion and religious law; ultimately neither guidance nor the implementation of justice can be compulsory. This issue is so important that, if we denied [people] choice in either realm, not only would guidance, ethical elevation and moving towards God be meaningless but the realization of justice would be impossible.

Justice must be justly implemented, otherwise it is oppression. Repeated human experience has also shown that reasonable and just implementation of justice is impossible without people's conscious and free choice and their sincerest, broadest and deepest participation. If justice is implemented by force and without people's wish and choice, even if it is motivated by love and compassion, it is doomed to fail. One important reason for the failure of the justice-seeking revolutions has been that the people's will, choice and dignity have been ignored. Karl Popper[46] says that whoever wants to create a paradise on earth, creates a hell. In some instances this assertion is correct, but we must also ask what the cause or causes were. Is it wrong to seek justice and pursue human ideals of equality and fraternity? Failure does not necessarily mean that it is wrong to have a justice-seeking ideology. As Gorbachov admits in his book *Perestroika*: 'Our gravest mistake was that we wanted socialism without democracy and without attention to people's will, opinion and choice.'

Religious democratic government
Considering the explanations offered, the question whether we can have a religious democratic government has a clear answer. If our explanations and arguments have so far been reasonable and acceptable, then it must be said that not only are Islam and democracy in the realm of state and government not incompatible, but, on the contrary, Muslim government cannot be undemocratic. That is to say, despotism, authoritarianism and, more specifically, ruling people without their consent, are in contradiction with the essence of religion, human free will, and Islamic texts and sources. Although the scope of the

---

[46] Popper's works have been widely read and discussed among post-revolutionary Iranian intellectuals; see Boroujerdi (1996: 163f.).

debate is wide, and many reasons can be offered in support of the democratic essence of the political system of Muslims, in the limited time available I shall mention only a few.

1 – In Islamic sources a special form of government has not been suggested.
Clearly there is no denying that the Koran and Islamic Sayings have not defined and recommended a fixed, definite and eternal form of government or political administration of society. When the Prophet established a government, in ruling and dealing with the affairs, large and small, of Medina, he employed his own personal acumen and tact, in the best possible way at the time. Even if we consider the Prophet's leadership to be an aspect of his prophethood, and therefore divine, there is still no doubt that the vast majority of the Prophet's social and political decisions came from his own discernment and discretion. If the Prophet had governed in another place, he certainly would have acted differently with regard to the way of running society and everyday decisions. Naturally, in conditions different from the time of the Prophet, Muslims can experience other modes of government. So, in Iran today, we have a republic, separation of powers, elections, parliament, etc.; none of these concepts and institutions existed at the beginning of Islam. Putting aside the theoretical and rational side of the issue, the form, organization, scope and practice of government are entirely matters of time and place, and cannot be otherwise. That is to say, one cannot conceive of a fixed form for government and state.

2 – Government is not a matter for religion and religious law
It is often claimed that government is [derived] from religion or religious rulings. But it is unclear what this means, and what is meant by saying that government is [derived] from religion. In Islam we have 'dogmas' (*'aqayid*) and 'rulings' (*ahkam*), which have been classified as 'religious principles' (*osul-e din*) and 'practices' (*foru'-e din*), and 'government' is not one of them. That is to say, government is mentioned neither among the 'religious principles' (oneness of God, resurrection, prophethood, justice, imamate)[47] nor among the 'practices' (prayers, fasting, hajj, etc.).

Even the imamate, as believed in by the Shia, has no connection with the phenomenon of government in the sense in which we are discussing it here. This is because, according to Shia belief, first, imamate

[47] *Towhid, mo'ad, nabovat, 'adl, emamat.* These are Shia *osul-e din*; *'adl* and *emamat* are not among those of the Sunni.

(as Ayatollah Motahhari says in his book, *Imamate and Leadership*)[48] is a broader concept than government and political leadership; secondly, although it is true that we believe political leadership also to have been the right of Imam Ali and subsequent Imams, in practice this never happened; besides, the imamate was confined to twelve persons, and this shows that the imamate, in the sense in which the Shia believe, is not the same as the phenomenon of government as a requirement of social life that always exists. It can of course be said that Islamic government – the Shia [type] – is committed to govern in accordance with the model of Imam Ali's rule and the teachings of the twelve Imams, and to follow the example of those blessed men and the Prophet. But it is clear that this has nothing to do with the notion of government as a matter of religious dogma; and no one has ever spoken of government in this sense.

Another point worth noting is that there is no definite and solid rational and textual evidence to support [the claim] that government is [one] of the religious rulings. For instance, there are Koranic verses about prayers, fasting, hajj, almsgiving, etc. Are there such verses or even Sayings available about government? Religious rulings are legislated through textual authority, and no one has the right, through his own understanding or *ijtihad*, to legislate a new matter in the name of religion and religious law. For instance, no one can declare a new form [of worship] as religious law alongside prayer, fasting, etc.; this would certainly be an illegal or heretical innovation, and for this reason in none of the social and jurisprudential schools have such additions or omissions occurred since the beginning of Islam. It is of course clear that *ijtihad* is not making new religious rulings but 'arriving at secondary religious rulings by means of textual evidence and reasoning'. In any case, in Islam, government has never been regarded as a religious matter. Of course, in our sources (including the *Nahj ol-Balagheh*),[49] there are myriad Sayings concerning the importance and role of government, the attributes of rulers, the duties of governors and their actions and conduct. But needless to say, these kinds of Sayings do not confirm that government is a [matter of] dogma, religious ruling or religious practice. Irrespective of all this, because of its form and content government is a human phenomenon, which is always evolving and is entirely defined by time and place; and thus it cannot come

---

[48] Motahhari (1985).
[49] Literally, *The Way of Eloquence*, a collection of sermons and letters by Ali, the first Shia Imam.

under dogmas (such as oneness of God, resurrection, etc.) or religious rulings (such as prayers, fasting, hajj and so on). That is to say, these two are not the same kind of thing; they cannot be compared. To compare, for example, prayer and government would be like comparing chalk and cheese – they have nothing in common. For this reason, in Islam, neither is government – despite its importance – located among *fiqh* rulings and religious dogmas, nor has any special type of government been recommended.

3 – The people are the source of power
The rational and textual origins of Islam indicate that, in our religious thought and tradition, the sources of power, government and the state are worldly and popular, not divine. This means no one can make an a priori and essential claim to be representing God or the Prophet in matters of government and the exercise of political power. The phenomena of government and power basically fall into the realm of the people's voluntary and chosen acts, and essentially cannot be otherwise. Throughout history, however, (for various reasons, including people's ignorance) people have rarely made use of their natural right. Even in exceptional cases, when an appointment (such as that of Ali as Commander of the Faithful at Ghadir)[50] occurred out of necessity, it was left to the people's vote and choice; hence the act of allegiance[51] took place. With respect to the Prophet of Islam, too, it is certain that he acquired leadership and government with the approval, invitation and sincere assistance of the people of Medina (the majority of whom at first were not yet even Muslims). Some points, therefore, are certain:
1 – Government, as a time- and place-bound phenomenon, is human and has a worldly origin. This is a basic rule and exceptions do not disprove the rule.
2 – Government is a contract, thus bilateral in any event. The two sides (government and people) have mutual rights and obligations (Imam Ali also explicitly referred to these reciprocal rights in Sermon 207 of *Nahj ol-Balagheh*).
3 – The imamate has been realized in twelve specific individuals.[52] This shows that, first, the imamate is not merely about leadership;

---

[50] See footnote 29 above.
[51] *Bey'at*, see footnote 28 above.
[52] In accordance with Twelver Shia dogma, the number of Imams was limited to 12, starting with Ali and ending with the 'Imam of Time', who went into Occultation.

secondly, if it was intended that God appoint leaders until the Day of Judgement, then limiting the numbers [of Imams to twelve] would be senseless and unnecessary, and anyway [the number of rulers] could not be specific and limited. Even if we believe that in the 'Era of Absence' the *fuqaha* are general deputies of the 'Imam of Time' and that the right to govern belongs to this group, still it is the people's choice and will that create political power and actualize it in practice.

In any case, until the people in a society have raised a person or persons to leadership and established political power, there is no government, no governor with the power to rule, and no legitimate exercise of power. Ultimately, in any time or place, Muslims create their desired government and choose properly qualified people to rule them; the legitimacy and acceptability of the government and the rulers comes from their election by the people, from nowhere else. Thus the responsibility for this election is with the people themselves, not with God, the Prophet or religion.

4 – Popular consultation and participation in the affairs of state and government are an eternal principle and a right
According to explicit Koranic verses (Shura, 38 and Al-'Imran, 159), in the affairs of government and administering the affairs of the people (though not of course in matters of revelation and legislating religious rulings), the Prophet is commanded and obliged to discuss and consult with the stakeholders [i.e. the people]. This consultation, of course, begins with the establishment of the state and the election of statesmen, extends to how the rulers should organize and take decisions, and how their work should be supervised, and ends eventually with [how] to dismiss rulers, and if necessary to change the political system.

Although the esteemed Prophet was not elected officially or by ballot, the first and second Aqaba pacts (especially the second),[53] are

---

[53] Aqaba is a place near Mecca where secret meetings took place between the Prophet and the representatives of two tribes (Aws and Khazraj) from the city of Yathrib, during which a pact was made, leading to the emigration of Muslims from Mecca to Yathrib (later named al-Medina, the City). The Prophet joined the migrants in AD 622, which became the starting date of the Muslim Hijri calendar. At the second meeting, in June that year, it was agreed that the Prophet would become an arbiter between the feuding tribes of Yathrib. This agreement defines the relationship between Muslims and tribes of Medina, and is preserved in a written document that is considered authentic. For a succinct account of the details of this agreement, see Ruthven (2000: 49-50).

indicative of the fact that the political authority of the Prophet was realized with the consent, support and acceptance of the people, not through the exercise of one-sided authority from above. Throughout the ten years [of his rule], the tradition of consultation and seeking people's views continued; and people's agreement was taken into account at least in important matters (especially in war and peace, which were the most important decisions at that time). Even the important issues of [the Prophet's] infallibility and the revelation coming to his aid (in some instances) did not preclude the Prophet's consultation [with people]. For this reason too, in social and political matters people often rose in opposition to the Prophet, and this tradition also existed in the era of Imam Ali; and no one at that time considered such opposition as irreligiosity or weakness of belief. This is because, in Islamic tradition, this has been the definite right of the people. At the same time, in the absence of the Prophet and [during the] deprivation of leadership by the [Imams], popular sovereignty and the rejection of theocracy are beyond question; this is really so evident that there is no need for argument. Thus, during the constitutional era, some of the great ulama like Akhund Khorasani,[54] issued the following fatwa:

> It is a [Shia] religious requirement that during the Era of Absence the government of the Muslims rests with the majority of the people.[55]

And this requirement is self-evident and cannot be denied. Even in the constitution of the Islamic Republic of Iran, the republican political system, founded on *velayat-e faqih*, is established and acquires legitimacy through the will and vote of the majority of the Muslims (even non-Muslims, since every Iranian citizen has the right to vote), and nothing else.

---

[54] Mohammad Kazem Khorasani (1839-1911) is particularly known for his innovative style of teaching the science of Islamic jurisprudence.
[55] *Tarikh-e Bidari-ye Iranian*, Part 2, p. 230 [Reference footnoted in original; Nazem ol-Eslam, 1970].

5 – The authority of common sense[56] is in the Sharia

If we accept that government is basically not the concern of religious dogma and law, but is a human phenomenon and [bound to] time and place, we must also admit that government comes in the domain of common sense, the custom and conditions of the age; thus it cannot be discussed and debated in the realm of religious law and *fiqh*. That is to say, decisions relating to type of government, its form and organization, who the leaders should be and how they should govern, how the people should supervise their work and dismiss them when necessary, and so on ... all such matters are clarified through discussion and making use of the experience of the wise in the course of history. In every era it must be asked: how can we now have a just government? The answer to this question does not come directly from the heart of the Koran, Sayings *(hadith)* and *fiqh*, but a just system can be established at any time and place by using common sense, human experience and tried and tested methods. Even if *fiqh* and the *fuqaha* want to provide an answer for it, they will have to rely on common sense and the customs and practices of the time. Thus the idea of *velayat-e faqih* was inserted in an already tested political system, that is a 'republic' and a parliamentary system; and almost all the democratic methods, tools and institutions of the world today have been accepted in this system. But at the same time, it must be said that the use of common sense is itself a religious principle; that is, a comprehensive and complete religion like Islam regards common sense as a source for *ijtihad*, decision-making and practice in the realm of social life.

We refrain from invoking other arguments, and return to the main point: Why do we consider Islamic government to be necessarily viable and achievable only on the condition of democracy? If the arguments we have introduced under the five headings above are acceptable, then it is clear that:

1. government as a phenomenon is not essentially religious,

2. the establishment of government is a requirement for Muslims,

3. government and government organizations are bound by time and place,

---

[56] *Sirah 'uqala* (lit. 'the way of the wise') is a technical term in Islamic jurisprudence and literature in the sense of recognizing the best decisions of humans as a source of law in issues where the sacred texts are silent or on issues outside the remit of the religious law; see Mohaqqeq-Damad (1996: 149).

4.   a just [political] system, compatible with religious values, at any time or place, is defined and [made] possible by using the experiences and traditions of the wise,

5.   Common sense and experience tell us that at the present time, the best, the most beneficial, the most Islamic, the most just, and finally the least harmful type of government organization is [achieved] by using democracy and democratic institutions; this is because:

5.1   the choice and electoral power of the believers are better reflected and expressed in this system and tradition (compared to a despotic system),

5.2   from the stage of the establishment of the political system to that of implementation and practice, the Muslim people have wider and more serious involvement and oversight, and ultimately the right to dismiss the rulers and change the system [rests] with the people,

5.3   the ethical, intellectual, scientific, economic and cultural development and progress of society is greater,

5.4   the political system will be more stable and durable, and basically less subject to chaos, revolution and destruction,

5.5   social and national unity will be achieved at a broader and deeper level, and class antagonism will be reduced,

5.6   independence of the Islamic country in the face of foreign interventions will become more possible, etc.

Nevertheless, I do not want to draw an idealized and utopian picture of a democratic society and government, or to say that democracy is the ultimate human ideal and has absolutely no flaws or shortcomings. This is never the case. Democracy is a great invention in the history of humankind, because people have finally, by trial and error, come up with a means of − in Aristotle's words − lessening the evils of governments and powers and organizing themselves [or their affairs] in a more rational and less harmful way. But it is natural that human work is always flawed and imperfect, and as a rule, the flaws of democracy too will gradually be overcome and someone will try out new ways in democracy.

The basic, essential and humane ideal of democracy is people's exercise of free will and conscious choice in their affairs. But how and in what form is this will exercised better and more fully? There exists no fixed and eternal form. The invention of liberal and parliamentary democracy was a significant step, but basic flaws still exist; and incidentally, Western thinkers have been more aware of these flaws than others and have addressed them. To overcome them, and in the hope of reaching a true and flawless democracy, 'social democracy' was devised and tried for a while, but that too was not so successful, and, at least in its Marxist form, it failed. We Muslims can devise a new model of democracy that is free from the flaws of liberal and social democracy; in that case, of course, all freedom seekers and democrats of the world would employ our model. At the same time, however, we must realize that we too are human and thus the democracy we devise will have flaws too, which we must remove through trial and error, to make it more righteous. But this is provided that:

  - first, we accept the validity of experience, and
  - secondly, we do not grant sanctity and eternity to a special model of government, and
  - thirdly, we do not forget that freedom, choice, the growth of consciousness and the achievement of people's freedom are Islamic ideological principles.

Our basic argument and claim is that the democratic method has so far been the most effective, the most logical and the most Islamic way of administering society. And Islam teaches us to make the best use of common sense, in life and in social and political organizations. Now if anyone objects to this claim and believes that there are better ways, they should give reasons and show us [the way]. If we are convinced, we will accept that way.

To avoid any misunderstandings, let me add that we do not claim that the government of the Prophet or Imam Ali was entirely compatible with the basis and methods of today's democracy (such as the parliamentary system, separation of powers, elections, parties, assembly, etc…), or that it operated in accordance with these criteria. Such a claim either stems from ignorance or is made for a purpose. As already said, the Prophet acted, like any ruler, within the context of the possibilities, conditions and known and tried traditions of the Arabian Peninsula; and of course his decisions and actions were based as far as possible on justice. Nothing else was or could be expected. It is exactly for this reason that we say that today we too are obliged to act in the light of the experience, possibilities and needs of our era and to create a better political system. But our point is that the ideal of democracy, as manifested in three principles (the principle of human choice and responsibility, the principle of the worldly basis of political power, and the principle of pluralism and popular participation), is validated and emphasized by the Koran and Sunna. And the rational and textual sources of our religion instruct us to use the best solutions. Our claim is that currently democracy is the best way, and if we object to existing democracies we must redress their shortcomings and reach newer and more Islamic forms of democracy.

Truly, those who categorically reject democracy and depict it as anti- Islamic, must say what their recommendation is. What political system are they offering in its place? If not the caliphate, whether in the Abbasid, Ottoman, or Saudi Arabian styles, what model of government do they have in mind?

Why religious government?

It may be asked: if this the case, why link government with religion? Why give it the adjective 'religious' or 'Islamic'?

The answer is that my understanding of religion, its role and functions is such that neither can religion and religious people be indifferent and unresponsive towards the government, its form and content, and the actions of the rulers, nor are governments capable of remaining indifferent and unresponsive towards religion, religiosity and the people's religious culture. Based on the definition we have already offered, religion must govern all aspects of a believer's life, and *towhid*, worship of God and religious ethics must run like blood in every vein of the believer's body. Basically, I (like others) do not regard religion as a cultural, historical and human phenomenon alongside other cultural and social phenomena. For instance, I do not say that in Iran there are three cultures: Islamic, Iranian and Western, and all have equal value.[57] Such an interpretation of religion is entirely sociological, and either ignores or overlooks its revelatory nature. In this perspective, religion is a human product [and] like other products; and religious practice, rulings and values too are basically analogous to human ones. Religion, of course, is influenced by human culture and itself becomes a culture alongside other cultures. But this does not mean that we [should] neglect the ideological essence and mission of religion, and substitute religious culture for religious ideology. The true and original purpose and mission of religion must be discovered, and used used for a critical approach to religious culture and history. In my view, guidance, ethics, and getting close to God are the essence of religion, and sincerity (that is, purity and transparency in the way of God) is the core of religiosity. But at the same time I believe that

[57] Eshkevari is referring to Soroush's 1990 lecture, 'The three cultures', given at Tarbiyat Modarres University in Tehran, and published a year later (Soroush 2000: 156-70).

without a just, religious, balanced and decent society, decent human life at a general level is not feasible.

The above claim is based both on text and reason as well as on tested human experience throughout the course of history. Basically the main reason for the monotheist prophets' conflict and confrontation (at times bloody) was in relation to this social dimension of religion, not in relation to their purely ethical, personal, intellectual and philosophical call to worship of God and unity of God. If it were otherwise, there would be no need for all that conflict, struggle and suffering. Which monotheist prophet did not struggle, to a greater or lesser extent, against his surrounding environment and the dominant political, social and cultural system of his society? I am not saying that every prophet struggled to gain political power, as most of them did not find the opportunity. I do say, however, that, as attested by the Koran and the history of the prophets, the call of the monotheist prophets did not occur in the realm of individual ethics and mere preaching, but rather all of them engaged in social struggle against current circumstances. Friends who attempt to depict the prophets as preachers and teachers of individual ethics and confine the scope of religiosity to individual matters and a personal inner relationship with God, in other words, to 'inner religious experience', had better analyse the indisputable struggles of the prophets (among them, the Prophet of Islam) and say what the Prophet of Islam's 23-year struggle was for, and finally what was his establishment of state and government for? Was it only to secure happiness in the hereafter, at the expense of accepting the existing polytheistic circumstances?[58]

'Justice' can be regarded in a broad and general sense as the 'social philosophy' of religion; the Koran is explicit about this, as already discussed. Justice is certainly not confined to the creation of a just and balanced world, but includes the realm of legislation, and according to the Koran implementing justice is closer than anything else to piety. Doubtless devotion and worship of God too are political, and therefore cover all realms of life, personal, social and economic.

Towhid has [several] aspects, beginning, in theological terms, with the unity of the essence, actions and attributes of the Divine Essence and extending to unity in worship and obedience; and unification in the realm of thought, action, ethics, politics and economics is essential to *towhid*. The prophets' conduct attests to this interpretation of *towhid*.

---

[58] These questions are explicitly addressed to Soroush, as well as to the points Bazargan raised in his last lecture.

In fact, the prophets' conduct is the interpreter of *towhid*. If this is so, we ask: can one be a monotheist and worship God without creating a *towhidi* society in line with religious ideals? A just and monotheist society is in all respects the necessary means and context for the development and personal ethical elevation of humanity. For this reason we believe that the prophets' plan was the creation of an 'ideal' and 'special society' to be gradually actualized by the believers as a 'necessary prelude'. This assertion, of course, is truer with respect to Islam. If we accept that guidance and the moral elevation of humankind are possible and desirable in the context of a 'special society', then it is apparent that social life, the correct and just regulation of collective relations, and giving people their rights, are only feasible under a just government and state, or, in Islamic terms, a 'compassionate state'. Particularly in today's world, where – by comparison with the past – government has become more law-bound and more limited in some aspects, its influence and impact on human fortunes have increased and deepened. How can religious people in this world be content to live under any government and any kind of political system and administration, and with any interpretation of justice, humanity and human rights? Can religion tolerate any interpretation of society, humanity, history, law and social relations, and remain indifferent and disinterested about human existence? It is strange that some have said that religion has no special orientation![59] Isn't 'Serve Allah and eschew Evil' (Nahl, 36) an orientation? Or is it [one] with no relation to society and the material and worldly life of the believers? It is odd that a Prophet who struggled and fought in bloody battles for twenty-three years, and in the course of ten years had more than seventy armed conflicts and raids on Qureysh commercial caravans, is sometimes depicted as a character who did nothing except kindness, peace, forgiveness and defence; that is to say, a prophet whose life contains only mercy but no violence. It is of course true that the Prophet did not seek war and violence, but whenever necessary he did defend himself and protect his ideals and his own existence with all his power and might and he did keep the arrogant Qureysh on their toes.

The issue is not the reasons for those conflicts, rather it is that in the life of the Prophet of Islam there were numerous conflicts, wars and long battles, and God too advises His prophet: 'Rouse the Believ-

---

[59] *Jahat*, literally 'direction'; Eshkevari uses it in the sense of ideology; his main target is the attempt by Soroush and his *Kiyan* circle to separate Islam from ideology.

ers to the fight' (Anfal, 65), and tells him to build up his military forces as much as he can in order to frighten the enemies (Anfal, 60). If a compassionate and benevolent prophet like Muhammad could have guided people and done justice with mere compassion and peace, without war and violence, he would certainly have done so. We too, if we could remain religious and fully realize our religion without engaging in conflict and battle, we should certainly do so. But the reality of life is something else. What do you do if your enemies will not stop injuring and oppressing you and want to destroy you? How can one logically give a fatwa: 'whatever the situation, surrender and make peace'? If we find ourselves in conditions like those of the Prophet and face those imperatives, is it wrong to have war, peace and a government system like that great man? The question is not whether Islam is a religion of war or a religion of peace; in reality Islam is both, but each has its proper, valid and correct place. Unfortunately, Islam is sometimes depicted as a religion of war and sometimes as religion of peace. Both are wrong and one-sided. If a religion says jihad is 'one of the gates of heaven' that God has opened to His special servants (Sermon 27, *Nahj ol-Balagheh*), how can it be regarded as only a religion of peace?

In short, complete and appropriate 'religious conduct' without 'religious society' and religious society without 'religious government', are impossible for believers. That is to say, religion will provide direction, doctrinal inspiration, and a guiding ideology for state and nation.

We must also add that, for believers, religious government is a practical and strategic imperative, not an ideological and doctrinal obligation – that is, government is by itself, separate and distinct from religion, and does not come under the domain of religion and religious ideology, doctrine and rulings. Therefore, we are making a case for religious government from a perspective external to religion, not from the inside.

But as for what kind of government this is, how far the religious element extends, what form it takes in practice and how it is organized, these and similar questions – however important – are beyond the scope of our present discussion. The wise, the thinkers, the believers must sit together and come up with a practical proposal for achieving their desired government in a framework of religion and democracy; and in time overcome its flaws and discover better ways for getting closer to religion and democracy.

As for a name and title for such a government, there is no insistence on the prefix 'Islamic'. We may call it the government of the faithful or the Muslims, or even not give it an epithet at all. 'A rose by any other name ...'[60] A title does not make a person, a state or a society religious, nor does its omission make any difference in reality and practice. But it is evident that titles denote content, and names represent what is named, and basically, in order to show the difference between an Islamic system and others, we need an expressive, realistic and suitable name. For the time being, I think 'Islamic democratic government' is the most suitable title. 'Islamic', because of the content, philosophy, viewpoint and doctrinal mission; and democratic because of its worldly and civil character, and its use of popular elections, public opinion and free will, and people's supervision of, and at times direct involvement in, all matters in accordance with laws and regulations. Like any other government, Islamic government depends on the people, thus it is accountable to the stakeholders, that is to say the people; and the rulers cannot say 'we are the representatives of God and religion and we are only accountable to God for our actions' (though they too must answer to God. For this reason, people consider they have the permanent right to dismiss the rulers and change the government and regime. Free-thinkers[61] (whether Muslim or non-Muslim) enjoy equal rights with others within the framework of law, and all can be present and participate in the state and legislative and political activities; in such a system there are no second-class citizens. This is so because an Islamic government is necessarily 'national', that is to say, when people live within defined geographical boundaries and enjoy common rights to the land, this means that all are members of one nation and all enjoy equal social rights. In other words, in Iran everyone is Iranian and, as such, has the right to engage in and supervise all governmental, political and social affairs of their country; no one is more Iranian than any one else. Of course, inevitably there are, and will be, differences in faith, views, race, ideology, class, and so on, but none of these are the basis for legal or political privilege for any person, class, or religious or social group. As long as the government is based on a believing and like-minded majority, [neither] the complete

---

[60] The Persian poetic proverb is *manteqi ra bahs az alfaz nist* (lit. the logician is not bothered by words).

[61] *Digar-andishan* (other-thinkers) is a term used in Iran for those who do not believe in the Islamic state. It has become a kind of euphemism for secularists. 'Free-thinkers' is an approximate equivalent.

freedom of others [nor] democracy will create any problem. If the Free-thinkers gain the majority by democratic means, they are entitled to establish their own democratic government, and in their government too Muslims are entitled to gain power by democratic means.

As long as democracy and freedom are maintained, no citizen (whether Muslim or non-Muslim) has the right to go outside the law and use force to gain political power. The Prophet of Islam did not resort to the sword in order to gain political power; and more clearly after him Imam Ali never used force, the sword, disorder or injustice in order to gain power and office, though he realized that he was more competent than anyone else. Nor did the subsequent Imams (especially Imam Sadeq[62] who had the opportunity to reach office) use such a method.

The final word is that Islamic government is a human, civil, pluralistic, and democratic [form of] government, relying on the views of the generality of Muslims (in practice, the majority). Its basic ideal is to dispense justice, so that, with the establishment of a healthy, just, free and prosperous society, ethical betterment and human and divine progress become possible for all.

---

[62] The sixth Imam, Ja'far Sadeq (d. 765) was a renowned *faqih*. He lived at a time of intense political upheavals that led to the overthrow of the Umayyad Caliphate and establishment of the Abbasid dynasty. It is said that he declined the offer of caliphate from Abu Salma, the political leader of the Abbasid revolt and instead devoted his energies to *fiqh* and theological studies. The Shia school of law is also known by his name, Ja'fari. See Momen (1985: 38).

4

'The Seminaries and Government'
The Relation between Religious Authority and Political Power

Editors' introduction

The seminaries and government' (*'howzeh va hokumat'*) was first published in three consecutive issues of the daily newspaper *Neshat* in spring 1999, at the height of the period of press liberalization. It is the transcript of a discussion between Eshkevari and a young journalist, Mohammad Quchani, about the consequences of the merger of the clerical establishment and political power in the Islamic Republic. Quchani, a political science graduate in his early twenties, was writing some of the most innovative and widely read political columns in the independent reformist press.[1] Here, he articulates the viewpoint of those reformists who reject an ideological reading of Islam.

Quchani reprinted the discussion in 2000 – after Eshkevari's arrest – in *Religious State, State Religion*, a compilation of transcripts of interviews with various political thinkers and activists.[2] Along the bottom of the front cover of the book are passport-sized pictures of the other interviewees (Abbas Abdi, Amir Mohebbian, Emadoddin Baghi, Majid Mohammadi and Fariborz Raisdana),[3] but the cover is dominated by a

---

[1] In May 2000, following the mass closure of reformist papers, Quchani was imprisoned for two months, then later released without trial. By 2004 he was chief editor of *Sharq*, a new reformist newspaper.

[2] Quchani (2000).

[3] Abdi, political activist, editor of *Salam* newspaper and member of the Mosharekat party, was a major reformist personality; he was arrested in autumn 2002 and in early 2005 was still in prison. Mohebbian was a columnist on *Resalat*, a conservative newspaper. Baghi is the journalist who exposed the 'serial murders'; sentenced to 3 years in prison, he was released in 2003, but his file remained 'open'; he started a new paper, *Jomhuriyat*, which was closed down; he founded the Association for the Defence of Political Prisoners.

pixellated photo of Eshkevari, who is clearly the main focus. In an Introduction with the title 'An intimation', Quchani narrates his encounters and debates with Eshkevari. He pays tribute to Eshkevari and his thought, and comments on his departure from Shariati's 'ideological reading of religion' and his rethinking of relations between religion and government. He recalls his conversations with Eshkevari. In one, Eshkevari spoke of his plan after the 2000 Majlis elections to 'kiss politics goodbye' and to 'devote himself to thinking'; in another, he 'compares the work of journalists and prophets'. Quchani concludes:

> [Eshkevari] was a 'thinker' not a 'politician'. Although he did not know that the Berlin Conference would turn out to be the biggest political event of his life, the discussions with him in this book verify that what Eshkevari said in that conference was based on deep thought not empty rhetoric. If the only achievement of this book is to establish this point, that is enough for me.[4]

As we shall see, the discussion framed a debate between the generation that made the revolution and the generation that inherited it. Islamists such as Eshkevari, who two decades earlier argued and fought for an Islamic state, were now finding themselves faced with questions posed by those (like Quchani) who came of age under the Islamic Republic. Important among these were: What went wrong in the revolution? Can a 'religious state' be democratic – is this not contradiction in terms? Eshkevari uses the interview to give his own version of the history of the revolution, and attempts to challenge and correct the version promoted by the conservatives. This was now possible because the reformist press had opened the space for discussion of previously

Mohammadi, a religious intellectual, was writing for the reformist press (see Chapter 5). Raisdana, professor of economics, is one of the most outspoken secular reformists.

[4] The first chapter in the book is a transcript of an earlier (November 1998) discussion with Eshkevari, 'Religion and the state', which covers much the same ground as Chapter 3 above, though now, in the aftermath of Khatami's 1997 election as president, Eshkevari clarifies the premises of his theory of government. On both occasions, another reformist journalist, Mohammad Hakimpur, was also present, but in the discussion transcribed here he remained silent, perhaps preferring not to be implicated in a dangerous discussion of *velayat-e faqih*.

taboo subjects. Indeed, criticisms of the conservative interpretation of the constitution and the theory of *velayat-e faqih* were already being widely voiced, following the lead of one of the principal architects of the theory, Ayatollah Montazeri.

Democratizing velayat-e faqih: *Montazeri's sermon*

In November 1997, after nearly ten years' absence from the political scene, during which he devoted himself to teaching in the Qom seminaries, Ayatollah Montazeri broke his silence. In a sermon delivered in Qom to a group of his supporters and seminary students on the occasion of the birthday of Imam Ali, Montazeri publicly voiced his disagreement with the ways in which the theory of *velayat-e faqih* had been translated into practice. In this sermon, later published as a pamphlet, Montazeri argues for *nezarat* (supervision) rather than *velayat* (rule, mandate, guardianship) by the *faqih*. He says that the *faqih*, who should be the most learned in religious knowledge, can only interfere in domains that are directly within his expertise – i.e. religious law, not the affairs of state. His role is that of supervision, to ensure that the Sharia is upheld and people's Islamic rights are respected by the state.

Here we reproduce those parts of Montazeri's sermon that touch directly on *velayat-e faqih*, and summarize the rest. Montazeri articulates what no other reformist has dared to say and provides a scathing criticism of the current Leader's qualifications and style of governance. What makes this critique important is that it comes from the heart of the clerical establishment and from the very *marja'* who has written books providing the theological and theoretical basis for the theory of *velayat* and arguing for its insertion in the constitution of the Islamic Republic. Montazeri still believes in the theory, but is now well aware of its undemocratic implications and wants to redress them.[5]

Montazeri's style is typical of the older seminarians: he is speaking to his students, making allusions to religious events familiar to his audience; the argument is not linear, and ideas are sometimes repeated several times.

He begins his sermon by making three points, to which he returns several times. First, Islam and politics are inseparable and the Muslims cannot remain indifferent to what is going on in their society; they must organize themselves, take their destiny into their own hands and

---

[5] See Moussavi (1992) for the attempt to democratize *velayat-e faqih* by Ne'matollah Salehi-Najafabadi, who seems to have been a major influence on Montazeri (see Buchta 2000: 93).

challenge injustice. The true Hezbollah ('party of God') are not those mob-supporters of the Islamic state who blindly follow slogans and allow themselves to be manipulated by the powerful. The Hezbollah, he says, 'work for the good of society'. Secondly, there must be a democratic basis for government, which is only possible when there are viable political parties, separation of powers, free elections and a free press. No one has the right to limit the scope of people's choice at election time and tell them whom they can choose. The media and the press belong to the people, not to government, and they must be free to reflect the people's views. Thirdly, people today are aware and well informed, they are educated, they cannot be governed by sheer force – or, as he puts it, 'by wielding clubs' – a reference to bands of thugs controlled by the conservatives. The time for dictatorship is over: 'government by the club will no longer work in this world.'[6]

Montazeri goes on to defend the uneasy fusion between theocracy and democracy in the constitution of the Islamic Republic that he helped to frame. But to honour the republican side of the state he now proposes to enhance the mandate of the elected institutions: the presidency and the Majlis.

> 'Republic' means 'government by the people.' Of course, I should also point out that while the people should have parties and organizations, be alert at the time of elections, and elect individuals independently on the basis of their own understanding and views, [they must not forget that] *velayat-e faqih* is enshrined in our constitution. But this does not mean that the *vali-ye faqih* is in charge of all affairs. In that case, 'republic' would no longer mean anything. But the *vali-ye faqih*, with the qualifications that are mentioned in the constitution, has specific duties that are in the constitution. His main duty, which is most important, is to oversee the movement of society and to see that the course of society does not deviate from the standards of Islam and justice. The *vali-ye faqih* is for this purpose.
>
> Now, since we want our country to be operated on the basis of Islam and religious law, all the people must participate. There should be political parties. There should be organizations ... Of course, the people bring the government to power. 'Government' means the head of the government, the president. The

6 Translation of Montazeri's sermon from *London Keyhan*, 4 December 1997, slightly modified. The original is available in Montazeri (2003: Appendix 254).

[Majlis] deputies should be brought to power by the people. No one has the right to interfere. If certain individuals sit down and play favouritism – even the Guardian Council – they will be violating the rights of the people … Moreover, the people themselves must bring the … president to power. Nevertheless, at the top there should be a person who is more knowledgeable of Islam and religious institutions than anyone else. This is because we are religious. Now, if it were the Prophet's time, the Prophet would be at the top. If it were Ali's time, Ali would be at the top. Ali himself says, enjoin good and prevent evil, people should be involved in all affairs, but [remember that] Ali is at the top; now that Ali or an infallible imam is not present, the *vali-ye faqih* is at the top.

He goes on to say that the most knowledgeable *faqih* who is at the top is not above the law and should not be indifferent to what people want; he must follow the example of Imam Ali's rule. Criticizing the intolerance of criticism in the Islamic Republic, he relates a Saying that he cited in his book on *velayat-e faqih*: Imam Ali used to go to the Kufa bazaar to remind the merchants of the importance of religion, saying 'first religion, then trade!' One day a group of Persian traders come; when they see Ali, one of them calls out 'here comes Big-belly!' Ali does not get angry and shout, 'arrest him!' but rather takes it in good spirit and jokes back: 'above is knowledge and below is food.'

Shifting back to the present time, Montazeri turns to his criticism of the *velayat-e faqih*: it has been corrupted in order to justify authoritarian rule and ignorance and to silence opposition.

Velayat-e faqih does not mean having a royal organization and ceremonial travels that cost billions and the like. These things are not compatible with the *vali-ye faqih*. As soon as something happens, the gentlemen [Khamene'i's supporters] call us 'anti-*velayat-e faqih*.' Anti-*velayat-e faqih*! God rest your father's soul, we were the ones who first raised the issue of the *velayat-e faqih* [for insertion in the constitution]. We were the ones who wrote books about it. Now, are we anti-*velayat-e faqih*? A group of kids who were not even embryos when we were doing all this now go around and say, anti-*velayat-e faqih*! Shame on you! What do you think you are doing? *Velayat-e faqih* – like the rule of the Commander of the Faithful [Imam Ali] – must supervise the country, supervise the parties, supervise the government, but not interfere everywhere. In the Islamic Republic, the government must be independent, that is, a government that is able to work.

He then addresses Khatami and urges him to use the people's vote to assert the government's authority and to reform the system:

> This is actually one of *my* criticisms of President Khatami ... when he was first elected, I sent him a message ... saying, 'if I were in your place, I would go to the Leader [Khamene'i] and say: "Your position is protected; respect for you is maintained. But 22 million people voted for me; and when these 22 million people voted for me, all of them knew that the Leader of the country had someone else in mind [Nateq-Nuri, the conservative candidate]. He himself, and everyone in his office, endorsed someone else. But did 22 million people come and vote for him? It meant that they did not agree with that organization. The vote of these 22 million people means, we do not agree with what you say. They have expectations of me, and if you want to interfere with my ministries, with my ministers and governors-general, and impose certain individuals on me, I cannot work. Hence, I will thank the people and resign. I will say to the people, they want to interfere in my work".' This is how he should have acted. People also had other expectations of the ministers.

Montazeri ends by addressing Khamene'i directly, reminding him that he is not qualified to be *marja'* and criticising his attempts to bring the seminaries under state control:

> You are not at the level and status to be a *marja'-e taqlid*. I have cautioned [you] before. It was at the time of the death of Ayat-ollah Araki. Through Ayatollah Mo'men, I sent [you] a message about several things. I read section seven of the message: 'Shia *marja'iyat* has always been an independent spiritual power, it is proper that you should not break this independence, and not make the seminaries dependent on government, because it will be detrimental to the future of Islam and Shiism. Despite the efforts of your agents it is certain that you will not achieve the scholarly status of the late Ayatollah Khomeini. Do not allow the sanctity and spirituality of the seminaries to be mixed up with the diplomatic affairs of [state] bodies ... It is in the interest of Islam, the seminaries, and yourself that your office announce

officially: "Because he has a great deal of work to do and is responsible for the administration of the country, he excuses himself from responding to religious questions; from now on, he will not answer religious questions, and officially religious scholarly inquiries and even minor religious fees should be sent to the seminaries, as before".' I sent this message on 13/08/1373 [4 November 1994], when Ayatollah Araki was just being taken to the hospital.

Montazeri is alluding to the time when, after the death of the Grand *Marja'* Ayatollah Araki, Khamene'i's supporters in Qom sought to promote him as a *marja'* – a move that met a great deal of internal resistance in the seminaries. This led to a crisis that was eventually resolved by a face-saving formula (just as Montazeri suggested): on 14 December, Khamene'i withdraw as candidate for *marja'iyat*, saying that the burden of leadership was too heavy to combine it with *marja'iyat*.[7]

He continues with his revelations, relating what Ayatollah Mo'men – a learned and respected high-ranking seminary cleric and a member of the Assembly of Experts – has told him about the way Khamene'i deals with religious questions:

Ayatollah Mo'men himself told me: One of these gentlemen [i.e. clerics] goes and sits in his office in Qom and answers questions in accordance with the opinion of Mr Khamene'i. I told him: 'He hasn't written a treatise *(resaleh)*. How can you issue religious edicts on the basis of his opinion?' He said: 'We answer on the basis of the writings of Ayatollah Khomeini.' I said: 'But the people, after all, want his opinion.' He said: 'They say that his edicts are like the edicts Khomeini; we answer on the basis of Khomeini's writing!'
Well, is it not degrading the Shia doctrine of *marja'iyat* when, the very night after the death of Ayatollah Araki, they brought a few people into the street in front of the Society of Seminary Teachers, just as they do now, then three or four people came from Tehran and, in fact, (those who were calling [Khamene'i] *marja'*) were not more than seven or eight people ... they degraded the doctrine of the Shia *marja'-e taqlid*; they made it infantile, with a

---

[7] For a detailed analysis, see Gieling (1997); for attempts to establish Khamene'i's religious leadership, see also Buchta (2000: 94-7).

bunch of kids from [the Ministry of] 'Intelligence' that they brought. These are the calamities that we see in this country.

Montazeri's sermon caused a political storm. The conservatives responded with an immediate show of force. Their newspapers mounted a vehement personal attack on Montazeri and printed the letter from Khomeini in which he dismissed Montazeri as his successor. After days of orchestrated demonstrations against Montazeri in Qom, on 19 November mobs attacked his house, chanting 'Death to the anti-*velayat-e faqih!*' Security forces took him to an unknown place. A few days later he was returned to his house but his classes were shut down and he was put under house arrest, which lasted until January 2003.[8]

Reassessing the revolution: Kadivar's critique and the discussion with Eshkevari

Montazeri's sermon revived the debate over what went wrong, and how and by whom an Islamic Republic should be ruled. He articulated a critique of the institution of *velayat-e faqih* that reformists within the government could not, and his proposal to bring the institution under the rule of law was also in line with the reformist agenda. The press was banned from discussing his views, but photocopies of the sermon circulated widely and its contents became public knowledge.

Though Khatami's own response was silence, by early 1999 the reformist press began to debate the issues raised in Montazeri's sermon and to cross the red lines the conservatives had drawn, provoking a strong reaction.

In February, Hojjat ol-Eslam Mohsen Kadivar, a student of Montazeri and the author of two books on *velayat-e faqih*,[9] was arrested

[8] On 13 January 2000, in a faxed interview with Geneive Abdo, the *Guardian* correspondent in Iran, Ayatollah Montazeri reiterates the points he made in his 1997 sermon that led to his house arrest. He makes a strong case for the separation of powers and for the independence of the clerical establishment from the state, and calls the 1989 constitutional amendments un-Islamic. He insists that the roles of the Leader and the Guardian Council should be limited to 'overseeing' and ensuring that 'the laws issued by parliament are of an Islamic nature; the Leader has no right to exercise absolute power' (Abdo 2001).

[9] Kadivar (1998). The second, *Hokumat-e Vela'i* (Government by Mandate), undermines the religious premise of the theory of *velayat-e faqih* by showing that eight of the ten Sayings (*hadith*) commonly invoked by its advocates are not

on the orders of the Special Clergy Court. At Kadivar's trial in April, the prosecution built its case on two statements. The first cited in the indictment echoes what Montazeri said a year before. In the course of an interview with *Khordad*,[10] Kadivar stated that the track-record of the revolution is not that glorious if seen in terms of people's demands and the promises articulated in the slogan that became the revolution's motif: Independence, Freedom, and Islamic Republic – the last, in his view, containing people's demand for the elimination of monarchical oppression and the establishment of Islamic justice. The revolution's balance sheet, Kadivar concludes, is positive only with respect to the first slogan, as Iran today is relatively independent of foreign powers. But the revolution only succeeded in transforming the face of monarchy in Iran; autocratic rule and monarchical relations have remained intact, and are reproduced in the form of the absolute *velayat-e faqih*. Not only are the people unable to choose the *vali-ye faqih* directly, they have no control over his style of governance and cannot dismiss him if he goes against their will. Like an absolute monarch, the *vali-ye faqih* occupies his position for life and is above the law.[11] As for freedom, Kadivar says that the revolution has failed Iranians. One of the prerequisites of freedom 'is freedom of opposition, that is, the degree to which those who oppose the government or the ways of its rulers can be active in society and can air their views … it is only in the past two years that we could experience a degree of relative freedom … it seems that we have a long way to go, and apart from these two past years, one could say that the record of our freedom in the past two decades was a failure.'[12]

authentic, and the rest do not validate the clerics' claim to political power (see Abrahamian 2001). Kadivar had already started to publish articles that formed the third volume (Kadivar 2002), starting with one published in *Rah-e Now* (September 1998) and continuing in *Aftab* (Sun), the journal that became the main forum of religious intellectualism after the closure of *Kiyan* in November 2000.

[10] The interview was published in three installments as Kadivar (1999a). The full text is also in Kadivar (1999b: 148-68).

[11] In Kadivar (2002) he makes the parallels between absolute *velayat-e faqih* and absolute monarchy explicit, with diagrams and tables for quick access. The book is an analysis of the practical consequences of basing a government on the conservative version of the theory of *velayat-e faqih*, where the *vali* derives his mandate from God and is only answerable to Him, and elected institutions are thus subject to his authority.

[12] From the indictment, in Kadivar (1999b: 40-41)

The second statement in Kadivar's indictment was made on 12 January in a speech on 'The religious prohibition of terrorism', given in the Hoseynabad mosque in the city of Isfahan (where Montazeri has the highest number of followers) in the presence of the Friday Prayer Leader, Ayatollah Taheri, a close ally of Montazeri. Kadivar refers to the assassinations of intellectuals, known as 'serial killings', that have scandalized the country over the preceding year. Arguing that Islam bans violence against those with whose views we disagree, he declares that condemning someone to death for apostasy, secretly and without open trial, is un-Islamic and 'an innovation that it has appeared in our time'.[13]

The court sentenced Kadivar to eighteen months' imprisonment for what it identified as 'propagation of lies and disturbance of the public mind', and 'propaganda against the Islamic Republic'.

It was at just this time that Quchani went to seek Eshkevari's views on the relation between the seminaries and government. Eshkevari offers a candid critique of the theory of *velayat-e faqih* and how it conflicts with both the Shia notion of religious authority or *marja'iyat* and the democratic and republican basis of a modern state.

'The seminaries and government'
Mohammad Quchani's introduction: In this conversation Hasan Yousefi Eshkevari talks of the relation between the two institutions, the seminaries and the government. We went to him with the assumption that in the past twenty years, the distance between the two institutions has been removed. We drew Yousefi Eshkevari's attention to the principal role of Ayatollah Khomeini's charisma in bringing about this closeness. He confirmed our hypothesis and, by scrutinizing the period of the generation between the victory of the revolution on 11 February 1979 and today [1999], tried to explore the positive and negative dimensions of the merging of [these two institutions]. Yousefi Eshkevari reminded us that at the beginning 'Islamic Republic' had a broader meaning than 'Clerical Republic'. In the course of the interview we realized that, contrary to the belief of some speakers who these days delight in criticizing the record of Mehdi Bazargan and often speak of the provisional government's plan to confine Ayatollah Khomeini to Qom [to remove him from politics in Tehran], such a narrative of history is not only distorted but an inversion of reality.

---

[13] From the indictment, in Kadivar (1999b: 41-42); for the text of the speech, see Kadivar (1999b: 169-99).

Mohammad Quchani: The subject of this discussion is relations between the seminaries and government. I begin with a question that refers to one of the sayings of Ayatollah Motahhari. In the book, A Discussion about the Marja'iyat and the Clergy,[14] *he says that one difference between Shia and Sunni clergy is the independence of the former. He points out that the Sheykh of Al-Azhar sits under a picture of Nasser, whereas in Shia seminaries we never sit under the picture of any [political] personality. It appears that this way of thinking continued during the revolution. Khomeini's emphasis was that the clergy should do supervisory work and not interfere with executive affairs. For instance, he even prevented Ayatollah Beheshti from running for the first presidential election. This way of thinking also continued in the early years of the revolution, but after a while the regime of the Islamic Republic − for whatever reason − came to the conclusion that it should use the clergy in the executive field. The history of the revolution shows that [the clergy's] share [of power] increased day by day. From a general perspective and by way of assessment, do you think that, at this point, the disappearance of the distance between the seminaries and government, and the seminarians' acquisition of a role in political power, have been on the whole beneficial or detrimental to the seminaries?*

Hasan Yousefi Eshkevari: In the Name of God the Merciful and Compassionate. I thank you for making this discussion possible. Without deciding in advance whether the phenomenon of the merger of the seminaries and government − or in a more precise sense, the active and increasing role of the clerics during the twenty years of the Islamic Republic − is negative or positive, I shall try to explain the consequences of this merger; and only then assess whether it is negative or positive and give you my opinion.

The establishment of the Islamic Republic with a virtual monopoly of government by clerics has had several consequences that one can say, from a future historical perspective, are not and will not be in the interest of the clerics.

The first consequence of the overwhelming power of the clerics in the Islamic Republic has been that it went contrary to the initial promise (...)[15] of the leaders of the revolution. While Ayatollah Khomeini was in Paris he expressed in his interviews something to the effect that, after his return to Iran, he would return to seminary work,

---

[14] Motahhari (1962) in Anjoman (1962); see introductory notes to Chapter 3, and Vahdat (2002: 178).

[15] The bracketed ellipsis here (and in other instances below) indicates something Eshkevari said that had to be censored for publication.

and that he didn't intend the clerics to gain power. These interviews are now published and can be referred to.

In other words, he said that it was not intended that government should be in hands of clerics. Apparently, judging from his statements, what he had in mind was for the clerics to have a kind of supervisory function, but not to be involved in executive work or in the political administration of society. Specifically, for instance, they were not to hold the posts of president, prime minister, provincial governor and so on.

Once he had come to Tehran [from Paris], after a month he moved to Qom, although at that time Bazargan, who was head of the provisional government, pressed him to stay in Tehran. In Bazargan's view, Khomeini's presence in Tehran could have helped solve many problems, but the latter initially did not accept this and went to Qom. When in Qom, as the Leader of the Revolution, Khomeini would receive many visits; the Revolutionary Council and the provisional government were always meeting with him, and ultimately all affairs were subject to his approval. Despite this, he lived in Qom as a *marja'*, not as ruler.

The role he assumed at that time was a natural one. He was the Leader of the Revolution and it was not possible to do things without the leadership's approval. Even if he had withdrawn, conditions and exigencies were such that, without his presence, things would not have moved. Problems in Tehran and in the government were increasing daily, and the authorities were constantly going to Qom to seek guidance from him. Sometimes immediate access to him was not possible. It was for this reason, I think, that, some time in August or September 1979, Mehdi Bazargan wrote and requested him to move to Tehran, because his presence there was needed in order to solve the problems. Khomeini did not respond and did not come to Tehran, and in effect did not agree to the request. Later, when he was transferred to Tehran because of heart problems, he stayed for some time at the Heart Hospital; and then he had to rest in Tehran for his convalescence. Anyway, the situation became such that he remained in Tehran.

My point is that Khomeini's thought indicates that when he moved to Tehran he was still acting according to the promise he had made. Later when the issue of the presidency came up, and Ayatollah Beheshti was a candidate, Khomeini did not accept his candidature. There was a lot of pressure for certain clerics to be candidates but Khomeini did not accept this.

One finds the same concern in Ayatollah Motahhari's statements. He too stressed after the revolution that the clergy must return to their clerical work. Likewise, Ayatollah Taleqani, who was one of the leaders of the revolution at the time, and whose statements were regarded as those of the collective leadership of the revolutionary regime, was also adamant on this point. Therefore, the totality of promises made to the people was that the clerics would do their own work and at most retain a high supervisory role. Otherwise, the affairs of society, government and political rule would be managed in accordance with the convention in other political systems of the world (that is, the democratic ones). I am referring to Ayatollah Motahhari's interview broadcast on television and published in the book, *About the Islamic Republic*.[16] In that interview, he was asked whether the *velayat-e faqih* did not contradict the national government and national sovereignty that we had been advocating since the Constitutional Revolution. He replied, no, they are complementary, not contradictory; the *faqih* is not a leader. The governing, political leadership of society, or in other words, the government, is in the hands of the people, who will elect their own president, prime minister and leader according to their own practice. The *velayat-e faqih* is the ideological leader and in effect has a kind of ideological supervisory role.

Never mind that the statement itself was vague, and that it did not say what 'supervision' entails. Does supervision take place within the context of the political structure of power, or is it something above it? These issues were not that clear at the time and contained [much] ambiguity (...)[17]

We know that the first draft of the constitution, which was written by the provisional government and then completed by the Revolutionary Council and which the Leader of the Revolution wanted to put to a referendum, did not include the principle of *velayat-e faqih*, that is, government by clergy. Khomeini himself had read it and had made a few objections that were supposed to be corrected in the Assembly [of Experts]. At the time, however, neither he nor others raised any objection as to why it did not include government by clergy.

If we put all this together, we see that the thinking, and the promise made to the people at the time, was that the clergy would not be in government – and certainly not that they would monopolize government. However, as events turned out, the idea of *velayat-e faqih*

---

[16] Motahhari (1981).
[17] Ellipsis in the original, see above.

was institutionalized (that is to say, somehow government by clergy was inserted into the constitution). Nevertheless, I believe that the inclusion of *velayat-e faqih* in the constitution did not by itself necessarily have to result in transforming the Islamic Republic into a clerical Republic (in Bazargan's words). In other words, we could have had the principle of *velayat-e faqih* without a clerical government. Anyway, for whatever reason, Khomeini himself eventually accepted the phenomenon of clerical government. Then gradually, especially after the events of 1981 and the dismissal of Bani-Sadr and developments that occurred after that, the course of events naturally – perhaps also a little unnaturally – led to the Islamic Republic being transformed into a clerical Republic.[18]

Therefore, the first consequence of the full entry of the clerics into the government of the Islamic Republic was the breaking of a promise. That is, a pledge given to the people before the revolution and during the revolutionary era was broken. For this reason, many political forces, both inside and outside the country, raise this as a major criticism and problem for the Islamic Republic.

The second consequence or problem connected with this issue was that the Islamic government rapidly became sectarian and *fiqhi*.[19] If we discuss this in theoretical and analytical terms, I think it will be evident that religious government is different from *fiqhi* government.

A religious government can be defined as one that is managed in accordance with a series of values and broad directives that are rooted in religion. These might be reflected in various articles of the constitution, nothing more; or at most some religious laws might be legislated and implemented as positive laws.

This is what was also done at the time of the constitutional movement. Then, when they wanted to write laws, they took civil laws from Shia *fiqh*, as Shia *fiqh* was very rich with respect to civil laws. But as for general principles of political thought and the political system, it provided no special model, and so they translated articles from the law codes of Belgium, England, France and other European countries. They had no alternative: there was nothing else available.

---

[18] For this period, see Abrahamian (1989), Bakhash (1984); for details, see Schirazi (1998).

[19] Literally 'juristic'; but intended in the sense of 'clerical', run by a *faqih*. See Editors' Introduction to Chapter 3 for Bazargan's and Soroush's critiques of ideological *fiqh*.

The same could have occurred in the Islamic regime, but it did not, and it was transformed into a *fiqhi* government. By '*fiqhi* government' I mean one in which all affairs, including decision-making in the executive, the legislative and the judicial powers, take place within the framework of *fiqh*. When everything is supposed to be done in accordance with *fiqh*, and when we approach legislation, the judiciary, the executive power and other matters from a *fiqh* perspective, then the result will be a clerical government. This is the inevitable result.

We could have had an Islamic Republic in which a set of general values under the broad rubric of Islamic government could have been realized and implemented – just as the same idea had already been raised in Pakistan and the Islamic Republic of Pakistan came into being. That is, they could have founded an Islamic Republic on the basis of a range of values and principles that exist in Islam.

We could even have bypassed these general laws and legislated minor laws in parliament. They could have then been put at the disposal of the judiciary, a judiciary that remained in the hands of the clerics, but clerics who were familiar not only with *fiqh* but also with contemporary legal concepts. In the past, many *fuqaha* claimed exclusive right to judgement in their field. In today's world, of course, this matter cannot be exclusive to the *fuqaha* and ulama, though part of our *fiqh* could have been nicely manifested in the judiciary – particularly as our *fiqh* is rich in terms of individual, penal, civil and family law and many other matters. The *fuqaha* have already worked in these areas and this could have been implemented in a relatively problem-free manner. However, this government very rapidly became a *fiqhi* government, and by the beginning of the 1980s it acquired various epithets, such as 'juristic Islam' (*eslam-e feqahati*) or 'treatise Islam' (*eslam-e resale'i*).

Fiqhi government has its own corollaries. One is sectarianism. When we speak of Islamic government (since Islam is a broad designation), we could include in the Islamic Republic, in the *fuqaha*'s terminology, a kind of comparative *fiqh* (*fiqh-e moqaren*) and make the Shia form dominant. Incidentally, had this happened then our *fiqh* could have become dynamic. By comparative *fiqh* is meant that both Shia and Sunni *fiqh* are utilized. This is the approach of the House of Closeness (*Dar ul-Taqrib*), pursued at the time of Ayatollah Borujerdi. It was his efforts that led Sheykh Muhammad Shaltut, the Mufti of Al-Azhar, to place the *fiqh* of Imami Shiism next to the four schools of Sunni *fiqh* and grant it official recognition. In Iran, next to these four *fiqh* schools we could have utilized Shia *fiqh* and thus have a collection of comparative *fiqh*. This could have led to more dynamic *fiqh* and the evolution of an Islamic *fiqh* that could have brought these two groups of Muslims closer together.

MQ: Our legal structure already contained Islamic and Shia fiqh ...

HYE: Correct, but when Islamic government becomes *fiqhi* government, it becomes sectarian. Because we are Imami Shia, so the *fiqh* of that sect must rule. Hence you see it stipulated in the constitution that the president must be Shia, and the official religion of the country is Twelver [Imami] Shiism, although these stipulations to an extent seem normal because of the Shia majority.

At that time many Sunni Iranians also criticized these stipulations; and these differences and criticisms have continued. In fact, as I recall, when the constitution was put to a referendum, many Sunnis did not want to vote. At that time, in a speech or a directive (addressed to the Kurds and other Sunnis) Ayatollah Khomeini promised that these problems would be dealt with in the constitutional amendments. However, this government became a Twelver Shia government, and the Sunnis, who are Muslims [too], had no role in the structure of this *fiqh*, and their own *fiqh* also became irrelevant. In practice too, although some [Majlis] deputies are elected by Sunni majority areas, in intellectual and doctrinal terms they have no role in law making. At the same time, this *fiqhi* government has created clashes and problems among the [Shia] clerics themselves who have different *fiqh* perspectives.

The third problem is that the full entry of clerics into the arena of government led to a degree of confrontation between the institution of *marja'iyat* and the institution of government. This is an important point, which should be considered and debated.

MQ: Why is this important?

HYE: The *marja'iyat* of the Shia is a thousand-year-old institution. A principal feature of the institution is the official acceptance of *ijtihad*; the Shia have always been proud that they, unlike the Sunnis, have left the door of *ijtihad* open. A second feature is that the Shia institution of *marja'iyat* has never been governmental. This gave a kind of independence to the *marja'iyat*, and in the course of its thousand-year history this independence enabled it to remain a support and refuge for the people whenever needed, and at certain historical junctures – though not always – to provide leadership for popular movements. The Tobacco Protest and the constitutional movement[20] are the two of most conspicuous and evident examples of this. One can also mention the role of popular clerical leadership in the National Movement (Mosaddeq), the role of [Ayatollah] Kashani and others, and also the role of clerics in the period of revolution, including Ayatollah Khomeini, Ayatollah Taleqani and others. They could organize a popular movement because they were truly independent from the institutions of government. They also had relative economic independence – as the clergy had always had its own specific sources of income, such as the Imam's share, religious dues, people's charities, donations and other endowments – which is to say that (unlike Sunni clerics) they did not receive government salaries. They were also politically independent; and especially after the Safavid era, the *marja'iyat* was an independent institution parallel to the political institution. Of course, because the two institutions were independent, sometimes they collided and clashes arose between them. If the clerics were strong, this confrontation would lead to the weakening of the monarchy – as was the case during the constitutional movement. If the monarchy were stronger, it would lead weaken the independence of the *marja'iyat*. In any case, this independence brought with it many blessings in the past. Before the revolution, our clerics, for instance Ayatollah Motahhari in his book, *A Discussion about the* Marja'iyat *and the Clergy*, or Dr Shariati in his speeches, always mentioned this as being a key to the power of Shia clerics, which was indeed the case.

However the very same clerics who yesterday were subjects have now become the rulers. The very same people who yesterday, in Motahhari's words, boasted of not sitting under anybody's picture and not needing permission from any ruler to speak their mind and issue fatwas, today not only are themselves linked to the government but have become the rulers. This is a fundamental change for the institution of *marja'iyat*.

Al-Azhar has been dependent on government throughout history, ever since it was established at the time of the Fatimids.[21] That is to say, it was a branch of a state institution. Thus you see that the political and intellectual inclinations found in Al-Azhar have always reflected political developments in the state. For instance, at the time of King Faruq, you see that his policies were endorsed by Al-Azhar. If

[20] For these, see Chapter 1.
[21] The Fatimid Caliphs ruled in Egypt between 969 and 1171.

Al-Azhar issues political or social fatwas, they always reflect the policies of the rulers. When the 1952 revolution took place in Egypt and the Free Officers emerged, first Naguib and later Nasser, and a socialist state came into power, Al-Azhar issued leftist and socialist fatwas. Then when [Anwar] Sadat came and policies changed, Al-Azhar also changed. But we did not have such a thing in Shiism. Of course, occasionally the [Shia clerics] toed the political line, for instance during Safavid or Qajar times. But at the same time they retained a relative independence for themselves.

MQ: You said that one of the reasons for the clergy's popularity was that they were independent of [state] power. You also gave instances of this. The question that arises is: given that these two structures [seminaries and government] have now become one, do you think the clergy retain the capacity and power to undertake the leadership of social movements in future?

HYE: Yes. I believe that in the past twenty years not all our present clerics have become governmental, nor has the institution of *marja'iyat*. Besides, our clergy are not unified and it can even be said that many of them have not yet been welded into the structure of the Islamic Republic and are not attuned to it.

MQ: But the people's perception of the future leadership capacity of the clergy is different.

HYE: It seems that the people's perception is not correct. That is to say, people are not familiar enough with the internal fabric of the clergy and what is going on in the seminaries.

MQ: Perhaps the official media are trying to spread this line [i.e. that all clerics are with the government].

HYE: This is one factor. Although the people, and even the intellectuals, had relations with the clerics before the revolution, they were not very familiar with the inner realities of clerical society.

I speak from experience, because not only am I myself a cleric but also both before and after the revolution I had relations with political and intellectual activists, and I still have. We notice that even people like Mehdi Bazargan, despite all the connections he had with the clerics (in childhood, in his family and at the time of his father Hajji Abbas-qoli Bazargan), did not have a good and accurate appreciation of the internal fabric of the clergy. The perception that people now have is not a correct and realistic one. At present it appears that one part of the clergy are totally traditional, that is, non-political, and, from a position faithful to traditional Shia political thought, they consider any involvement with politics to be incorrect. They do not accept a religious government, that is a *fiqhi* one, and consider [government] to be the sole prerogative of the Infallible Imam. They say that when the Infallible Imam is absent, we cannot have an Islamic and *fiqhi* government.

Someone like Na'ini, in his *Tanbih al-Ummah*,[22] did not consider constitutional government to be Islamic – of course, Islamic in the sense of *fiqhi*. From this perspective and position, some of our clerics agree neither with *velayat-e faqih* nor with the Islamic Republic; but, for whatever reason, they remain silent and raise no objection.

There were other clerics who were involved in the revolution. They believe in political Islam and even in *velayat-e faqih* and accept the totality of the constitution, the framework of the regime of the Islamic Republic. But they do not agree with certain interpretations of *velayat-e faqih* or with the performance of the clerics in the Islamic Republic. Some of them, we see, are regarded today as dissident clerics, for instance Ayatollah Montazeri, who was himself one of the founders of *velayat-e faqih*. He still says that he believes in *velayat-e faqih* but at the same time his interpretation of *velayat-e faqih* is different. As the research of [my] friend Kadivar indicates, so far eight theories of Islamic government, in the sense of *velayat-e faqih*, have emerged in Iran. This shows that the fabric of our clergy has not become monochrome and it cannot be said that the clergy collectively are coterminous with the Islamic Republic.

Let me mention another point: apart from these two groups (that is, the traditional clerics and the political clerics who are still faithful to the revolution or were players in the revolution but now relate to the Islamic Republic from a critical and dissident position), a third group is now emerging. These are young clerics who have a novel and more modernist way of thinking, which is different from that of the two other groups. They entered the seminaries or came of age after the revolution. One example is Mohsen Kadivar, who is in effect a product of this period. Kadivar's approach is not unique to him; a sizable group in the seminaries are coming round to his way of thinking. Therefore, it cannot be said now that all clerics have become one with the Islamic Republic.

[22] Na'ini (1955). See Chapter 1 above.

Hence in response to your question as to whether clerics can still be movement-creators and continue to play their historical role, my answer is affirmative. Society showed this in the elections for the fifth Majlis, and particularly with the presidential election and even the council elections. In spite of all their criticisms of the clergy (especially of the ruling clergy), people have not yet become absolutely anti-clerical. This depends on who a cleric is and what his position is. A person like Mr Khatami was both a cleric and for ten years a minister in this regime; nobody regarded him as being outside the system of the Islamic Republic. But he won such a high vote because he offered a more modernist and reformist vision and his statements addressed the people's needs or were compatible with their demands. I think that if Mr Khatami stands again as a candidate for election as president, not only will he win but his share of the vote will increase. This demonstrates that people still accept clerics; remember that in Tehran Abdollah Nuri won the highest vote. We can interpret this as [meaning that] people judge an individual cleric on his merits.

MQ: Meaning that people attach greater importance to a public figure's political stance than to whether he is a cleric or not?

HYE: Yes. Besides, the good will that existed during the revolution is no longer there. That is, people no longer say, let us vote for whoever is a cleric. Instead people consider his ideas and thinking, his track record and his approach – not whether he wears a clerical robe or not – and this shows that someone who is a cleric can still become a [political] player. Especially since, given that a cleric wears a cloak and speaks in the name of religion, and that our masses are religious, people listen more to him. I'm speaking of the masses, not of the elite and intellectuals. I have found this through experience. This goes against the analysis of some who say that people in the Islamic Republic have quite turned their backs on religion and the clergy. I do not believe this to be the case.

Therefore, with respect to the discussion of *marja'iyat* and government, I was saying that, with the establishment of the Islamic Republic and the merging of a section of the clergy with government, the institution of *marja'iyat*, which had been following a certain trajectory, has now entered another historical phase. That is, the clergy's second millennium is going to be different from their first. Even in the first millennium, the history of the clergy can be divided into five or six distinct phases. However, if we take a broad view, my belief is that from the fourth century onwards, i.e. from the start of the Greater

Occultation in the year 329,[23] when the ulama became players in intellectual, social and political fields, until 11 February [1979], the clergy and our institution of *marja'iyat* on the whole followed one path. With the Islamic Republic, and the clergy's merging with it, it seems that, at least theoretically, our clergy have taken the opposite course.

MQ: Does the situation that prevailed in the seminaries in the past still continue?

HYE: Yes, it now continues officially in the Islamic Republic. But new political and intellectuals positions are also emerging among the clerics. These may play a role later on.

I mean that, from a historical perspective, with the advent of the Islamic Republic – the enactment of *velayat-e faqih*, the coming to power of the clerics and their assumption of all responsibilities (executive, judiciary, legislative) – the clergy entered a new phase. Of course, it was not necessarily intended that the clerics should head the executive branch, but in practice this is what happened.

And above all, there is the Leadership,[24] which is above all other powers, [the incumbent] holding the supreme leadership; and in present conditions it is impossible for him to be a non-cleric. Ideologically speaking, the Leader does not have to be a cleric; that is to say, it is not necessary that the *faqih* should wear a clerical robe. In theory there is no reason that a non-cleric cannot also possess the qualifications for leadership and be elected as Leader. In reality, however, such a thing is not possible.

Our thousand-year-old institution of the *marja'iyat* today, in some cases at least, is in conflict with government; and since it is now merged with government, the conflicts too have become evident. This conflict goes back to the very issue of independence. That is to say, our past independent clerics thought in certain ways and recognized a certain distinctiveness for themselves. For instance, suppose anyone who wanted to choose a *marja'* could do it personally, or could ask expert and informed people in order to identify the most learned.

---

[23] The year 329 AH/941 CE marked the end of the Lesser Occultation, which lasted about one hundred years, during which the Twelfth Imam was in contact with his followers through four messengers. For the doctrine of Occultation, see Momen (1985: 161-71).

[24] Eshkevari uses the office (*rahbari*, leadership) to imply the incumbent (*rahbar*); see Chapter 1.

Especially since the time of Sheykh Ansari,[25] when the issue of being 'most learned' arose, most people have chosen their *marja'* in this way. But now you see that the institution of *marja'iyat* wants to retain its independence; and in the Islamic Republic this is something that is accepted, especially after the dismissal of Ayatollah Montazeri, when *marja'iyat* as a condition [for leadership] was dropped from the constitution (...)[26] Therefore *marja'iyat* as condition for leadership was dropped and only *ijtihad* remained. After this, we see that the conflict with government has come to the surface. On the one hand, the government, because of its religious and clerical composition, wants to subordinate the *marja'iyat* institution to itself – which is in direct contradiction to the thousand-year independence of the clergy and the *marja'iyat*. On the other hand, the *marja'iyat*, because of its claim to independence, wants to subordinate the government to itself. They [the *maraji'*] say, we want to remain independent in Qom; we want people to choose their *marja'* in the traditional way; we want each *marja'* to have his own followers, to receive the Imam's share, issue fatwas, etc. – exactly in the old style. These demands contradict some of the elements, decisions and institutions of government.

Let us consider the Imam's share. In the past one of the indisputable *fiqh* principles was that every follower paid the Imam's share to the *marja'* he followed. Now if this Imam's share is paid to the *maraji'* – which is still done – they gradually acquire economic power; and what happened in the first millennium will happen in the Islamic Republic. If this happens, then the independence of the clergy (be it economic, political, cultural, or the freedom to issue fatwas) will eventually lead to a situation in which one day some cleric will issue a fatwa that directly opposes the policies of the Islamic Republic.

Suppose that in the past [before the revolution] one of the *maraji'* believed that taxation is forbidden, whereas these days a government cannot function without taxation. Now what should his followers (...) do? If they want to pay tax, they will be going against the fatwa of their *marja'*. If they do not want to pay tax, the government will make them pay, because when the taxman comes he does not ask: 'who is your

25 Sheykh Morteza Ansari (d. 1864) became sole *marja'* in 1850; well known for his innovative teaching methods, he was the author of two texts (*al-Makasib* and *Rasa'il*) that are still taught in Shia seminaries.
26 Ellipsis in the original. The omitted passage probably referred to the present Leader (Ayatollah Khamene'i)'s lack of religious qualifications to be a *marja'*, and also to the disputes that led to the dismissal of Ayatollah Montazeri.

marja?' He takes the tax according to the law, and you must pay. Thus one has to pay both tax and religious dues. But can religious dues be considered a tax? This is debated among the *fuqaha*. Ayatollah Khomeini himself finally did not allow it. He was the founder of the Islamic Republic and advocated a religious and *fiqhi* government but he did not allow religious dues to be considered as [state] tax. It was for this reason that when he died there were 800 million toman in the account that he left to the seminaries. The newspapers confirmed that Hajji Sayyid Ahmad [Khomeini's son] delivered this amount to the seminaries.[27]

This independence has some conditions that do not fit well with a centralized power. It was different if, as in the past, the state was divided into secular and religious elements. In the past, ever since the time of the Safavids, a kind of division of labour between the ulama and the kings emerged naturally. Now this division has broken down. In short, because of its [political] nature on the one hand, and because of its religious and *fiqhi* nature on the other, the government believes that all social, political, and economic affairs of society, and all decisions that must be taken in relation to society, must come under government control, because it is a religious government. It has a *vali-ye faqih*, a *mujtahid* is at the head of the regime, there are a Guardian Council, an Expediency Council and a Majlis, which are all religious, and government acts accordingly. On the basis of this theory, and because of the circumstances, the institution of *marja'iyat* must necessarily come under the government. Whereas, if the traditional *marja'iyat* wants to remain independent, the government will somehow be subordinated to it, and it seems that in future this conflict will become [increasingly] problematic.

MQ: Can't you suggest a middle way? Isn't there one?

HYE: One must dominate the other. The government could turn the seminaries and the *marja'iyat* into something like Al-Azhar; that is, the head of the seminaries would be appointed by the Leader, and [the *maraji'*] could not issue independent fatwas, and matters such as the follower's relation to his *marja'* and paying him the Imam's share and religious dues would be abandoned. Or there could be an assembly of *fuqaha* for issuing religious fatwas, which would pertain only to personal

[27] This consisted of religious dues paid to Khomeini as *marja'* by his followers. At the time, it was equivalent to about US$ 5 million.

and ritual matters. This could happen only if these two institutions [*marja'iyat* and government] were merged, as [Ayatollah] Mo'men[28] suggested a few years ago. He proposed that no *marja'* should be entitled to issue fatwas regarding administrative, social, political and economic matters, as these all fall in the domain of government.

Once, we had both secular and religious [elements in the] government, but now this makes no sense, according to current theory, as after all we have only one government and it claims to be religious. Therefore, if these two institutions are unified, we must say: let *maraji'* exist, but people should follow them only in ritual acts that do not concern government, such as prayers, fasting and pilgrimage. If they want to issue fatwas [on other matters], there should be a Fatwa House or a Fatwa Council. This council must have a head who is appointed by the highest government authority, i.e. the Leader, and issue its fatwas in a framework of clearly defined regulations – exactly as in Al-Azhar – and not as in the past, when a *marja'* like Mirza-ye Shirazi could emerge, who could bring the country to a standstill with one fatwa,[29] or Khomeini himself, who could do the same. In this case, such *maraji'* cannot appear.

MQ: To what extent is this in line with the theory of a fiqhi *Council that Ayatollah Taleqani proposed in his book?*

HYE: If it is to be like Al-Azhar, it would be possible. Of course, at that time (1340/1961), the debate was not about [Islamic] government or politics. The point was: why should there be ten or twenty *maraji'* whose fatwas are very similar and whose treatises are like carbon copies of each other?

In 1961, after the death of Ayatollah Borujerdi, when there was a Grand *Marja'* [succession] crisis, Ayatollah Taleqani and another cleric proposed this theory; Ayatollah Motahhari too, in his book, initially more or less supported this view: that the *fuqaha* should form a consultative assembly and merge their fatwas.

In my view, of course, this is not feasible. If it happened, it would contradict another *fiqhi* principle; *ijtihad* would come under government control, and lose its autonomy. Ayatollah Montazeri, and also some of Motahhari's fellow-thinkers, are trying to solve the problem by saying that the clerics and even the *vali-ye faqih* should have a super-

---

[28] See Editors' Introduction to this chapter, above.
[29] In the Tobacco Protest of 1891.

visory role (*nezarat*). In other words, Islamic supervision is correct, but the clergy and the Leader have no right to interfere in executive affairs, merely to supervise. Thus no problem would emerge in practice, and freedom, democracy and political parties could do their work. But what is the nature of this supervision? This issue has not been clarified – at least it is not that clear in Mr Kadivar's theory.[30]

A further problem is the relation between [the institution of] *marja'iyat* and individual *maraji'*, and the institution of *velayat-e faqih*. What sort of relationship will these two have? Will it be as individuals? When they are individuals, the relation between follower and followed means something. But once a Fatwa Council is created and there is a collectivity that issues fatwas, the relationship between follower and followed becomes meaningless. Besides, who will get the Imam's share? The council, or each individual *marja*? Or simply the government?

The issue of the autonomy of the *marja'iyat* creates another problem. Suppose there are ten *fuqaha* sitting in the council and issuing fatwas. What if one of them reaches the conclusion that the [council's] opinion is not correct and that his is correct, that is, there are nine against one?

In this situation, if, for instance, I come to the conclusion, according to the Shia [principle of] free *ijtihad*, that God's ruling is this, on the basis of what religious argument should I [put aside my own *ijtihad* and] follow the opinion of the other nine? Surely *taqlid* [following the rulings of others] is forbidden for a *mujtahid*? Then, if someone asks me my opinion, I must say that my opinion is different from the other nine. That is, if I have the right to express my opinion. In that case, a new division will emerge in government and decision-making, and myriad problems will be created in society.

Whichever of these two ideas [that the *marja'iyat* obeys the state, or that the state follows the *marja'iyat*] we accept, we will have problems. Each way has certain consequences that are not easily resolved, unless matters take their natural course and eventually, however events develop in future, many of the fundamentals accepted in the past will be gradually transformed. Without a transformation of the fundamentals (e.g. the autonomy of *ijtihad*, the relation between a *marja'-e taqlid* and his followers, the *khoms* [one-fifth tax] and the Imam's share, following the most learned, and independence in *ijtihad*), the conflict between the institution of *marja'iyat* and religious government is insoluble.

---

[30] Kadivar has since come down on the side of democracy, see Epilogue.

MQ: Two other models can be invoked and discussed. First, a point that I want to link to this discussion is that leadership in this government comes about in a charismatic way. We see its exemplar in the person of Ayatollah Khomeini. As you mentioned, religious marja'iyat *and political [authority] were combined in the person of Khomeini. It seems that if such a distinctly charismatic personality should emerge in the political future of Iran, then this conflict [between political and religious authority] could be resolved. My question is whether you can foresee a repetition of this occurrence in the future? The problem is that even if such a situation occurs it will not last — just as it did not outlast Khomeini and we saw how after him the division re-opened.*

Secondly, another model that I think can be considered (which, while traditional, takes a totally modern form) is a plurality of maraji'; *they could be elected by their followers and brought into the arena of civil and democratic competition. I mean that, by separating parts of the public and private realms from each other, and by reducing the role of the state in people's private lives, we can in practice create a situation where people can choose one from among various* fiqh *schools and theories (just as political parties are elected in the modern world). This [chosen] 'theory' rules for a certain time and then space is opened for other [competing] theories. Of course such a rule would be confined to the public realm; if it were to include the private realm, in practice [personal] freedoms would be curtailed.*

HYE: You know that charismatic personalities, embodying those features that Max Weber detailed and which we now have in mind, never emerge in normal, predictable conditions and common contexts. People with special talents and unique personal attributes emerge in exceptional conditions caused by political, social and cultural change; a particularly magnetic charismatic personality emerges to play a specific historical role.

If our [political] landscape in future retains the normal routine of the Islamic regime, then there is no reason for such a personality to emerge. In fact the conditions for the emergence of such a personality will not be there. A charismatic personality is basically a revolutionary and rebellious character, angry about the present condition of society. Such a person does not emerge in ordinary situations, unless there are changes and developments in the course of which some dissident cleric protests against the current situation and emerges as a charismatic character. However, since the Islamic Republic is still evolving, and rapid changes and developments can still happen, it is possible that another Ayatollah Khomeini could arise in this Islamic Republic. But this person will no longer be an ordinary personality who fits the normal routine of the Islamic Republic.

As for your second point, this is a very important one and may in effect be regarded as a positive aspect of setting up the *marja'iyat* and a plurality of sources of religious authority alongside the government. If this event happens in this form then the *marja'iyat* can become a solid institution of civil society – given that it also has historical roots and that each *marja'* has a broad constituency and can lead various social groups with his ideas. This prevents the emergence of dictatorship and to some extent impedes the unification of religion and government; or, in Na'ini's words, prevents religious despotism. This is the positive side of the issue.

However, for such a situation to occur and for the institution of *marja'iyat* and the plurality of *maraji'* to be treated as institutions of civil society as we define it today, it is necessary for many matters to change and many issues to be clarified.

The first thing that must be clarified is that the *maraji'* should abandon their claim that they have the right to [issue] fatwas on all affairs. This is the same theory as that proposed by Ayatollah Mo'men. This is so because, as we have already said, we have only one government, which has certain mandates; after all, it makes policies, legislates and interferes in all aspects in our lives; today all our affairs are subject to government control.

MQ: Can't [the maraji'*] claim the right to declare public and social rulings but make their enactment of them subject to the consensus of the majority?*

HYE: This theory is not compatible with our *fiqhi* and doctrinal premises, because when a *marja'-e taqlid* issues a fatwa, he is declaring God's ruling and his followers believe that he has expressed God's ruling.

MQ: You mean, it would change the understanding that [the marja'*] alone declares God's rulings?*

HYE: It is no longer Shia *ijtihad*. In the tradition of the *marja'iyat*, we have cases like Mirza-ye Shirazi who said, 'today the consumption of tobacco is war against the twelfth Imam ...'

*MQ: If Mirza-ye Shirazi had no followers, how could he implement this ruling? In fact the [literal] reading of this view is that theoretically any [*marja'*] can recognize for himself the right to interpret God's ruling but enforcement in such cases will be subject to the people's vote. That is, in practice, this can become a publicly accepted doctrine in the social realm [i.e. people vote which religious rulings should be*

enforced]. I am expressing the modern interpretation of this matter, I am not dis-
cussing it from a traditional perspective and I do not wish to criticize fiqhi *premises*
but simply to reproduce them for the new circumstances.

I think it is possible [for a marja'*] to put this in the form of a proposal to*
society and stand by it, and say: 'this is God's ruling and I am declaring it'; but to
leave its actualization to people's vote.

HYE: Look, that fatwa is understandable and acceptable given those
premises. That is, a *mujtahid* deduces God's ruling on the basis of *fiqhi*
arguments and then declares it. Those who follow him are duty-bound
to carry out that ruling, and this is the framework that we have inherited from the past. If someone like Mirza-ye Shirazi came and banned
something, it could be said that this was exceptional. Consider ordinary fatwas such as those [banning] things like fish or music.[31] At
present there are many scholars who [still] consider music to be forbidden. Well, what should their followers do?

MQ: When this issue has an impact on the public sphere then it creates a [legal]
conflict.

HYE: That's just it. That's what I am saying. I say the conflict that has
emerged between the *marja'iyat* and government – and is expanding
day by day – stems from this cause.

MQ: In practice, therefore, our fuqaha, *like politicians, or politicians in a modern*
society, must accept that the realm of government is not a realm for a plurality of
decision-making [authorities] and ultimately one view must dominate, even if the
deciding factors differ.

HYE: And that view is [that of] the Islamic ruler. Even when it is said
that people today must now pay [religious] dues to the Leader, this is a
correct and logical statement, as far the political side of the government is concerned. For there is no reason for billions of tomans to go
to [*maraji'* in] Najaf, Qom, Tehran, and for [the *maraji'*] to spend it on
their own programmes, regardless of all other criteria and regulations.
All this must go to the state treasury.

---

[31] He is referring to two controversial fatwas by which Ayatollah Khomeini in
1985 removed the ban on listening to music, and fishing and eating one type of
fish.

MQ: Therefore, if the marja'iyat *wants to retain its independence, it seems that it cannot do this without the aid of modern methods; and if it wants to do this it should submit itself to reconstruction.*

HYE: Certainly. That is, the theoretical premises of *ijtihad* as well as our institution of *marja'iyat* must be rethought, along with the practical organization and regulation of existing relations within the clergy. In other words, the issue of *taqlid*, free *ijtihad*, God's rulings, the Imam's share, and so on, must all be reconsidered. The realm of *fiqh* and fatwas must also be restricted.

If the *marja'iyat* wants to remain meaningful, the *maraji'* too must revise their own intellectual premises – our *fiqh* concepts, matters that we have so far regarded as fixed principles of *fiqh*. Internal relations among the clergy must also undergo fundamental revision.

I am not, of course, suggesting that this should happen, and I am certainly not saying that this is a good thing. I am saying that if the clash between the *marja'iyat* and government is to be resolved, then the *maraji'* must limit the scope of their work. That is to say, they must confine the field of fatwa to the realm of personal and ritual matters; i.e. those things that will not clash with government.

If a *marja'* wants to say paying tax is forbidden, this is [trespassing] on the realm of government.

MQ: Won't this end in the secularization of the realm of religion – or at least of fiqh?

HYE: This is basically the dilemma of a religious government. Before the revolution, without a role in government, we lived in the clouds with our ideals, so we did not appreciate these difficulties. But after the revolution, these problems arose as events unfolded.

In 1980 or 1981 I wrote an article about *velayat-e faqih*. I endorsed the principle, which then, in my view, was incontestable. But I [also] pointed out the problems that might arise in future. I raised the issue of the future of the *marja'iyat* and asked these questions: what kind of relationship will the *marja'iyat* have with government in future? Should the *maraji'* obey the ruler? If so, this is pointless and compromises the whole institution of the *marja'iyat*. Should government obey the *maraji'*, this would be problematic too. We do not have one single *marja'*. We might have a hundred of them. Then each of them issues his specific fatwas. Their fatwas sometimes trespass on the realm of government.

Besides, not all *maraji'* are under the Islamic Republic. According to our former way of thinking, fatwas and relations between a *marja'* and his followers recognize no geographical boundaries. Had it not been for the present political situation in Iraq and Saddam's massacres [of the Shia authorities], some religious authorities would certainly have emigrated after the revolution from Iran to Najaf; and today the Najaf seminaries would have been powerful.

During the constitutional movement, and in other cases, Akhund Khorasani issued a fatwa from Najaf in support of constitutionalism. Now what if the Najaf seminary were [still] powerful and individuals like al-Hakim, Akhund Khorasani, Sayyid Abol-Hasan Esfahani, and Borujerdi[32] resided there and issued fatwas from there for their followers – assuming that a majority of [Iranian] people were their followers? What would have happened? There would have been constant clashes and chaos.

That is why, in my view, the traditional fabric of our *marja'iyat* as it existed in the past, with those principles, premises, and structure of relations, cannot come under government. Nor can government become subordinate to it, because in this government an Islamic Leader has been installed to speak in the name of Islam and to declare its rulings, so there is no reason for this Leader to defer to a *marja'*. Even if he were to obey a *marja'*, which *marja'* should he obey?

For instance, suppose we grant the *maraji'* also the right to express their views on foreign policy. One might say that it is mandatory to resume relations with America, and another might say that it is haram and tantamount to 'war against the twelfth Imam'. This is the case right now among our high-ranking clerics, but it is of little consequence, as the *marja'iyat* has little influence. During the constitutional movement, some *maraji'* supported it, considering it to be defending the twelfth Imam.

As long as there is revolt, struggle and revolution, these issues are unimportant; like secondary issues, such as touching the earth twice or thrice for ablution when there is no water, they will not create problems. They are just so many social institutions that do not clash.

But if all these *maraji'* have the same right to issue fatwas in all the people's affairs, domestic and international, cultural and political, economic and so on … Like right now in the Islamic Republic, this is even extended to endorsing candidates for elections, parties and

---

[32] These were the sole *maraji'* of the Shia world in the 20th century: Akhund Khorasani (1839-1911), Sayyid Abol-Hasan Esfahani (1867-1946), Hoseyn ibn Ali Tabataba'i Borujerdi (1875-1961), Sayyid Mohsen ibn Madi al-Tabataba'i al-Hakim (1889-1970).

groups. For instance, one *marja'* may say it is recommended to vote for Mr A and another that the recommendation and the religious ruling is to vote for Mr B. All this causes conflict, unless, as I already said, we limit the realm of the *marja'iyat* and confine it to personal issues.

Even if the *maraji'* were to form political parties, we would still have problems. Political parties that exist in the world are civil institutions; they do not issue God's rulings. Political parties in the world have a programme for their supporters that they declare and their supporters approve; they might be against another party, which is no problem. But they do not accuse each other of heresy and do not say 'this is what God says'. However, if one *marja'* forms one party and another *marja'* forms another party, both want to lead their parties from a position of issuing religious fatwas and interpreting God's commands.

Incidentally, all this has been tried in the Islamic Republic. After the revolution, you saw the creation of the Islamic Republican Party whose founders were five high-ranking clerics, all of whom were supporters of the Leader of the Revolution and had revolutionary credentials. On the other side, supporters of Ayatollah Shariat-madari – with either his knowledge or his approval – formed an opposition party named the Islamic People's Republican Party. Each party conducted its activities under the auspices of one *marja'* [Khomeini and Shariat-madari respectively]. In 1979-80 there were clashes between them. The second party carried out certain activities in Azarbaijan, occupied the television station and so on. Eventually, the problem was solved by dissolving the party, arresting its members, and executing some of its leaders.

MQ: I think if the 'rules of the game' had been accepted in that case, and if it had been left to a popular vote, without using any leverage to subjugate the other side, perhaps this experience would have succeeded. But in that case the rules of the game were not followed.

HYE: Correct. But what are 'the rules of the game'? If 'the rules of the game' were followed [as] in a modern society, we wouldn't have a problem. The problem is that these 'rules of the game' are not compatible with those of *fiqh* thinking, with the relations between the *marja'* and his followers and with God's ruling.

MQ: But if they were rethought, as you said...

HYE: Yes, provided all of them are rethought.

MQ: I suppose it is not necessary for the scope of fiqh *to be narrowed. It can be kept broad and even extended to the public realm, but then left to popular choice. If the people choose the views of one of two* fuqaha, *then the other should confine himself to issuing personal rulings for his followers, so that on another occasion and through a free discourse his views might prevail.*

HYE: That's fine. But in view of the kind of premises that we have ...

MQ: No, provided these premises change.

HYE: Well, in that case, basically the question is, why do we need to have these *maraji'* gentlemen intervene in these affairs? What do they want to put to people's vote?

When a *marja'* issues fatwas, and says that prayers and fasting and so on are obligatory, in the same manner he will issue fatwas as to whether paying tax is haram or halal. On this basis, as a follower of this *marja'*, I believe that if I act in accordance to his fatwa, I have pleased God, and if I do not, I am committing a sin. This point is important.

MQ: Perhaps our fiqh *must be narrowed.*

HYE: Yes, the only possible solution is the theory of Ayatollah Mo'men, that *maraji'* should confine their fatwas to [personal] ritual and non-social rulings. If this happens, then the conflict will also disappear. But of course in this case we would no longer have the institution of *marja'iyat*. We would have to take back all we have said in the course of a thousand years about Shia *marja'iyat* (i.e. their power, independence, the impact of their words on people, etc.).

Nevertheless, if there are going to be multiple *maraji'*, and their fatwas are to be wide-ranging and cover all aspects of people's lives, this is not compatible with the modern notion of government.

Modern government does not tolerate a plurality of power centres. Consider Sheykh Fazlollah [Nuri]'s criticism of constitutionalism, which now also applies to the Islamic Republic. Many of his arguments were sound if we take *fiqh* fundamentals into account. For instance, it is now stated in the constitution [of the Islamic Republic] that all are equal before the law. But are men's and women's rights equal? Are *dhimmi* and non-*dhimmi* equal? Are slaves and masters equal? Are *harbi* and non-*harbi* equal? They all have different rulings [under *fiqh*].[33]

You see that the problems go back to a set of basic and fundamental issues, and as long as these are not resolved, the problems will not be resolved.

During the era of Reza Shah these contradictions became clearer. All our reformers, from the time of Amir Kabir[34] onward, have tried to reduce the power of the clergy. Right now the objection that is levelled at them [by the Islamists] is that they said that 'religion should be separate from politics'. But they were not saying that religion should be separate from politics, rather they simply wanted to separate government from the clergy. This was one of the main objectives of Amir Kabir – and he was opposed. Later, when Mirza Hoseyn Khan Sepah-Salar did the same thing, an outcry arose from the ulama. Then when Mirza Ali Khan Amin ad-Dowleh came and wanted to introduce the same reforms, he too clashed with the ulama. When Naseroddin Shah returned from his journey [to Europe], Mirza Hoseyn Khan was accompanying him; Hajji Molla Ali Kani and another of the Tehran ulama issued a fatwa that it was forbidden for Mirza Hoseyn Khan to take over government. They stopped Naseroddin Shah in Bandar Anzali and said that unless he dismissed his minister he had no right to come to Tehran. He dismissed the Sepah-Salar right there and made him governor of Gilan, and then came to Tehran. When he arrived, he first went to see Molla Ali Kani in order to appease him. Of course, in those times these things happened less often, since the clergy did not want the government.

When Reza Shah – according to one interpretation –sought to impose a modern government, for instance by establishing the judiciary, this raised an outcry among the clergy, who said: 'judgement is our affair, and now you have gone and brought a foreign-educated nobody and made him minister of justice'. Or take the religious endowments, which have always been one source of economic power for the clergy and our *maraji'*. All our reformers since the time of Amir Kabir have tried to bring the endowments under state control. You cannot do this under religious law, because the endowed property must be managed according to the will of the endower. This person

---

[33] These are all *fiqh* categories: *dhimmi* are protected non-Muslims; *harbi* are those who wage war against Islam.

[34] Mirza Taqi Khan Amir Kabir, Naseroddin Shah Qajar's famous 'reformist' prime minister from 1848 to 1851.

appointed a custodian (who was usually at that time from among the clergy) to administer the endowment in accordance with his wishes. In a modern state, however, this cannot be done.

Therefore, in Western states, in any modern state, and in what we have today in the world, we have a separation of powers: there are civil institutions, independent political parties, and so on, and all these operate outside the realm of religious fatwas. Here too there will be no problem if a cleric, as a citizen, wishes to form a political party, engage in political and electoral activities and become a deputy or a minister. That is to say, I, a cleric, have as many rights as you, a non-cleric. This means accepting 'the rules of the game'. However the clerical system of thinking and [the kinds of] relations [that exist] between a religious authority and his followers can only be properly realized in the premodern era. In today's conditions, even in the context of our current constitution, their realization is not possible. When I say that such clashes will persist, it is for this reason. Note that each of the existing *maraji'* has his own opinions. Why should the one who is sitting in a corner in Najaf, and considers himself – according to his own criteria – to be more learned than the Leader of the Islamic Republic, follow somebody else's fatwa?

Changing those [doctrinal and *fiqhi*] premises is not going to be an easy task. That way of thinking took shape over the course of a thousand years, and all its elements are in harmony. By contrast, new ways of thinking and developments in the Islamic Republic have not yet acquired a stable form. That is to say, the roles of the *maraji'*, the state, the leadership, the heads of the [executive, legislative and judiciary] powers, the president, the leaders of political parties, and ordinary people – none of these are yet clear; and they are not yet in harmony. For instance, it is not clear yet whether there should be political parties or not.

According to today's definition, political parties have their own programmes, which they announce; and people vote for those programmes in elections. When a party is elected, it forms the government and carries out its programmes. However in the Islamic Republic we see that the supporters of absolute *velayat-e faqih* say explicitly, 'We do accept political parties, but they must all come under the Leader.' That is to say, the Leader is General Secretary of all political parties. These then are not political parties in the modern sense. It is a contradiction in terms and a contradiction in essence. In my view, these problems cannot be resolved by means of superficial reforms.

MQ: Do you think the questions raised in our conversation have been addressed by [advocates of] the school of thought in the seminaries known as 'Critical Traditionalists', such as Mohsen Kadivar and Ayatollah Montazeri? Have they been able to provide an answer?

HYE: As far as I am familiar with the views of Ayatollah Montazeri and Kadivar, they want to keep the institution of *marja'iyat* independent, to uphold the government and the state of the Islamic Republic in accordance with the law, and to create a kind of understanding and co-operation between these two institutions. Of course, in the short term this is not a bad idea for resolving problems and reducing tensions. For the time being, this line of argument should be followed and these efforts too are positive. But they have not yet arrived at these levels of the debate [on the essential structure of *marja'iyat*]. Ayatollah Montazeri has not concerned himself with these debates. Mr Kadivar, who has been dealing with these debates in a rather more theoretical way, either has not yet reached these levels of the debate or has not answered them. In his interviews and books, by following the theories of Sayyid Muhammad Baqer Sadr[35] and Ayatollah Montazeri, and to a certain extent those of Ayatollah Motahhari, he tries to resolve the problem by [arguing] that the clergy, even the *vali-ye faqih*, have a supervisory role [not a mandate to rule]. That is, Islamic 'supervision' is correct but the clergy and the Leader have no right of executive intervention; they merely oversee. Thus in practice there will be no problem, and freedom, democracy and political parties will function.

But what is the nature of this supervision? This has not been clarified, or at least in the theories of Mr Kadivar it is not that evident.

The other issue is the nature of relations between the [institution of] *marja'iyat* and the *maraji'* and the institution of the leadership. What sort of relations should these two have? Which of these two has the final word in the regime of the Islamic Republic? As far as I know, this question remains unanswered in Kadivar's writings.[36]

---

[35] The modernist Shia *faqih* based in Iraq who was executed on Saddam Hossein's orders in 1980. For his life and views, see Mallat (1993, 1994: 251-72).

[36] See Epilogue for recent work by Kadivar.

5

From the Berlin Conference:
Religious Intellectualism and its Discontents

Editors' introduction

The Berlin Conference of April 2000 marked a turning point in the brief period of liberalization of the press and of public discussion that peaked with the landslide reformist victory in the February 2000 elections to the sixth Majlis. There was an atmosphere of excitement and optimism that reforms could go ahead, now that both the executive and the legislative powers were in the hands of the reformist government.

This chapter contains Eshkevari's three contributions to the conference. They represent Eshkevari's most open expression of his views on key issues, but they led to his being one of the prominent victims of the conservative clampdown on the press and the intellectuals that began in the immediate aftermath of the Berlin Conference. All three texts were published in a book published soon after the conference, entitled *Berlin Conference, Service or Subversion*,[1] which contains a day-to-day report of the conference and its coverage by the Iranian press, with a vivid account of each session and of the exchanges between participants from Iran and the exiled opponents of the regime who have disrupted some of the sessions.

At a major political trial the previous November, some of the issues discussed by Eshkevari in Berlin were also raised. This public trial exposed the deep rift among the clerics, the two competing visions of Islamic law, in short, the crisis of theocracy in the Islamic Republic.

Irreconcilable differences: the trial of Abdollah Nuri

In November 1999, the debate over relations between Islam and democracy – now framed more precisely in terms of whether the right to rule rests with the clergy or the people – moved to a new level with

---

[1] Zakariya'i (2000).

the trial of Abdollah Nuri. A veteran revolutionary who had been Ayatollah Khomeini's representative in the *Pasdaran*, Nuri is a cleric with impeccable religious and revolutionary credentials. In 1997 he joined Khatami's new cabinet as Minister of Interior, a post he once occupied in Rafsanjani's government. From the outset he showed that he was serious about reform and was not a man of compromise, which dismayed and angered the conservatives; as a priority, they planned to silence him.

In June 1998, the conservatives who dominated the Majlis successfully impeached Nuri and removed him from Khatami's cabinet. But this neither silenced Nuri nor eliminated him from the political scene. He joined the forces of 'civil society' and launched a newspaper, *Khordad*, named after the Iranian month in which Khatami was elected. He became even bolder in his criticisms of the conservatives, and his popularity increased. In the municipal council elections, which took place for the first time ever in February 1999, Nuri stood as a candidate for Tehran, and topped the poll. Fearing his popularity, and in order to pre-empt a repetition of this success in the February 2000 Majlis elections, the conservatives now had him brought before the Special Clergy Court and convicted on various charges.

But this move back-fired. Nuri's trial turned into a head-on public clash between the two competing ideologies. In the course of his defence – reported in detail by the reformist newspapers – Nuri effectively used the trial to raise the stakes. He made a strong case for democracy and articulated the views of the radical reformists, which they would not have dared to utter during their election campaign. Despite his conviction, his defence was immediately published as a book, *The Hemlock of Reform*,[2] which became a runaway bestseller and the unofficial reformist manifesto for the forthcoming Majlis elections.

As one commentator put it:

> For many of Iran's 65 million people, the trial has assumed the significance Americans attached to the Scopes trial in 1927 [sic – 1925], or people in England to the treason trial of Sir Thomas More during the reign of Henry VIII – a moment when a courtroom becomes a testing ground for irreconcilable views about

---

[2] Nuri (1999).

the future of a society and its beliefs, with huge social, philosophical and political stakes resting on the outcome.[3]

The prosecutor's 44-page indictment of Nuri – and, by implication, of
the entire reformist agenda – summarizes the charges under three
headings:

1. Insulting and slandering the regime's authorities and institutions, spreading lies with the intention of disturbing the
   public mind or causing harm, and propaganda activity
   against the regime.
2. Contradicting [Khomeini's] perspectives and insulting His
   Excellency.
3. Publishing materials opposed to religious tenets and insulting
   religious sanctities.[4]

The trial lasted for six sessions. During the first two, Nuri challenged
the legality of the Special Clergy Court and its competence to try press
offences. In the other four sessions, he dealt with the specific charges
brought by the prosecutor – a catalogue of 'just about everything [the
hard-line clerics] dislike in the reformers' more tolerant social
philosophy'.[5] The charges focused on articles written by reformist
writers and published in Nuri's paper *Khordad*, which the conservatives
considered to threaten their position by discussing topics that should
not be addressed in public: propagation of Ayatollah Montazeri's
political views, criticism of the theory of *velayat-e faqih*, questioning the
course of the revolution, and implicating the religious authorities in the
serial killings of political dissidents. Among the offending articles were
the interviews with Mohsen Kadivar.[6]

Nuri begins his defence with a Koranic verse that reminds the
court of the transitory nature of power,[7] and then speaks of his despair

---

[3] Burns (1999). Burns' reports of the trial in *The New York Times* admirably
convey both the atmosphere and the importance of the issues at stake.
[4] Nuri (1999: 15): preamble to Indictment.
[5] Burns (1999).
[6] See Editors' Introduction to Chapter 4, above.
[7] 'Such days (of varying fortunes) we give to men and men by turns: that Allah
many know those that believe, and that he make take to Himself from your
ranks martyr-witnesses (to Truth)' (Al-Imran, 140).

at the course the Islamic Republic has taken and the immense rift that has developed among the clerics.

> What has happened is that today one cleric claims that another cleric's actions constitute vilification, defamation and dissemination of lies, aiming to damage the regime and Islam, that his actions are hostile to religion and Islam and religious authority. If this gentleman [the prosecutor] is telling the truth, pity the clergy to which I belong! And if this gentleman is lying, pity the clergy to which he belongs! ... If the revolution after twenty years produces a person like me, then pity this revolution; and if it produces a person like this gentleman, then pity this revolution! If a representative of the *vali-ye faqih* after twenty years ends up in my situation, then pity this *velayat*; and if he ends up like this gentleman, then pity this *velayat*. If, after a life of study and preaching, the product of our religion is a person like me, pity this religion and if it produces a person like him, pity this religion![8]

Here we shall focus on Nuri's defence of the two articles that the prosecutor invokes as 'evidence' of his having published materials opposed to religion. As we shall see, they share the same premises and put forward similar arguments to those articulated by Eshkevari in the Berlin Conference. The exchanges between the prosecutor and Nuri encapsulate their different approaches to Islam and the state.

The project of religious intellectualism
An article, 'A look at the liberation project of religious intellectualism', by the investigative journalist Akbar Ganji, appeared in *Khordad* in March 1999.[9] Attacking a theory of religion that calls for unquestioning belief and the suspension of reason, Ganji argues for a rational approach to religion and politics. He explicitly refutes two of the tenets of the conservatives' vision of Islam: absolute obedience to religious law and the *fuqaha*, and the inseparability of Islam and the state.

The prosecution finds Ganji's article to be 'opposing Islam' on two counts. The first is that it privileges rationalism at the expense of religion:

8 Nuri (1999: 20).
9 Ganji (1999a).

Citing Kant, the German philosopher, on the conflict between rationalism and religion, the writer says: 'leaving the state of minority and reaching enlightenment involves three processes: first, rejection of the god/master-servant relation (rejection of the guardian [i.e. *velayat-e faqih*]); secondly, rejection of tradition as a source of reference; and thirdly, independence of "reason-based" institutions from "religion-based" institutions.' This statement explicitly rejects unquestioning obedience to God and the acceptance of what religion brings, which are among the essentials of religion; it depicts reason in opposition to religion, and thereby limits the teaching of religion. The writer continues by introducing rationalism as a newcomer that competes with religion, and eventually [speaks of the need] to rationalize religion not in order to understand and defend it but in order to diminish it and reject some religious statements that he finds unacceptable.

The second count is Ganji's critique of clerical rule and his advocacy of the separation of religion and state.

In another part of the article the writer says: 'power corrupts and absolute power corrupts absolutely. Power needs legitimacy. What better than an ideological reading of religion to justify and legitimize absolute power? Absolute power not only benefits from religion for its own legitimacy but also makes religion a state matter and takes in hand the guidance of the people. State religion is a tool for domination and for consolidating the power of one class [the clergy], and is the opiate of the masses.'

The prosecution sees such criticism of state religion as tantamount to an attack on Khomeini and the Islamic Republic:

In this vein, *Khordad* also questions the basis of Islamic government [by calling it] 'absolute government', declares it to be on a par with absolute corruption, and defines state religion as a tool for stupefying the masses and for government by one class. This is a patent contradiction of the political philosophy of Islam, and in particular of the way that Ayatollah Khomeini has depicted it. At the end of the article, continuing his attack on state religion, which is in effect an attack on 'the Islamic Republic', the writer opposes Khomeini's view, according to which religion and politics are not separate, and follows Western and westernized writers and analysts who advocate the principle of separation of religion from politics; and he says: 'thus, the separation of the institution of religion from the state is one of the requirements of the project of religious intellectualism.'[10]

In his defence of Ganji's article, Nuri rejects the charge of 'questioning the basis of Islamic government' and makes the case for freedom of speech by referring to Article 23 of the constitution, which explicitly forbids 'investigation of opinion'; therefore, the indictment has broken the law as it treats a citizen's right to express his opinion as a crime.

Secondly, even if it is true that the article says there is 'conflict between rationalism and religion', this is not a crime. Many religious-minded people have said it – for instance Allameh Mohammad Baqer Majlesi[11] rejects reason as deficient by comparison with revelation and the text. Nuri refers to Allameh Tabataba'i's critique of Majlesi, and quotes Tabataba'i on Majlesi's antagonism to philosophers and theologians, which was so strong that it drove him to reject their work entirely.

Thirdly, Nuri contends, the prosecutor has misrepresented Ganji's main point:

Of course, the writer's point was not to defend the conflict between reason and religion, but to argue for a rational approach to religion and the need for critical understanding – a point that has been ignored wittingly or unwittingly.

Nuri then turns to the charge of 'rejecting the unquestioning obedience to God and acceptance of what religion brings', which the indictment defines as 'among the essentials of religion', and makes a case for a different kind of religiosity.

The whole article is in the service of religiosity at a high level, making a relation between human beings and God and removing the obstacles that hinder devotion to and faith in God. The writer says that one of the obstacles to the worship of God and

---

[10] Nuri (1999: 225-7).
[11] Majlesi, a prominent and powerful Shia scholar, initiated a campaign against Sunnis, Sufis and mystical philosophers in the last decades of the Safavid era.

the experience of divinity is when certain people play god and create god/master-servant relations among humans. His suggestion is that these earthly gods must be put aside to make room for worship of the true God. He declares religious despotism to be one of the obstacles to religiosity and the worship of God.[12]

The writers of the indictment have taken the author's opposition to 'state religion' as [arguing for] the separation of religion and politics. The author is scared of state religion, not of religious government. What the article condemns is state religion, not religious government. He says that the state does not have the right to interfere with religion and to impose one reading of religion on society. The study and propagation of religion are the work of the ulama, *fuqaha*, mystics, philosophers, exegetes and seminaries; the state has no right to pour religion, like a decree, into a uniform cast and to impose it on others.

Not only is opposing 'state religion' not a crime, it is the duty of any religious and concerned person who strives to maintain the health and independence of religion. The effect of state religion was not and is not anything but the reduction of religion to an instrument for justifying the power and the actions of the powerful. In the notion of a 'religious state', religion is a guide for the state, but in the notion of 'state religion', religion becomes a cheap tool to extend the domination of its advocates.

Nuri ends his defence of Ganji's article by giving his own reading of the sentence quoted at the conclusion of the indictment: 'thus, the separation of the institution of religion from the state is one of the requirements of the project of religious intellectualism.'

This sentence clearly argues for the independence of religious institutions (seminaries, mosques, and so on) from the state, not for the separation of religion from politics. Whether Islamic rulings are political or not, and whether religion is separate from politics, [are questions that] have nothing to do with creating a state religion. Religion and politics are not separate from each other, but religion must not become identified with the state. The learned and the religious leaders in the seminaries are not

[12] The point made here echoes Soroush's argument in a series of talks delivered in 1990, and later published as a collection (Soroush 1994: see in particular, Lesson 8, dated 17.1.1369, p. 194).

state employees. Politics has no right to interfere with religiosity, religion cannot be organized in accordance with political interests, and religion cannot be read and interpreted according to the wish of state officials.[13]

The term 'secularism' is implicit but not uttered here, indicating the limits that still exist as to what can be publicly discussed and debated. As we shall see, Eshkevari breaches these limits in his development of the same argument in Berlin.

Hijab *and apostasy: Sharia or life-style*

The second article in the indictment, 'Morality, gaiety and life-style', by Mohammad Majid Mohammadi,[14] contains a critique of compulsory hijab, along the same lines as those aired by other reformist papers such as *Neshat* at more or less the same time (spring 1999).[15] Critical of an ideological understanding of religion, Mohammadi argues that what is taken to be a divine rule at one time is nothing more than the life-style and values of a certain group, speaking in the name of religion. Pointing out the danger and futility of making an ideology of one's life-style and imposing it on the rest of the society, he makes a case for tolerance, and concludes by arguing that people should be able to choose how they live as long as they stay within the limits of religion, law and ethics.

Tolerance of different ideas and ways of life, and the right to choose, which Mohammadi and other writers were promoting in the reformist press, are the very arguments that conservatives saw as undermining the foundation of their Islamic ideology. The article is thus evidence that Nuri has questioned and denied what is for them one of the essentials of religion: the rule of hijab.

The prosecutor begins by citing passages that he considers to be blasphemous and opposed to Islamic principles. For example:

---

[13] Nuri (1999: 227-9).

[14] Mohammadi (1999). Mohammadi no longer regards himself as a religious intellectual; by 2003 he was living in New York; in his writings (in Persian), which appear regularly at *www.gooya.com*, he openly criticizes the Leader and the people around him, and addresses issues such as the Islamic Republic's intolerance of homosexuality.

[15] See Mir-Hosseini (2002b).

If a section of society has separate quarters at home for men and women, if they favour chador and hijab, if they disapprove of men and women mingling in a gathering ... if they don't listen to music ... if they don't shave their beards ... all these must be considered as a life-style peculiar to them ... But other social groups also have the right to live differently, within the limits defined by ethics (not by the life-style of a certain group) ...

In Islamic law it is said that believing women must cover their hair and body but nowhere does it say that women should be forced to do so if they don't have firm belief or if they have none at all. What is done in terms of imposing hijab as a kind of dress code in Iran today, even on non-Muslims and foreigners, is as [im]moral as Reza Shah's ban on hijab in the past.

The political rulers, and any group who consider themselves to be followers of Sharia, are only allowed to defend the rights of those who wear hijab and believe in it; they do not have the right to impose hijab or any style of dressing, eating or conduct on others, because this constitutes a violation of the rights of others; and finally, the life-style of one group in society cannot be imposed on others in the name of religion and morality. Having power (in the sense of having the Guardian Council, a majority in parliament, control of the police force and a monopoly over Iranian Radio and TV and the judiciary) cannot be a justification for imposing one's life-style on others in the name of morality and law ...

Therefore those who seek to make life-style an ideological issue, having made religion, *fiqh* and mysticism ideological, must be aware that people's lives and tastes are not like religious belief or legal and mystical opinions, where parts that do not conform with the ideology can easily be put aside.[16]

Having cited the offending passages, the prosecutor states the five charges against Nuri, which sum up the argument of the anti-reformists who insist on keeping intact the ideological hold of *fiqh*. Here is a paraphrase:

1. By publishing this article, Nuri has openly ridiculed religious groups and those who follow the religious law; accused them of

16 Nuri (1999: 206-208).

imposing their life-style on the rest of society; and compared their actions to Reza Shah's banning of hijab.

2. *Khordad* newspaper, besides ridiculing and slandering the religious segment of society, accuses the regime and the authorities who control the Guardian Council, the judiciary, Radio and TV and the police forces, of imposing a certain life-style. It thereby questions the actions of the *vali-ye faqih* who, according to the constitution, is responsible for appointments to these bodies.

3. The message of this supposedly scientific and sociological article is to insist that people should have freedom in taste and life-style and [be able to] choose what to eat and wear; nobody has the right to interfere. This kind of thinking is in open contradiction to the Islamic duty of 'promotion of virtue and prohibition of vice' which is one of the essentials of religion, and Article 8 of the constitution recognizes it as a collective duty. We can say with confidence that the writer of the article, because of this rejection, has become an apostate, and Mr Nuri, by publishing the article, is spreading propaganda against the essentials of religion.

4. By separating life-style from religion and allowing people to choose, and by placing issues such as observing hijab, listening to music, mingling of the sexes, wearing a beard and so on in the realm of 'life-style', this article is implicitly propagating social corruption and immorality in society. In so doing, this article has put these matters, which all or most *fuqaha* consider forbidden, into the realm of debate. This is a subtle propagation of permissiveness (*ebahigari*), which is clear evidence of 'cultural invasion'.

5. One of our glories is that Islam is an all-inclusive religion, and *fiqh*, with its many chapters and broad net, covers all human action in private life, family and society. It is one of the essentials of Islam that all human actions fall into one of the five categories of ruling (*ahkam-e khamseh*): obligatory, commendable, neutral, reprehensible or forbidden.[17] By denying this essential of our religion, the author of the article and the director of *Khordad* are trying to separate religion from people's private lives, and to

---

[17] In *fiqh*, all human acts are classed, first, as *halal* (permissible) or *haram* (forbidden). Permissible acts are then subdivided into obligatory, commendable, neutral, and permitted but disapproved.

pave the way for permissiveness and social and moral corruption.[18]

What the prosecutor calls *ebahigari* and we have glossed as 'permissiveness', is nothing less than the tolerance of different views,
personal freedom, and pluralism that the reformists advocate. The old
guard see it as a threat, as it requires loosening the hold of *fiqh* over
every aspect of the individual's private and public life.

In his defence, Nuri makes the case for such a loosening, on both
political and religious grounds. He starts by pointing out how the
indictment has misunderstood and misrepresented the article by citing
passages selectively and out of context. He continues:

> The main point of the article is that, in the context of religion
> and its 'five categories', which all religious people in society
> admit and follow, it is possible to have different life-styles. It does
> not say that, in order to achieve these different styles, the five
> categories must necessarily be put aside ... The problem is that
> there are those who deny the existence of different life-styles,
> who not only consider their own life-style to be the only relig-
> iously correct one, but also do not allow any sociological dis-
> cussion of this issue, on the grounds of 'entering forbidden
> zones'.[19]

Nuri then reminds the court of the existence of *fiqh* arguments for not
imposing hijab on non-believing women and non-Muslims. But he
does not elaborate; instead he grounds his defence of different life-
styles in the old conflict between tradition and modernity, and points
out how, in the past hundred years, aspects of traditionalism have been
taken to be part of religious law, and aspects of modernity have been
rejected in the name of religion. What is considered to be religious law,
Nuri argues, is often nothing more than tradition. He recalls that,
before the revolution, many clerics and religious families considered
television and radio – and even, until a decade ago, video – to be
against religious law. Women were also denied the right to social and
political participation, as their right to vote was argued to be against
Sharia. But after the revolution, all this, once forbidden on religious
grounds, became permissible. He then suggests:

[18] Nuri (1999: 208-110).
[19] Nuri (1999: 212).

In order to increase social harmony, and to reduce political tensions that are rooted in different life-styles, the solution is to sever the link between religious law and a particular life-style, so that different life-styles can co-exist in harmony in the context of law and morality. Defining divine laws according to one's own taste is neither in the interest of religion (as it decreases the numbers of its followers) nor in the interest of religious people (as it increases tension in society and deprives them of a peaceful and harmonious life).[20]

Finally, Nuri rejects the charge of apostasy. He asks the court on what grounds the writers of the indictment dare to issue apostasy judgements so freely. According to the fatwas of many *fuqaha*, including Ayatollah Khomeini, an apostate is a person who denies the principles of Unity of God and Prophethood.

Suppose the article has presented an unorthodox and incorrect point of view, does freedom of expression mean only the freedom to express views that are totally correct? If something printed in a newspaper is incorrect without harming the principles of Islam, the correct way to deal with it is through debate and critical analysis, not court and trial.[21]

In the court's judgement, the charge of apostasy was dropped and the jury – composed of conservative clerics – exonerated Nuri from the charges of 'publication of material opposing Islam and insulting religious beliefs' and 'insulting Ayatollah Khomeini'. But he was found guilty of propagating Ayatollah Montazeri's views, and publishing material 'disturbing the public mind,' and sentenced to five years in prison.

As noted in Chapter 1, Nuri's trial marked a new phase in the struggle between conservatives and reformists. The subsequent February 2000 Majlis elections showed decisively that the people supported the reformist vision of Islam and government. Parliament came under the control of reformists, many of whom had been radical Islamists in the early 1980s but now were thinking along the same lines as the 'liberals' they had defeated then. Following the elections, the conservatives, having lost public support, instituted a severe backlash.

---

[20] Nuri (1999: 216).
[21] Nuri (1999: 220).

Their main priority was to silence the reformists and to eliminate key figures from the political scene. In May, on the Leader's orders, there were mass closures of reformist papers: an excuse was found in the April Berlin Conference.

Eshkevari's speeches in Berlin

The background to the conference has been outlined in Chapter 1. In the audience were members of Iranian exiled opposition groups, who protested at not being represented among the speakers. They staged demonstrations outside the conference building, holding placards saying: 'Separation of religion from state!', 'Abolish stoning!', 'Abolish compulsory hijab', 'Why is the opposition outside [Iran] not present?'

For the opening session (7 April, p.m.) about two thousand turned up at the main conference hall, which had space for only 500, so the proceedings were broadcast on CCTV. Before proceedings opened, two groups from the audience – the Workers' Communist Party (WCP), based in Sweden, and the Berlin Exiled Women of Iran Against Fundamentalism (BEWIAF) – took centre stage and performed a set of pre-planned actions intended to prevent the conference from starting. The chair of the first panel ('Iran after the Elections') was Ahmad Taheri; the speakers were Ezzatollah Sahabi, Mehrangiz Kar, Sayyid Kazem Kardavani, Akbar Ganji, and Eshkevari. As the speakers came forward, the audience reacted. Some welcomed them with applause, but there were a few chants of 'Death to the Islamic Republic'. As the chair introduced Eshkevari, protesters chanted: 'Akhund (cleric) get lost!' When the session was about to start, Shadi Amin of BEWIAF asked for a minute's silence in memory of the thousands of victims of the Islamic Republic. Then others opened up the black chadors they were wearing, inside which were slogans against the meeting and the Islamic Republic. Some members of the audience tried to stop the protesters. This led to a scuffle and the police were called. Amin was escorted outside, shouting. The organizers tried to calm the situation; they accepted the protesters' demand, and announced a one-minute silence.[22]

The protests reached a peak during the second day of the conference. To calm the situation, the organizers enlisted the help of participants from Iran who enjoyed respect among the opposition abroad: Shahla Lahiji, Mahmud Dowlatabadi and Kazem Kardavani, secular

---

[22] Three different narratives of what happened in this session were posted on the Internet at the time; see Zakariya'i (2000: 50-58).

intellectuals who have now joined the reformists. The organizers also tried to reach an agreement with the protesters and to accommodate their main objection: not being given a voice. A representative of one dissident group – Mina Asadi of the WCP – declared 'we will not take part in a panel and sit with people whose hands are stained with the blood of thousands.' The organizers agreed to give the protesters fifteen minutes to express their views, but it soon became evident that they were interested only in disrupting the meeting. Asadi went to the rostrum as the first opposition representative; she said that they were only prepared to listen to participants who had not been among the leaders of the Islamic Republic; they would disrupt anyone who defended Khatami. Then she told the audience, if they opposed taking part in the conference they should show it by chanting 'Death to the Islamic Republic'. The chants followed and the agreement collapsed.[23] The day's programme went ahead, but faced constant disruption, such as a woman wearing a Walkman and performing an erotic Persian dance, and another wearing nothing but a bikini and a headscarf as a gesture of protest against 'the oppression of women in Iran'. Some speakers were unable to deliver their papers in full, including Eshkevari, who left the session when a man undressed to reveal his torture scars while shouting slogans against the Islamic Republic.

For the third day, the organizers decided not to allow members of the two disruptive groups into the conference building. Cards were distributed and the remaining sessions were held in relative peace; but they turned into a confrontation between secular and religious reformists. Eshkevari was invited to join the panel on women's rights; he was not on the schedule to speak, but Mehrangiz Kar insisted that it was imperative to hear the views of the 'New Religious Thinkers'. This was the context for the third text, the one that brings Eshkevari a charge of heresy for defending a Muslim women's right to wear what she wants.

The first text in this chapter is a transcript of Eshkevari's presentation at the first session, on 'Iran after the Elections'. The second is the full version of the paper he was unable to deliver in full at the disrupted session on 'Islamic Reformism and Modern Civil Society'. The third is a transcript of his contribution to a session on 'Women's Rights and the Women's Movement'.

These texts build on the ones in previous chapters, and show how Eshkevari presents his vision of democratic Islam to an often-hostile audience outside Iran. At times their reactions impelled him to go

[23] Zakariya'i (2000: 132-33).

further than he had done before. At various moments during the conference, the participants from Iran clashed; the exiled opposition forced the secularists to separate themselves from the religious reformists, holding them responsible for the failure of the revolution and the course taken by the Islamic Republic.

'Iran after the elections'[24]

In the name of God [some booing]. I thank all the friends and compatriots who live here [some booing and shouting]. Inside Iran we are the victims of intolerance, and we expected those who are outside Iran struggling for freedom and popular democracy to behave in a democratic manner [majority applause, some protest]. Thanks so much. At least we hope not to face the same attitude we have to deal with in Iran every day and every week [majority applause, some protest].

What I want to say in this short time is that Iran has never been so ready to enter the realm of democracy, especially to institutionalize democracy. Because among the general public, and in particular among the intellectual, political and cultural elite, there has never been such a strong and deep awareness, such democratic and reformist demands, such a public will and the necessary consensus for [having] freedom and democracy and [attaining them by] peaceful and rational means. Of course it is the case that many conditions must be met before entering on the stage of democracy and realizing a democratic system of government. The most important among them are: the necessary public understanding of modern conceptions of society, humanity, free will, freedom, democracy, the rights of individuals, the state, the nation and so on.

Other conditions include the formation of social groups, the growth of class, group and national consciousness, increased urbanization, the expansion of urban classes, improved welfare for deprived groups and the people, the development of the intellectual and political elite to the extent that they can become intellectual, organizational and political guides for classes and groups. Although these conditions and factors have not been fully realized, and in particular we are still far behind with respect to social and economic development, the groundwork for them has been prepared to a greater extent than ever before.

---

[24] Translated from transcript in Zakariya'i (2000: 64-7). In this section, square brackets are used both for editorial insertions (e.g. [applause]) in the transcript, and our own insertions in the translation.

In the course of a hundred years of struggle against despotism and cultural, social and political backwardness, and after many setbacks, today freedom, democracy and citizens' rights have become more important for us than ever before. In the past, neither the people nor even the intellectuals and the political elite gave much priority to democracy – at least, they did not place the necessary value on the means for attaining the goal of democracy. But both [the end and the means] have now become important for all.

The experience of the past twenty years has convinced everyone that freedom, democracy, and ensuring the rights of citizens are preconditions for any kind of social, economic, scientific and cultural change. The developments that began about four years ago during the elections to the fifth Majlis are good evidence of this important change. The presidential elections three years ago, the council elections, and the recent Majlis elections show that the people and the intellectual, social and political elite, whatever their [political] orientations, have reached a degree of awareness and understanding of historical necessity that, with all their being, they desire freedom, democracy and justice. In particular, everyone has agreed to reject the path of exclusion, the path of violence and despotism in any shape – even in the garb of religion, revolution or some other disguise [applause]. They want fundamental and structural change [applause] in all matters through peaceful and democratic means. The important point is that now Mr Khatami's government genuinely supports reforms and wants as far as possible, given the limits, to help institutionalize freedom, law and democracy. Of course, they have made considerable efforts in this respect. But what gives hope is that popular demands have now become so resolute and extensive that no obstacle can impede their progress. Even if Mr Khatami [some applause] for some reason should be defeated in his work, the process will certainly continue [applause]. This time, not only has democracy become the first priority, but there is a great and unprecedented consensus on this among intellectuals and the intellectual and political elites in Iran. But this does not mean that after the elections and the victory of the reformists all problems and obstacles have been removed. The conservative faction and the guardians of despotism will certainly [attempt] sabotage and will continue to concoct various conspiracies. But in my view the historical age of despotism in Iran has come to an end for ever [wild applause]; different forms [applause continues] of despotism and violence no longer have any credibility among the people; their efforts to sabotage the reforms will only irritate the people and have the useful effect of intensifying their demand for democracy.

Anyway, in my view the future prospect for the Iranian nation is clear, and what more than anything gives cause for hope is that this time progress towards democracy is steady and measured and in the context of a broad national and popular movement. It has been said that [to achieve] social change you must not think of the shortest but of the surest way, even if it is longer and harder [applause]. Nowhere in the world has democracy been realized overnight without people being educated and made aware by top-down means. No important event will happen until people's awareness reaches an adequate level, the ground is laid and democracy becomes a deep and general demand. Democracy will not last until civil institutions are created.

Apart from conservative plots, however, there are serious concerns about the future of reforms. One of these concerns is the disputes and lack of planning among the reformists in the government and in the new Majlis. Another is a possible division within the reformist faction that may become deeper. Thirdly, some of those within the Second Khordad Front who are demanding reform, may, for various reasons – such as a lack of the necessary commitment to freedom and demo-cracy, or because they see people's demands as superficial, or seeking to promote their own class or factional interests, or out of political or sectarian conservatism – abandon the people and sacrifice democracy to their own factional interests. Another worry is sabotage by opport-unist and undemocratic elements in the opposition [applause] who may be prepared to sacrifice democracy to the interests of a group or for the sake of tired and unfashionable ideologies [majority applause, some booing].

Anyway [applause continues] the difficult progress towards demo-cracy will continue and with the aid of honest and loyal intellectual and political leaders, in particular the brave writers and the powerful press in Iran – never has the press been so poweful and enlightening in Iran – the people will move towards the final stages of democracy. So let us arise to help people and let us arise to help each other [loud applause] [some chanting of 'Death to the Islamic Republic'].

* * * * *

Questioner: I have a question for Mr Eshkevari. Given that all the opposition [groups] outside Iran, all the friends present here, are for the separation of religion from the state, and given that [voicing] such a demand in the Islamic Republic brings punishment, what is your view as a cleric? Do you think we should have the combination of religion and state? Or will the clerics eventually go back to the mosques [applause]?

With respect to velayat-e faqih, *the friends [i.e. speakers from Iran], and also all those elected to the sixth Majlis, have declared their commitment to* velayat-e faqih,[25] *and some to the Absolute* vali-ye faqih; *I wanted to ask Mr Eshkevari whether or not he supports the release of the founder of the theory of* velayat-e faqih, *that is Ayatollah Montazeri. What is your view? Generally, how do you see this theory and how do you justify it – as clerics do so well?*[26]

HYE: Before I respond to our friend's specific question addressed to me, I want [to deal with] the issue that was implied in the questions of many ladies and gentlemen, that is about Islam and the suggestion that only non-religious individuals have been victims in Iran. Of course I do not have time for an extended discussion of this issue. I do not want here to defend a specific religion or a specific way of thought. I only want to remind our friends of one reality; that is, oppression, violence and despotism do not recognize frontiers; so in Iran after the revolution we witnessed a savage and bloody repression. In this respect, all groups, all ideologies, all currents and all individuals became victims. So it was certainly not the case that only a certain group [was oppressed] and that only Islam [was responsible]. If you hold only Islam responsible ... I claim that in Iran, Islamic groups, Islamic individuals and religious dignitaries even at the level of religious *maraji'* – who should be respected more than anybody else in the Islamic Republic – have been oppressed and abused more than any other group in the past twenty years [audience babble]. This is a reality. Every one in Iran knows it, acknowledges it. If necessary, dozens of instances and cases can be cited. One instance is the treatment of Ayatollah Montazeri, who was referred to here. [As for] the slogan being chanted here: 'Free the political prisoners'; well of course [we aren't talking about] those who were imprisoned in the past, theirs is a separate story. Anyway, when you say, 'Free the political prisoners', you mean the present ones. If this is so, then at present among the political prisoners in Iran we have two prominent clerics: Mohsen Kadivar and Abdollah Nuri. They are clerics and religious and they too are victims. What is important is to rise and oppose any kind of

[25] The questioner is referring to the screening of candidates by the Guardian Council, implying that there is no place in Iranian politics for those who oppose a religious state.

[26] Zakariya'i (2000: 78).

violence under any name, and any kind of despotism and oppression under any name and any dogma. It's not a matter of religious or non-religious, left or right, this or that ideology. I wanted to add that I do not agree with part of what Mr Ganji said here,[27] but since there is no time, I will not deal with it. We are not talking about this or that group. Despotism does not make any exemptions when it comes to violence.

As for the specific question that our friend asked me, concerning the issue of religion and state or religion and the clergy; if I understood him correctly – because unfortunately there was so much noise that one could not hear the questions properly – my response is one that I have given time and again in Iran, in my speeches, writings and publications; it is that I do not consider government to be the concern of religion and religious law. Therefore, I oppose *fiqhi* government, clerical government, and in general government by an individual or by a class, under whatever name it comes – Islam, Marxism, socialism, nationalism. I am against it. I believe that government is a human matter [applause]; it is human [not divine]; therefore government must have a democratic base. That is, government must first emerge from the votes and desires of the people; second, in the exercise of power it must use democratic methods. So, even if a government had a demo-cratic and popular base at the time of its inception, if it does not

[27] Earlier in the same panel, in response to questioners who accused him of being part of the reign of terror in the early Islamic Republic, Ganji said that what happened after the revolution was the result of discourses that dominated the Iran of the 1970s. These discourses, he said, were produced by three groups of intellectuals: Marxists/leftists, such as those in the Tudeh party and the Fedayan Guerrilla Organization; secular intellectuals, such as Daryush Shayegan and Ehsan Naraghi; and religious intellectuals, such as Jalal Al-Ahmad and Ali Shariati. Their discourses, he said, had the following features in common: they were revolutionary, thus they sought change by violent means; they were highly ideological; they were strongly anti-western and anti-imperialist; they were not democratic, using but not theorizing the slogans of freedom and democracy; they sought to create an utopia; they advocated a kind of 'return to self' – for Shariati and Al-Ahmad this was an Islamic self, for secularists like Shayegan and Naraghi it was an Asiatic self opposed to the West, and for the leftists it was a classless self. Ganji concluded that, given these features, it was natural for events after the revolution to take a violent turn, and that violence is an inseparable part of any revolution, as Hannah Arendt clearly showed in her book on revolution. Ganji's remarks were loudly challenged by some in the audience (Zakariya'i 2000: 83-4).

employ democratic methods in the exercise of power and governance, then it is not democratic. I will explain this in detail, if I get a chance in the next session when I talk about reformist Islam [applause].[28]

'Reformist Islam and modern society'[29]

In the name of God. Let me begin with a note on modern society. Modern society has basically emerged in a historical continuum from older, traditional society; it is thus [at] a more evolved stage. In at least some areas, however, modern society is also in opposition to pre-modern society. Broadly, human history can perhaps be divided into two periods: 'traditional' and 'modern'.

The old world was ruled by one interpretation of humanity's place in the universe, and the modern world by another. By listing the components of modernity and the modern world one can to an extent understand some of the differences and some of the general discrepancies between the two worlds.

The most important components of modernity are:

1.   Humanism in the sense of anthropo-centrism and locating humanity at the core of nature, history and society;

2.   A belief in the equal creation of all humans and their equal humanity;

3.   A belief in the natural and equal rights of all humans (whatever their opinions)

4.   [Demand for] personal and social liberties in the civil realm;

5.   Separation of religion and state;

6.   A critical, and of course often an instrumental rationality.[30]

Perhaps the most important component of the modern world is a critical and revolutionary approach towards humankind, society, and history, as well as a strong conviction of the basic principle of 'change'. Perhaps Marx's statement – 'the philosophers have only *interpreted* the world. The point, however, is to *change* it' – represents modernity's basic essence. In Kant's famous words, 'to dare to know' is also, in another way, representative of the spirit of the new world. Western civil society too is the product of this [way of] thinking and [this] revolutionary process, and contrasts with the various societies and systems, traditional and modern, that are incompatible with demo-

[28] Zakariya'i (2000: 87-8).
[29] Zakariya'i (2000: 324-332).
[30] Here the audience disruptions began (Zakariya'i 2000: 134).

cracy, such as tribal, despotic, patriarchal, racist and populist systems. The Universal Declaration of Human Rights of 1948 is somehow the product of the human and social developments in the new West.

But perhaps in the noblest sense, civil society is the independent popular institutions that stand as a buffer between citizens and the state and defend citizens' rights against all forms of aggression on the part of the elite and powerful.

As for Islam, what is the relation of Islamic thought and law with modernity and the new age? As a religion of the pre-modern era, does Islam categorically oppose modernity and its theoretical and practical elements? Or does Islam agree with it, or agree with it only on certain conditions, or…?

Before answering this question, a note on the history of the contemporary Islamic movement is in order. The new Islamic movement came into being about 150 years ago when Muslims encountered new Western civilization and its developments. Muslims, who had once created the most progressive civilization and culture in the East, suddenly, in the second half of the nineteenth century, found themselves confronted by the two different faces of Europe. One was its advanced science, civilization and culture, the other was domination and colonialism. They found themselves impotent against both. Certain questions arose: What was the secret of the backwardness of Muslims and the progress of Westerners? What must now be done? And how could weakness be turned into power? Now, a century later, one can discern three Islamic reactions, three kinds of response to the basic issue of backwardness, or, to put it differently, to the important issue of the kind of relation [that Muslims have] with the 'new' West. These are: traditional Islam, fundamentalist Islam, and modernist or reformist Islam.

Traditionalist Muslims are non-political, follow Islam and the heritage of the forebears uncritically, and oppose many of the products of modernity. They have no faith in compatibility between Islam and modernization, and they also make no serious effort to reconcile them.[31] Meanwhile they pursue a peaceful existence alongside the achievements of the [modern] world, perhaps in the hope that one day the modern world will return to the truth of religion and its lost spirituality. Fundamentalist Muslims, who are traditionalists in some respects but whose Islam is political and militant, either see the

---

[31] At this point Eshkevari had to stop, as hecklers would not allow the session to continue (Zakariya'i, p. 135).

achievements of the modern world as entirely anti-religious or find modernity so problematic that it is beyond redemption. Instead, they rely on the 'veracity', 'universality' and 'completeness' of the religion of Islam. With an intense sense of religious nostalgia, they want, by reviving political Islam 'through the revival of an Islamic caliphate', and by jihad against the West and all the infidels, to [re]create a power similar to that of the Umayyads and Abbasids and the early Ottoman Caliphs. For them, political power and militarism are a basic necessity, to compensate for decline, backwardness and powerlessness.

Modernist Muslims, while welcoming developments in the modern world, neither see the old Islamic tradition and knowledge as entirely worthy of following, nor do they surrender absolutely to modernity. In fact they challenge and criticize the legacy of both and desire the progress and evolution of the positive and renewable aspects of each. On the one hand, they are rationalists whose rational action is a logical continuation of the Mu'tazili[32] and Shia intellectual-theological traditions and of the philosophical traditions of thinkers such as Farabi and even Molla Sadra Shirazi. On the other hand, they are influenced more than anything else by the modern world's tradition of critical thought, and its revolutionary and evolutionary approach. With these two resources, they are criticizing, analysing and scrutinizing tradition and modernity. This trend is sharply distinct from both the traditionalists and the fundamentalists. In the realm of [religious] thought, it advocates reform; and also, at the practical level, it seeks the reconstruction of social and religious institutions. For thinkers of this trend, rethinking and modernism in the realm of Islam have priority over any kind of modernism in political and social development; in effect, they consider social reform and the improvement of institutions to be possible and fruitful through the reconstruction of religious thought. It can be said that Muslim modernists and reformists all over the Muslim world pursue their project of reform in five phases:

1.   Critique of tradition and a refinement and distillation of the cultural sources of Islam

---

[32] A school of Islamic theology that advocated the role of reason and belief in the absolute necessity of God's justice and human free will. It came to prominence during the early stages of the Abbasid Caliphate; especially during the reign of Al-Ma'mun (813-33) who made it the dominant school. Later it was pushed to the margins under another Abbasid Caliph, Al-Mutawakkil (847-61), who adopted an anti-Mu'tazali policy, and it eventually lost ground to the 'Ashari school.

2.   Critique of modernity

3.   Assimilation and adaptation of the positive working principles or elements of tradition and modernity

4.   Combining and blending these adaptable elements

5.   Designing a kind of indigenous modernity (Oriental-Islamic)

Thinkers such as Sayyid Jamaloddin Asadabadi (known as Afghani),[33] Muhammad Abduh of Egypt,[34] Muhammad Iqbal of Lahore,[35] are among the pioneers of the last century's Islamic reformism. Encyclopaedias on the world of Islam include lengthy articles under the entry of 'reform', which deal with reformist developments in Egypt, India, Pakistan, Turkey, Iran and the Arab Middle East, and the ideas of their theoreticians.

The destiny and history of religious reformism in Iran are not separate from its story in the world of Islam. With the onset of the constitutional movement in Iran in 1906 the evolution of the bases of religious thought received more attention. People like Mirza Mohammad Hoseyn Na'ini, one of the constitutionalist and reformist clerics of Najaf, by writing the important book *Tanbih al-Ummah*, made a considerable practical and scientific contribution to the reform of religious thought and social reforms. But the most influential religious reformists appeared after World War II (after 1940). The epistemological source of reformist Islam lay outside the traditional religious seminaries and was largely based in the universities. From the very beginning, some of the more predisposed clerics came under its influence, and they too, at certain junctures, supported religious or social reform. After 1941,[36] intellectuals such as Mehdi Bazargan, Dr Yadollah Sahabi and Dr Mohammad Nakhshab, and an enlightened *mujtahid* like Ayatollah Sayyid Mahmud Taleqani, began an intellectual revolution in the seminaries and society. By advocating a social and reformist Islam that fights despotism and colonialism and rejects all kinds of religious superstitions and non-rational beliefs, they paved the

---

[33] In 1997, to mark the centenary of Afghani's death and examine his heritage, Eshkevari talked to a number of contemporary Islamic thinkers in Iran; a collection of these discussions appeared as a book (Eshkevari 1997b). For a succinct account of Afghani's life and thought, see Keddie (1994: 11-29).

[34] See Haddad (1994: 30-63).

[35] For a recent study of Iqbal, see Masud (2003).

[36] The year of the occupation of Iran by Allied forces and Reza Shah's abdication in favour of his son, Mohammad Reza.

way for significant religious reforms in Iran. During the next four decades, the universities and some young seminary students in Tehran and Qom and other places became the main audience for this movement, and they took its message deep into the cities and villages. In particular the emergence of the renowned Muslim intellectual Dr Ali Shariati, and the learned intellectual work of the distinguished religious scholar Ayatollah Morteza Motahhari in the field of traditional Islamic and Shia thought, played an important role in the expansion of the project of religious reform in recent years. The rapid expansion of these new Islamic developments led to the Islamic Revolution of 1979. If we examine the slogans and ideals raised in the Islamic Revolution, we see clearly that they all came from a reconstructed, modernist and reformist Islam that had no precedent in the seminaries or in a traditional *fiqh*. Freedom, independence, democracy, justice, development, human rights, civil society were among the most important promises of reformist Islam, and a major part of them are reflected in the constitution of the Islamic Republic.

If we consider these points, it is evident that reformist Islam is not a new phenomenon. In the course of a century it sometimes acted in a radical and revolutionary way and sometimes, in other circumstances, pursued its objectives in a calmer and more peaceful way. In its basic essence, Islam, and Shiism in particular, is reformist in the most comprehensive sense of the word.

It is for this reason that prophets are called 'reformer' (*muslih*) in the Koran (as is the case for instance in Sura A'raf, 170; Sura Hud, 88, etc.) and their mission and role are considered to be 'reformation'. In the Koran, the essence of religiosity and of religious conduct is a 'reformed act'. For this reason, until now all Muslim reformers have considered their reformist and corrective actions – whether in the field of religious thought and eradicating superstition, or improving social conditions for Muslims, or cultivating ethics and spirituality in the realm of the personal lives of believers – to be totally based on and derived from the Koran and Sunna. They engage in all these efforts as religious acts in order to please God and His Prophet. While this reformism has acquired more importance in recent times under the impact of modern developments and pressing social needs, this does not diminish its religious validity and credibility. In fact, Muslim reformers today do nothing other than this. By excavating historical Islam from the dust of time, superstition and non-religious and irrational thoughts and customs, and by reviving and reconstructing it in line with scientific knowledge and the experience of today's advanced humanity, they are once again intent on helping humankind, and Muslims in particular, to improve their personal, ethical and social lives. The slogans 'return to Islam' and 'return to the Koran' have no other meaning than this. Specifically, the present reformers of Iran are yesterday's revolutionaries, who of course, by changing some paradigms, are in fact pursuing the same unrealized ideals, but at a deeper level and in more subtle ways. Their main political goal in the short term is to change the general administration of the country from a conservative and theocratic position to a democratic one, through peaceful and legal means.

Although Muslim reformists comprise a broad spectrum and there exist serious intellectual disagreements among them on some issues, nevertheless there is a relative consensus or agreement among their principal spokespersons. Some of the points of agreement pertain to the following important issues:

1. A belief in 'Islamic protestantism' and the realization of an 'Islamic renaissance'. In fact this implies the renewal and reconstruction of religious thought, rethinking the whole system of 'Muslimness', in Iqbal of Lahore's word, and the achievement of social reform through the reform of religious thought.

2. A distinction between fundamental religious principles and religious knowledge. The unerring fundamental principles derived from the Book and the Sunna are fixed and essential and humans have no hand in them. But religious knowledge, in the sense of the human understanding of the texts and the fundamental principles, is elementary and broad, and thus relative. It is only methods that can be [judged as] correct or incorrect, while no understanding can be absolute or complete. Why? Basically because 'the highest understanding' in interpretations is impossible, though one can attain correct or incorrect understandings and justified or unjustified understandings, or a fuller understanding. For this reason, in the eyes of the new Muslim thinkers, history, knowledge and the inherited traditions of religion are not the same as the religion itself. Today the hermeneutic approach to religion and religious sources has gained considerable acceptance.

3. An emphasis on the principle of *ijtihad*, in the sense of the renewal and reconstruction of religious thought, religious dogma and religious practices as the engine of a deep and fundamental movement in Islamic thought and culture. *Ijtihad* makes the critique of both tradition and modernity possible, and it also empowers reformers to design an independent Islamic renaissance and to introduce reforms. Without *ijtihad*, religiosity is neither possible nor useful in modern times; nor is

there the likelihood of benefiting from science, technology and other achievements of human experience. Of course, by *ijtihad* I do not mean merely *ijtihad* in its current *fiqh* sense.[37]

4. Denial of an intermediary between God and people, and denial of an official, custodial religious establishment. Following the principles of freedom of choice, free will and the direct responsibility that every Muslim has for his/her choices, and the rejection of any intermediary between the creator and the created, the new Muslim thinkers consider that there can be no official establishment that functions as sole representative and interpreter of religion (as exists in Christianity).

Although the the reformists acknowledge the need for scholars and experts of religious knowledge, the clerics and the official religious institutions have fiercely opposed this idea [the denial of an intermediary]; which has therefore become a major bone of contention between the reformists [on the one hand], and the conservatives, traditionalists and fundamentalists [on the other].

5. Planning a kind of Islamic humanism, [having] a firm conviction in human 'discernment', and discovering in humans elements such as will-power, creativity, free choice, freedom, the power and the right to choose. Although humans are after all God's servants and their perfection is attained in the selfless service of God, a human being enjoys a status and rights that have been largely ignored in traditional Islamic thought. The pivotal base of reformism and the reformists' religious understanding is their new anthropology.

6. A belief that humans have natural, inalienable and unconditional rights. Humans are respected regardless of their faith, and likewise all people enjoy equal human rights (Articles 1 & 2 of the Declaration of Human Rights). There is no distinction in terms of humanity among various groups of individuals, peoples and nations. For this reason, intellectual and political pluralism and pluralism on other levels are commendable, because these pluralities are after all due to divine will and they have emerged within the context of the project of creation, not outside it.

Toleration and acceptance are, therefore, a religious principle whose negation is [tantamount to] opposing the project of creation; so a religious person [who tolerates other viewpoints] is not doing a favour [but merely doing his duty].

---

[37] He means the need to revise the *osul al-fiqh*, that is, the methodology by which *fiqh* rulings are derived from the sacred sources.

7. A belief in democracy, the realization of rule by the people and popular sovereignty in civil affairs. All new-thinking reformist Muslims believe in the temporal origin of power and that the legitimacy of political rule should be attained through public consent and demand. Although this can be regarded as a kind of 'social contract', it is a contract that is allowed and legitimated on the basis of the transfer of divine sovereignty to humanity. Therefore, autocratic and despotic or race- and class-based governments are categorically condemned; and, as Na'ini said one hundred years ago, 'despotism is an act of heresy and it is a religious duty to [do] jihad against it in order to establish democracy.'

8. Opposition to state religion, and consequently [a belief in the] total and unconditional freedom of every religion and every ideology, freedom of speech and belief within the framework of the democratic laws and regulations of society. Religion and government are essentially two different institutions and their merger is in the interest neither of religion nor of freedom and democracy. Religion and politics, however, cannot be separated from each other.

9. A belief in the mutability of the social laws of Islam. In the view of the majority of the defenders of reformist Islam, the obvious and fixed theoretical and practical principles of religion are eternal, and their transcendence can be defended on rational and intellectual premises. But social rulings (such as penal, economic or governmental laws) are in essence mutable and inevitably change with the change in the subject matter or philosophy of the rulings. For instance, in present conditions, the penal laws and some of the rights of women are in need of fundamental and *ijtihadi* revision. Of course, more than anything else, this kind of *ijtihad* is contingent on the reform of the premises and methodology of traditional religious studies.

10. Relations with the West will be based on 'difference' and 'mutual understanding' (*tafavot va tafahom*). Much has been and can be said about new West. But on the whole Muslim reformists recognize the new West and the modern world as an advanced phase in human history, and consider the utilization of its experience to be a rational and practical necessity and in line with Islamic premises: indeed the Koran recommends this, and the Prophet of Islam and Muslims at the beginning of Islam did just this too.

Another point worth mentioning is that at present there are two major tendencies among Muslim reformists. Perhaps one can say that the first tendency is more inclined toward liberal democracy, the second is the Islamic left, which is more akin to social democracy. The

Islamic left has a more critical approach (one similar perhaps to that of the Frankfurt Critical School) towards the West and modernity. This tendency considers rationality and acting rationally to be the basis of religiosity, but in the sphere of politics it is inclined more towards conceptual rationality than instrumental rationality. It therefore favours understanding and participatory democracy, based on understanding, dialogue and negotiation; and with respect to a style of governing, it regards the method of [ruling through] councils and the expansion of independent popular institutions to be more advanced and humane and closer to democracy. But perhaps the main distinction between the two trends [of Muslim reformism] lies in their social approach to religion. The first group is more inclined towards a private Islam.[38] The second sees Islam as a social movement and wants to bring about social reforms in Muslim societies by means of a social and reformist Islam.[39]

'Women's rights and the women's movement'[40]

In the name of God. Here at least in this one case my rights, as a man, are half of those of the ladies. The ladies spoke for 20 minutes but Ms Omidpour[41] told me I had only five minutes; I said that five minutes is one quarter [of twenty], and I should have at least half the rights [of the women] and speak for ten minutes. Of course I am joking: we are only guests and the ladies had the right to speak. But the issue they raised [on the reformist stance on women's rights] is the most natural question in this kind of debate. Because the debate (...)[42] one of the issues that Muslim reformists [have to face] is this key question of women's rights in Islam, and more specifically in the Koran. What is the place, in today's world, of these laws or some of the regulations that exist in Islam with respect to women's rights? Should they be enforced literally or not? If they should be enforced, are they enforceable or not? If they are to be changed, should they all be changed or only some of them? If we say they must change, we must have good reasons; and if we do not want them changed, we must also have good reasons.

---

[38] He means the *Kiyan* school and those close to Soroush's line of thought.

[39] He means those who follow Shariati's line and the Nationalist-Religious Alliance, with which he is associated himself.

[40] Zakariya'i, 226-33.

[41] The chair. The previous speakers were Mehrangiz Kar and Shahla Sherkat.

[42] Something missing on the tape [original footnote].

In any case, there are so many questions about this issue that in these few minutes I evidently cannot address them all, not even one of them [adequately]. But in this short time, let me give an introduction, which is a general discussion and contains perhaps a general response to the question. Friends, pay attention. The ulama, or the theologians and *fuqaha*, have always divided Islam into several fields. What is more common in our time however, and is taken more seriously by New Religious Thinkers, is a general schema in which Islam is divided into three parts or dimensions.

The first realm, which we may call worldview, is that of bases of belief or dogma. The second realm is that of basic values, which in Iran we also refer to as ideology. The third realm comprises [religious] rulings. In terms of their mutability or immutability, and where they stand in relation to tradition and modernity, these [three realms] are not equivalent. I very much regret that there is no time to elaborate this.[43] They are not equivalent; thus, only the dimension of dogma is eternal. What are the dogmas of Islam? Belief in God, belief in the oneness of God, belief in resurrection, belief in the vital importance of the Koran; some of these matters are spoken of as the principles and indisputable doctrines of Islam. Now if I want to speak in more technical terms, I can say that these statements can be proved or disproved, but they cannot be relativized. What does this mean? It means that if God exists, He always existed; and if God does not exist, He never existed. If God is one, He is always one, and if God is not then He never has been. It cannot be stated that God existed in the early stages of human life but not in later stages; that God existed in the era of feudalism but not in the era of capitalism; under capitalism but not under socialism; that God exists in the era of modernity but that in post-modern times God becomes meaningless.

Anyway, [these statements] can be proved or disproved but they cannot be relativized. We say the same with regard to the realm of basic values. This is so because basic values are really general concepts, which are in essence verifiable, but not relative. (I would say more but I am afraid that if I carry on the chairperson will soon tell me that my time is up).

But as for the realm of rulings, that is sub-divided into two categories.[44] First are rulings about worship, which are immutable. Take for instance prayers, fasting, pilgrimage, alms-giving and certain other

---

[43] See Chapter 3.
[44] *'Ibadat*, worship, and *mu'amilat*, contracts; see Chapter 1.

things [that are part of worship]: at least, as a general principle as regards worship, these are not mutable. Why not? I cannot give an explanation here as there is no time. I shall merely mention one point, which is that these are programmes devised in religion for the religious conduct of Muslims, for their spiritual and moral training; they are the minimal not maximal requirements of worship. Worship is very broad and extensive. There are minimal practices of worship for the spiritual training of a religious person, and they are not dependent on specific conditions of place and time. For this reason, if prayer is useful for humanity in the time of modernity – 'remembrance of God keeps [one] from shameful and unjust deeds'[45] – then it is also useful at all times, post-modern, pre-modern, traditional, etc.

Now as for the issue of women's rights, it falls into the second category of rulings. I would claim ... of course it is not easy to sub-stantiate this claim, and requires a lot of time to explain. ... I would claim that these social rulings of Islam are mutable in essence and by their very nature, even if parts of them come from the Koran [applause] – Please let us not spend the ten minutes this way! – Why do we say they are changeable? Since we often have this debate in Iran; and I have also dealt with it in my speeches and writings. In gen-eral, I have six broad arguments for my theory, but I don't have the opportunity now to outline them all, as there is no time. I shall only mention two arguments, in general terms:

In *fiqh* ... (excuse me if I have to use some Islamic clerical termin-ology; there is no alternative, and after all I am a cleric – though I feel for the interpreters who have to translate this for our German friends) [applause]. In Islamic *fiqh* we have a principle that says that the ruling follows the subject matter (*hokm tabe' mowzu' ast*). This is an obvious, rational principle. It is discussed in the Science of the Principles [*osul al-fiqh*], and the scholars have also discussed it extensively. What does it mean? It means that when a subject matter changes, the ruling too will change. But if the subject matter remains unchanged, the ruling will not change. I shall give an example to illustrate the importance of this matter. I am not talking about religious intellectuals. I won't return to what our brother Dr Pahlevan said about the New Religious Thinking. But let me just make this clear to him. From the way he spoke (no offence intended), I realized that he had not yet read a single page

45 Koran, 29 (The Spider), 45.

about the New Religious Thinking. For me this was indeed regrettable.[46] [Some cheers, some booing].

Let me illustrate my point with an example drawn from Ayatollah Motahhari, not from a religious intellectual [like] Bazargan or Shariati. Motahhari was principally a seminary cleric, who relied on traditional [religious] knowledge and was insistent on retaining its sources. Before the revolution, debates over capitalism and socialism were very important; in his book, *Foundations of Islamic Economics*, published after the revolution, Motahhari makes the point that capitalism was a newly created problem, a totally new problem, and thus required a new solution. This is not a light statement. Those familiar with Islamic issues know that this is no small matter. It is thus ironic for friends outside Iran if I say that – as they might not know – after the revolution, in spite of the unkind treatment he received, Shariati's books were not pulped. They were restricted and banned, but they were not pulped. Yet 100,000 copies of *Foundations of Islamic Economics* were pulped – despite the fact that Ayatollah Khomeini even said that all [Motahhari]'s works, without exception, were good for the Islamic Republic. Why? Again, specialists may know that, if our clerics and our seminaries had accepted this statement, then at least half of our *fiqh* laws would become irrelevant [lacking a subject matter]. That is why some of the gentlemen [clerics] disagreed; and they went to ask Khomeini what to do. As usual he appointed a three-man commission to investigate [laughter]. The three men were: Mahdavi Kani, Hashemi Rafsanjani and Musavi Ardabili. (I am sorry I'm taking such a long time, but sit back and let me tell you the rest of the story). These three got together – this is very symbolic and interesting – and each gave his opinion on the matter.[47] True to form, Mahdavi Kani put his foot down, and said 'this book must be destroyed and pulped, nothing

[46] In an earlier panel Changiz Pahlevan, a secular intellectual, launched an attack on the project of religious reformism in Iran, accusing religious intellectuals of having no one capable of producing ideas and of simply copying and stealing the work of secular intellectuals like himself who have been excluded from the power structure and have had no public platform on which to air their ideas (Zakariya'i, p. 194).

[47] The story encapsulates the main tendencies in the early years of the Islamic Republic and the ways in which Khomeini dealt with problems and attempted to create consensus. Mahdavi Kani represents the right, Musavi Ardabili the left, and Hashemi Rafsanjani the pragmatists within the clerical establishment. For those years and these characters, see Bakhash (1984); for the factional politics, see Moslem (2002: 41-81) and Chapter 1 above.

in it is acceptable.' So it is not only non-religious intellectuals that are censored in the Islamic Republic: Motahhari too was censored. Musavi Ardabili, who had leftist inclinations in those days, said: 'no, this book is good. It is publishable, we can add footnotes and give some explanations.' Hashemi Rafsanjani's line is interesting. He said: 'yes, this book is good and bad; some parts can be accepted and others cannot; if it is published with an introduction that removes its poison, then it is good.' That is Mr Rafsanjani's special approach [laughter and applause]. I apologize [for the diversion].

My first argument [for the mutability of social rulings] – as there is little time to expand – is that when the subject matter changes, the ruling also changes. I ask Shia and Sunni ulama and *fuqaha* – as it is not only in Iran, but all Muslims have this problem. Now the answers that have been offered, I don't care whether they are correct or not, but this point has been raised … I would ask these ulama whether today the 'woman question' … or other rulings about cutting off the hands of thieves, wearing hijab, women serving as judges, inheritance rules and so many other issues of women's rights, are these 'subject matters' or not? Are they essentially changeable or not? Have they been changed before today, or not? Here we need specialists and experts. We must sit and discuss with them, to ascertain whether these matters have changed or not. I suspect that they cannot claim that these [subjects] never change. That would be an empty claim that could not be supported. Therefore the [ulama] must admit that these matters change. If they accept this, that these are changeable subject matters, half the problem is solved. Then we reach the second stage and say, 'very well, have these matters changed today or not?' If we reach the conclusion, from a technical point of view and with strong, open and clear arguments, that these matters have indeed changed today, then the rulings on them must also change. I have simplified a complex discussion here, but I think it is very clear.

My second argument is that the Prophet of Islam received his mission thirteen years before establishing his government in Medina. Of the social rulings (I am leaving aside rulings on worship) that the Prophet implemented during his government in Medina, almost 99 percent were endorsed or approved.[48] What does this mean? This means that the Arabs of Arabia were already living by these laws and

---

[48] The *fuqaha* classify the laws (*ahkam*) made by the Prophet as either 'approved' (*emza'i/ta'yidi*) or 'leglislated' (*ta'sisi*, foundational); only the latter were completely new. See Mohaqqeq-Damad (2003: 4-8).

the Prophet did not introduce them. The prophet did not legislate the laws relating to women, nor the penal laws, nor many others. The Arabs were already observing them. The Prophet accepted a majority of them exactly as they were, and only a few with reforms and amendments. That is why the *fuqaha* say that these are not 'legislated' but 'approved' rulings. Another implication of this statement is that (friends please pay attention, especially the foreign friends who are perhaps less familiar with this) if the Prophet had established his government in Ctesiphon, Reyy, Nishapur[49] or Cairo – sorry, there was no Cairo then, but suppose it was in Athens or somewhere else in the world – what would he have done? Yes ... I want to say that it is not certain that you would be content;[50] the point is that one cannot make such definite statements [applause]. If the Prophet had appeared somewhere else, he certainly would have sanctioned the laws of that place. For this is a matter of custom and has nothing to do with religion and the basis of Sharia; perhaps some rulings are derived from divine revelation, but, based on this argument, I claim that from the beginning these laws were never meant to be eternal, they were to resolve the Prophet's difficulties at that time and in that place. (I apologise and will confine myself to the issue of women's rights) [applause].

I think [the issue is clear] in this brief summary, though it leaves much room for ambiguities and questions. I believe that, just as all social laws are changeable, so are the laws relating to women's rights. There must however be scientific and expert discussion. As for these difficulties which are constantly raised in Iran, my personal conviction is that, with a legal perspective alone, even if the sixth, the seventh or eighth parliaments come, nothing much will be solved. In the words of Sohrab Sepehri,[51] 'eyes must be washed' and we must learn to see the issues in a different way. That is, we must look for the root causes [applause]. I am sorry, but misogyny is not confined to Muslims, nor to Iranians. Sometimes in Iran I say that we have many turban-less mullahs – that is to say, we have many intellectuals and Western-

---

[49] Three cities of the Persian Empire.

[50] He is alluding to the anti-Arab sentiments of some Iranians who see Islam and Islamic law as the main cause of the fall of the Persian Empire (the leading world civilization before the Arab invasion in the seventh century) and of the backwardness of Iran.

[51] A pre-revolutionary New Wave poet who become very popular after the revolution.

educated people [who think like mullahs]. (When I was in America, a lady came to me, complaining about her husband. She said: 'we've been living in America for 35 years. I studied here. I met my husband and married him here. He is a distinguished physician and a Muslim. He tells me that, according to the law of Islam, I have no right to leave home without his permission. He was not educated in the seminaries; he hasn't been to Qom or Najaf; he studied in America.')

So this is not a dispute between mullahs and modernists or between Qom and Paris. This is a dispute that has been going on in Iran for one hundred years. Unfortunately it has been [treated as] a red herring; it is also a dispute about form [not substance]. Let me state my view on the issue of hijab and then finish. This is a question that is frequently asked here too. I believe that [the hijab ruling] is essentially changeable. Dress is a [matter of] custom. It is a cultural [issue] related to a specific time and place. What are [the rules] on wearing or not wearing hijab? [They are to be determined] on the basis of the link between a ruling and its subject matter that I spoke about earlier. But perhaps this argument seems too deviant, too heretical; and many do not accept it. Let me stress my second argument. Let us suppose that [the ruling for hijab] is not changeable. At the very least it is a personal issue; that is, one can choose to wear hijab or not [applause]. Now, however, things have got to the point that not only Iranians but also foreigners who come to interview us, whenever we get to a discussion of reform, say that today's reformists were yesterday's revolutionaries [i.e. that they were responsible for the imposition of hijab]. I just want to say that in 1977-79 I did not imagine that hijab would become compulsory. I was not educated at Harvard or the Sorbonne but I studied for 15 years in Qom and I was involved in the struggle. I was not on the margins, but I was a follower of these gentlemen [the clerical leaders of the revolution]. At that time it was never anticipated that we would have the slogan 'either a head-scarf or a head-smack' (ya ru-sari ya tu-sari). The same gentlemen who are now in power know that it was not compulsory for about a year after the revolution. I am therefore saying that from the beginning hijab was not supposed to be compulsory [applause]. We are not saying anything new [applause]. Deliver what you promised us in the first year of the revolution! We do not want anything more than what you promised us in 1979. In short, we now live in a different era. The issues of family, women's rights, relations between men and women, hijab, inheritance, whether women must be maintained, custody of children and many other issues that we have in Islamic *fiqh* – Shia or non-Shia – must all be reconstructed from the foundations.

For the information of our brother Changiz Pahlevan, I quote a phrase from Iqbal of Lahore. For us Muslim intellectuals, Iqbal is the father of religious intellectualism. He said it seventy years ago and I don't think he copied it – or at least he didn't copy it from Iranian intellectuals. So I finish with what Iqbal declared seventy years ago: 'the time has now come for us Muslims to review the whole system of our Muslimness'. That is all. [Extended applause]

* * * * *

Questioner One: I want to comment very briefly on what Mr Eshkevari said. I come from a clerical family and I know this rule [i.e. new subject matter calls for new rulings]. Our problem is not simply to change the ruling following a change in the subject matter. The problem for us women is the problem of a thousand-year-old patriarchy [applause]. (As a feminist in Europe) women's problems in Iran can only be resolved when we take this matter into account: this is the philosophical question of whether the chicken or the egg came first. We cannot wait [words in German]; this is just my point, that because of thousands of years of despotism we cannot wait for the subject matter to change so that the laws can change. And this applies not only to Islam and the religious government, but to every government that wants to deal with the question of women. Marxists and leftist governments too have not offered women anything better. So my question is thus, in a society like Iran in which women have been oppressed for hundreds of years, how can we wait for them first to rise and then attain their rights. It is the duty of a modern society to change the laws in accordance with social data that exist today in the world, not on the basis of the desires of a class which for years…. [in German]. Many thanks.

Questioner Two: Equal rights for women is a topic that is always debated. We all know that equal rights means [establishing] some new relations, on the basis of [new] laws. In Mr Eshkevari's remarks and in those by all [Muslim] New Thinkers, there is no discussion of the value hierarchy of Islam. That is, in Islam there is a value hierarchy that will never allow [the creation of] equality, of equal rights. At the top is God, then the Prophet and his offspring, and recently the velayat-e faqih and also the elite; and a role for everyone is defined from top to bottom. In this hierarchy there is a role for women and there is a role for men. For this reason, and with this ideology and value system, I think it is not possible to define equal rights for them [women] from the bottom up ...[52]

HYE: Unfortunately, in post-revolutionary Iran our situation has been such that, twenty-odd years after a revolution that was going to bring us democracy, freedom and welfare, that was going to make us a model for the world, here we are, sitting and talking about the most trivial matters. It is indeed regrettable that we still want to discuss whether someone must wear a scarf or not. On the other hand, our Islamists in Iran can only boast 'yes we are Muslims'; as one gentleman said before the revolution (perhaps our Iranian friends may remember), 'Hey, world! You may have a *qamar-e masnu'i* (satellite), but we have *Qamar-e Bani Hashemi*'[53] [laughter and applause]. This is unfortunately the state of our society.

A question was addressed to me to the effect that in Islam there is a set of values that do not allow equal rights for women to emerge. In my few minutes of talk (in which of course I overshot my time, for which I apologize to the chairperson) I wanted to answer this very question. I wanted to say that this value hierarchy that you are describing is a hierarchy that was constructed in the course of the history of Islam. By 'constructed' I do not mean that there was a conspiracy and someone wanted it to be like this. An idea, a thought, a religion, a religious school always first has a truth, a message, which then unfolds, evolves and changes in the course of historical development. Therefore we always divide Islam into 'Islam of Truth' and 'Islam of History'. The same can be said of Christianity, of Judaism, and of Marxism. It is well known that Marx said, 'Sir, I am Marx but I am not Marxist.' Therefore one can be Marx but not a Marxist; Marxism is different from Marx [and his thought]. That is why I said in my talk that not only this sixth Majlis but even a sixtieth Majlis[54] – if it comes – will not be able to do any fundamental work. I am not suggesting that legislation must not change; lawyers must make their efforts and women too must try their best.

---

[52] Zakariya'i (2000: 235-6). The rest of the question is addressed to Ms Sherkat and deals with hijab.

[53] *Qamar*, 'moon', is a personal name; the pun also contrasts the 'artificiality' of the satellite with the nobility of the Bani Hashem tribe.

[54] At this time, the conservatives were planning to annul the results of the sixth parliamentary elections, in which they were comprehensively defeated.

Here in parentheses I must say that I do not see this as merely a male-female issue. Why? Because in my experience I have realized that perhaps most of our women think like men; thus even if all 290 seats in Majlis were taken by women, I don't see much hope that women would be able to enact [equal] laws for themselves [applause]. Approaches to these issues are often largely emotional rather than truly discerning and rational; [and thus] society's culture will not change so soon. In response to your question, I want to say briefly that all our efforts must be geared towards changing these hierarchical values that do not, as you say, allow equal rights for women. And you are right about the hierarchy and that, with the existing foundations and assumptions, all our efforts must be directed towards revising the whole system of Muslimness. In other words, without a kind of hermeneutical approach (which these days has become fashionable in Iran), and without a reconstruction and rereading of religious thought, whether by men or by women, whether in Majlis or by this or that group, then everything becomes a political dispute. [Regardless of] whether there should be hijab or not, if someone wears a scarf, she becomes the epitome of backwardness, and if she takes off her scarf, or – I sincerely beg your pardon – if she strips naked in a gathering of a thousand people, then she becomes the epitome of freedom and democracy.[55] Let me say just one more thing. In the constitutional period, a poet composed a sarcastic quatrain, which, after one hundred years, still speaks to our condition. The context was the dispute between clerics and modernists. The poet uses the name Motaqaddem ['the senior one'] to refer to religious scholars:[56]

> Motaqaddem is proud of his robes; his turban has gone to his
>   head;
> A tie and a hat and a hairstyle do the same for Motajadded.
> The first in falsity's founded, in deceit the other is based,
> The first one's food is too salty, the other one's has no taste.

[applause][57]

[55] He is referring to the earlier disruptions.
[56] Motajadded means 'the modern one', as evident in his Western-style clothes.
[57] Zakariya'i, pp. 239-41.

Epilogue

After Berlin

On 6 August 2000, on his return to Iran, Eshkevari was arrested. On 7 and 15 October he appeared before the Special Clergy Court on the following charges:

(i) Apostasy, by denial of the essentials of religion and of the eternity of Islam; this was because he had discussed the mutability of social laws in Islam, and in particular had opposed compulsory hijab for women;

(ii) 'Waging armed war against God', conspiracy to overthrow the system of the Islamic Republic, 'corruption on earth', and taking action endangering national security; all of this arose from participation in the Berlin Conference;

(iii) Spreading lies with a view to disturbing the public mind, and propaganda against the regime;

(iv) Insulting Ayatollah Khomeini and the clergy by his presence at the Berlin Conference where actions occurred disrespectful to Islam.

Judgment was issued on 21 December; Eshkevari was convicted on all counts, sentenced to death (presumably on the first two charges), two years in prison (on the third), and defrocking (on the fourth).

Eshkevari lodged an appeal the same month. The decision came in autumn 2001, revoking his death sentence but confirming the other sentences. In late summer 2002 his case was reviewed by another branch of the court, which sentenced him to four years in prison for insulting the sanctities and one year for taking part in the Berlin Conference and propaganda against the regime; the other charges were dropped.[1]

The charges and penalties meted out to the Berlin participants were legally arbitrary, reflecting rather the degree of anger and anxiety they had aroused in the judiciary and their conservative backers. Some

---

[1] Personal communication with Eshkevari, August 2004.

were arrested immediately, others summoned to the court and released on bail; all were tried, some were exonerated, others convicted. The harshest treatment went to Eshkevari, Akbar Ganji, Ezzatollah Sahabi and the student leader, Reza Afshari, who all spent long periods in solitary confinement; the last two were released in 2002, the first two were still in prison in early 2005.

The conservatives had blamed the reformist press for their heavy losses in the February 2000 Majlis elections, and used the Berlin Conference as a pretext for bringing the 'Tehran Spring' to a close. They now severely muzzled the press and began a systematic persecution of leading reformists, both outsiders and insiders.[2] By early 2005, some 200 reformist newspapers and journals had been closed and scores of reformists had been detained, many of them being still in prison. Among other groups, the judiciary came down heavily on the National-ist-Religious Alliance, with which Eshkevari is associated. After a series of raids, arrests and trials, in July 2002 a Tehran revolutionary court charged the Liberation Movement with attempting to overthrow the Islamic Republic, and declared 'illegal' the party founded forty years before by Mehdi Bazargan and Ayatollah Taleqani to oppose the shah's regime and to promote an Islamic polity.

Unlike the persecutions of the 1980s, however, there was now a limit to what could be done to suppress the voices of dissent. Every time the judiciary prosecuted a critic, he or she became a popular hero; and even when they were jailed, their ideas continued to reach the public. At the same time, progressive clerics and other voices within the power structure, Khatami and his ministers, and some members of parliament continued to articulate the public demand for reform.

Stalemate and dual government

The 2000 Majlis elections demonstrated the popular support for the reformists and gave them control of both the executive and legislative powers. Yet they soon proved unable to fulfill their electoral promises, which eventually cost them the support of the public. The first blow to the credibility of the new Majlis — which called itself the Majlis of Reform — came when it tried to undo the draconian Press Law that the previous Majlis had passed in its final days in order to curb the

---

[2] For useful summaries and analysis of relevant events since 2000, see HRW (2003), ICG (2002, 2003), Gheissari and Nasr (2004), Baktiari (2005), Kermani (2005).

reformist press. Soon after the inauguration of the new Majlis in June 2000, reformist deputies presented a bill to amend the Press Law, but the Leader wrote to the Majles Speaker, Mehdi Karrubi, that the bill was not in the interests of the system.

This was the first time in the Islamic Republic that the Leader had interfered directly in a Majlis debate. It not only put the leadership (and the conservatives) on a collision course with the Majlis, but it also opened a rift among the reformist deputies. The more radical ones wanted to ignore the Leader's letter; others (including Karrubi) said that it was a governmental ruling (*hokm-e hokumati*) and must be obeyed; the latter prevailed, debate was blocked, and the bill was dropped.

From then on, the unelected bodies frustrated all the legislation of the 'Majlis of Reform'. Before 2000, Khatami's failures to implement reform could be, and were, blamed on his inability to control the Majlis. This was no longer possible. But the hopes for reform were still high, and Khatami's re-election in June 2001 with over 77 percent of the vote kept the reformists in charge of government ministries. It was then that the tensions between religiosity and secularism and between absolutism and democracy not only became more apparent, they fused into one clear cleavage in the state. The two sides – the unelected and elected bodies – came to represent starkly opposed ideologies (religious absolutism versus liberal pluralism), modes of governance (theocracy versus democracy), and methods (violence versus tolerance).

The resultant situation was a stalemate, a 'dual state' (*hakemiyat-e do-ganeh*) that lasted until the next Majlis elections in 2004. It became almost a 'civil war', where members of the unelected state institutions (under the control of *velayat-e faqih*) saw their survival and their hold on power as dependent on preventing the elected institutions carrying out their policies and their agenda. Neither side was strong enough to prevail; a no-win situation for both the reformists in government and parliament and their conservative opponents who controlled the unelected bodies. The dilemma for the conservatives was that the more they resisted the popular demand for reform and change, the more these were radicalized. The reformists' predicament was that the more they compromised with anti-reformist forces in the hope of achieving gradual change, the more they risked losing the leadership of the reformist movement to its radical elements.

By the time of the February 2003 council elections, the stalemate produced what the reformists had feared most: voter apathy. These were the freest elections so far, and for the first time since 1984 the Nationalist-Religious Alliance was able to field candidates, eligibility being entirely a matter for the Ministry of the Interior. Yet in the larger cities, people did not turn out; in Tehran, the turnout was as low as 14 percent. The conservatives regained control of the councils in the major cities, though not in the villages and small towns.

For the Majlis elections the following year, the Guardian Council disqualified a large number of reformist candidates, including 80 sitting members, such as Mohammad Reza Khatami (head of the Mosharekat party and brother of the president). The reformists protested, members organized a sit-in, there was talk of President Khatami's resignation, but to no avail. The election went ahead without the participation of the largest reformist parties.

The conservatives won the election, but victory came at a price: in order to appeal to the popular legitimacy on which the Islamic Republic was founded, they had to appropriate the reformist platform, at least its rhetoric. Running under the banner of 'Renovators' (*Abadgaran*), they now promised to implement 'religious democracy', economic reforms and prosperity, and to respect the rule of law and young people's desire for change, diversity and fun. They even refrained from putting the names of their better-known personalities on their lists of candidates, so as not to evoke sour memories. The turnout of around 50 percent was not as low as the reformists had warned, but the lowest for any Majlis election in the Islamic Republic. In some constituencies there was no competition, as all reformist candidates were disqualified. To make up for its lack of popular mandate, conservatives called the new Majlis the 'Majlis of Unity' or the 'Majlis of the Imam of Time'. The reformists termed it the 'Leader's Majlis' (*majles-e rahbari*) and referred to its members as 'let-ins' (*rah-yaftegan*), that is, selected rather than elected to represent the will of the people.

'Islam' or 'Republic'?

In 1997, when Khatami was elected, the idea of reform was as unformed as was the idea of an Islamic Republic after the victory of the revolution. Eight years on, the reformist phase of the Islamic Republic seemed to be over, but the demand for democracy will undoubtedly continue. Khatami and his reformist allies may have met with many political setbacks, lost many battles and failed to bring any tangible change in the structures of power, they nevertheless succeeded in their central aims of democratizing the political culture and changing the Islamic political discourses. They tried to do this by separating Islam from despotism, and by creating an Islamic worldview that is both modern and democratic. This is the language that speaks to the first generation of Iranians to have come of age in the Islamic Republic, who are now demanding their full citizenship rights.

In 1989, the tension between the two competing notions of religious authority was partially managed by amending the constitution and divorcing *velayat* from *marja'iyat*. A decade later, the main issue emerged more clearly as the cleavage between democratic pluralism and theocratic despotism. The 2004 Majles elections showed the difficulty of reaching a compromise. The underlying tension between *eslamiyat* and *jomhuriyat* was out in the open.

By early 2005, the reformists divided into three broad groups. One believed in the continuing validity of the two assumptions underlying the original notion of 'Islamic Republic' as enshrined in the constitution: that if people are given free choice they will choose 'Islam', and that what makes a state Islamic is the implementation of the Sharia. They supported some kind of *velayat-e faqih* and argued for democratization from within. This group included almost all the reformist clerics within the government like Khatami and Karrubi, as well as those outside, like Ayatollah Montazeri. In his memoirs, published on the Internet in autumn 2000,[3] Montazeri (then still under house arrest) gave an honest and candid account of the thinking behind the granting of so much power to *velayat-e faqih* in the constitution, and how it was shaped by anxiety about republicanism and the possibility of the abuse of power by a secular government, as happened during the Pahlavi era. Montazeri admits he had been naïve to imagine that men of God and the religious establishment would not be prone to such abuse.[4]

Many other senior clerics have come out in support of the reformist movement, and have openly criticized the policies and tactics of the conservative establishment and the Leadership. For example, in July 2002, Ayatollah Jalaloddin Taheri, appointed by Khomeini Friday Prayer Leader of Isfahan in 1979, and an ally of Montazeri, resigned. His letter of resignation was an outright condemnation of the

---

[3] His followers and family members in Qom put a major part (786 out of 1600 pages) of his Memoirs on the Internet (Montazeri 2000). The site was closed down several times but each time reappeared; the publication and distribution of the memoirs is strictly forbidden in Iran, but the text has been printed abroad by several publishing houses affiliated with different exiled opposition groups.

[4] In January 2003, the ban on Montazeri was lifted, and he resumed his lessons.

Leader's office for resisting reformist efforts to create a system of checks and balances that could bring about accountability and the rule of law and put an end to the corruption and excesses of the ruling clerics. He no longer wanted to be part of an unjust, corrupt and despotic rule that was 'marrying the ill-tempered, ugly hag of violence to religion.' The reformist press was banned from publishing the letter, yet it was widely circulated and welcomed.

The second broad group of reformists sees the original assumptions as no longer viable after the death of Khomeini; *velayat-e faqih* was a position only he could fill; some, like Eshkevari and Mojtahed-Shabestari, have questioned whether it is the role of Islamic government to implement the Sharia.[5] Others, like Kadivar, categorically reject the 'religious democracy' that the conservatives – now speaking in the language of Khatami – have promised to foster through reforms. 'The illusion of compatibility of the *velayat-e faqih* with democracy', Kadivar wrote in April 2003, 'is due to lack of familiarity with jurisprudential terminology on the one hand, and the theory of democracy on the other.'[6]

The third group, outside government circles, has called for more drastic change – for a secular democracy. In spring 2002, while still in prison, Akbar Ganji published on the internet a short book completed in prison, *Manifesto of Republicanism: Republicanism versus Constitutionalism.*[7] He offers a way out of the political impasse in which the reformists find themselves. Attributing their failure to a lack of theoretical clarity, he asks for conceptual clarification and a change of strategy. The reformists must make democracy their first priority, recognize that what they are struggling against is 'religious despotism', that there is no way to achieve democracy within the bounds of the constitution of the Islamic Republic, which sanctions dual sovereignty and makes the will of the people ultimately subordinate to the *velayat-e faqih*. The reformists, he suggests, must now pursue their struggle for democracy outside the formal structures of the state, rely on the people and ask for a referendum for a constitution that can bring about a 'fully-fledged republic' (*jomhuri-ye tamam-ayyar*). Quoting Ayatollah Khomeini's famous statement in 1978, when attacking the despotism of the shah's regime, that every generation has the right to choose its political destiny, Ganji says

---

[5] See Mojtahed-Shabestari (2000).

[6] Kadivar (2002).

[7] Ganji (2002).

that if the last generation said no to monarchy this generation has the same right to say no to the Islamic Republic.[8]

The reformists in government received Ganji's manifesto in silence, but it was an instant success with student groups – and with secularists outside and inside Iran. In the hands of the conservatives, though, it became another stick with which to beat the reformists, as revealing their real intention to do away with the Islamic side of the state.

Then again, in June 2002, on the twenty-fifth anniversary of the death of Ali Shariati, at a talk in the University of Hamadan (a city in western Iran), Hashem Aghajari (war-wounded professor and member of a radical reformist group) called for an Islamic Protestantism to rescue Islam from the clerical hierarchy. Criticizing the Shia concept of *taqlid* ('imitation', following a high-ranking *mujtahid* as *marja'*), Aghajari declared: 'people are not monkeys to imitate a *mujtahid*'; they can find their own way in matters of religion by going back to the sources. In November Aghajari was arrested, convicted of apostasy in a Hamadan court, and sentenced to flogging, imprisonment and death. This led to massive demonstrations in campuses all over the country. The students demanded a referendum, brandishing pictures of Ganji and Nuri; the protests were much louder, their slogans more radical than in July 1999, but this time the police reined in the vigilantes. The crisis was resolved by the intervention of the Leader, who asked the judiciary to review the sentence. The judiciary dragged its feet, but eventually backed down, and Aghajari was freed in 2004.

The struggle goes on

Eshkevari's writings between 1995 and 2000 are part of the ongoing debate among Muslims over the nature of the relation between religion and politics. An important effect of this debate may be the creation of its subject: 'Islamic democracy' or 'democratic Islam'.

The democracy debate is neither new to the Muslim world nor confined to Iran. In Iran, as we noted in Chapter 1, it began in earnest with the Constitutional Revolution of 1906. A century later, the debate is as alive as it was then, carrying a heavy legacy of painful experiences, bitter struggles, unresolved tensions, numerous failures – and lessons learnt. It was no coincidence that in August 2004 Khatami's reformist government – in its last year – celebrated the centenary of the Constitutional Revolution two years early. When asked, why not

[8] Ganji (2002).

wait for another two years, parliamentary vice-president Hojjat ol-Eslam Abtahi responded: 'since this is the last year of Khatami's presidency we thought it appropriate to bring the occasion forward.'[9] The premature celebration became the occasion for the reformists to draw parallels between the two Iranian revolutions of the twentieth century. *Sharq*, one of the few reformist papers still appearing, published a special supplement on constitutionalism which included barely veiled comparisons between the absolute monarchy of 1906 and the absolute *velayat-e faqih* of 2004.[10]

There are indeed remarkable similarities between the demands of the reformists today and those of the constitutionalists a century ago, as well as between the absolute power at the disposal of the shah then and the Leader now. But there are also significant differences in the contexts in which these demands were made, and the ways in which this absolute power was exercised and translated into policies. Iran of the early twentieth century was highly rural and feudal; 90 percent of the population were illiterate; the demand for democracy came from an elite for whom Europe was the source of reference. The people of Iran in the early twenty-first century are predominantly urban, educated and young; the twentieth-century experiences of both the secularizing and modernizing dictatorship of the Pahlavis (1924-79) and the clerical rule of the Islamic Republic have left most Iranians feeling jaded by ideology and betrayed by both monarchical and clerical absolutisms. This is what Eshkevari acknowledged in his speech at the Berlin Conference: 'even if Khatami … should be defeated in his work… this time not only has democracy become the first priority, but there is an unprecedented consensus among the intellectual and the political elites … the historical time of despotism is over in Iran.'

Just before this book went to press, in an extraordinary and unpredicted turnaround, the June 2005 presidential election was won by the former Tehran mayor, Dr Mahmud Ahmadinejad, on a platform of social justice, economic reform and a campaign against corruption. Supported by the leadership and radical elements among the conservatives, his landslide victory was widely interpreted as a rejection of his main opponent on the ballot, former president Hashemi Rafsanjani, who had campaigned as a reformist but was widely suspected of cynical opportunism. Some observers feared that Ahmadinejad's election marked the end of the reform movement, and that the relatively liberal

---

[9] *Sharq* 256, 14 Mordad 1383 (4 August 2004).
[10] Ibid.

cultural and social climate enjoyed under Khatami's reformist government would quickly change for the worse. Others suggested that the conservatives, with the end of the 'dual state', and with all the organs of government in their hands, would now take responsibility for a programme of effective reform, if only to restore their popular legitimacy. Either way, the struggle for democracy in Iran has entered a new phase; it has by no means ended, but there is a long and difficult road ahead.

Appendix

Hasan Yousefi Eshkevari, 2000-2004

The sentence of the Special Clergy Court neither ended the development of Eshkevari's ideas nor prevented his writings from reaching the public. In Autumn 2000, a selection of his articles published in the reformist press in its heyday appeared as a book, *Remembering the Days* (2000d). In the preface, dated just before his arrest, Eshkevari speaks of the reform movement as a peaceful and democratic continuation of the revolutions of 1906 and 1979.

Three other books reveal his intellectual preoccupations since his arrest. *A Critique of Religious Discourse* (2004b) is a translation (from Arabic) of the controversial work by the Islamic modernist Nasr Abu Zaid that led to his exile from Egypt. A friend gave Eshkevari the book as a present in July 2000 when he spent some time in Paris after the Berlin Conference. It was one of the books that he took with him when he was arrested in August, and it took him three months to translate. A colleague checked the translation, but the book did not appear for four years as the publisher took a long time to get the publication permit. Nasr Abu Zaid wrote a new introduction for the Persian edition.

Eshkevari wrote the other two books during the hundred days he spent in solitary confinement in spring 2001, when he was allowed only a copy of the Koran and pen and paper.[1] In the preface to *Solitary Reflections: A Prelude to Iranian Hermeneutics* (2003b), he says that, to keep his sanity, he decided to write down his thinking on the major questions raised in the science of hermeneutics about which he had been reading and thinking before his arrest.

After finishing *Solitary Reflections*, Eshkevari started *Letters from Prison to my Daughter* (2004a). In the preface, he describes how solitary confinement confronted him with his inner self, quoting Ali Shariati that at the moment of death and in solitary confinement one becomes one

---

[1] This was in connection with one of the major offensives against members of the Nationalist-Religious Alliance.

with oneself. He also writes of how he has become even more convinced of the rightness of the path he has chosen, and of his desperate need to be with his family and to tell them what he is going through. Knowing that his interrogators would scrutinize whatever he wrote, he practiced self-censorship, but also decided to fulfil one of his ambitions: to write an analytical history of early Islam and Iran. This was something that he had wanted to do since 1978 when, inspired by his guru Shariati, he came to understand the importance of history and of developing an analytical understanding of relations between history and religion. He started the project in November 1999, on the day of *be'sat* (when the Prophet received his mission), and his children, in particular his son Ruhollah, were to work with him. All came to a sudden halt with the Berlin Conference. Now in prison, he decided to continue the work in the shape of 60 letters addressed to his daughter Zahra, following Nehru's example. Each letter, while narrating some early historical episode, contains something of his feelings at the time, his desperation, his hopes for the future, his certainty in his faith and his longing for his family and the outside world.

In addition to these three books, several of his articles have appeared in what is left of the reformist press. Important among them are: a review in *Aftab* of the Persian translation (from the French) of Abd al-Raziq's book under the title 'Islam and sources of power';[2] 'Bazargan's last views: fears and warnings'; and articles on the Islamic and constitutional movements in *Sharq*.[3]

Following a report in *Sharq* about the June 2004 meeting of the Society for Iranian Studies in Bethesda, mentioning a paper we presented about this book, Eshkevari's son Ruhollah made contact with us by e-mail, and we sent him a copy of the paper. Ruhollah expressed his father's appreciation of what we were doing but also wanted to correct some minor errors; for example, *Sharq* incorrectly quoted us as saying that Eshkevari was a member of the Liberation Movement. We had a number of exchanges through Ruhollah, in which we managed to clarify a number of points on the background and also on the translation. Ziba arranged to speak to his father on one of his monthly five-day furloughs from prison. In early August, when we had finished a first draft of the book, she had a telephone conversation with Eshkevari. He modestly denied there was anything original in his work. She asked him what he was now working on, and whether there had been

---

[2] *Aftab*, Farvardin 1381, No 14, pp. 40-43.
[3] Eshkevari (2003a, 2004c).

a major change in his perspective since 1995 when he wrote 'Islamic democratic government' (Chapter 3). He said he had just finished writing a book on religious reformation and Islamic protestantism, consisting of three parts. In the first, he surveys religious reformation in Europe up to the eighteenth century, focusing on Luther and Calvin; this part is descriptive and examines the impact of these new religious ideas on developments in the new West. In the second part, he turns to the Islamic world, with a focus on Iran, to explore the role of religious reforms from constitutionalism to the present. The third part takes a critical look at religious intellectualism; the main question addressed is whether or not a religious reformation in Islam is possible. He went on to say that, although he rejects governmental Islam, he believes in social Islam; religion has social, cultural and political functions, and if it is going to have a part in government it must be through democratic means.

As for whether there had been any major shift in his thinking, he said that the only major change concerned his understanding of gender: he no longer saw gender roles as divinely ordained, but as social constructions. It was this that led him to argue for a change in hijab regulations, bringing down the wrath of the Special Clergy Court. 'My outlook on gender was limited to my own narrow experience of the life style I had seen in Qom and around me, but when I started to read about the women's rights movement and to travel, I realized that there are other ways and values, especially when I came to encounter believing Muslim women without hijab in the USA.'[4] The laws are not divine, he said, but man-made; laws that existed at the beginning of Islam can be changed in time; therefore the notion of religious government based on a 'divine and eternal law' is basically flawed. The commands of religion can be reflected in the laws that people make in line with their needs and those of time and place.

---

[4] In his book *Rereading of the Story of Creation* (1998a), based on lectures given between 1990 and 1996, Eshkevari reproduces the 'neo-traditionalist' argument for 'gender complementarity' (see Mir-Hosseini 1999), but his change of perspective is already evident in an interview published in *Zanan* (March 2000), where he points out that there is almost no mention of the subject of women in the works of prominent Muslim intellectuals such as Bazargan.

Bibliography

Works by Eshkevari
[Some publication details were not available]
1974. *'Ellal-e Jara'em va Rah-haye Mobarezeh ba Anha* (Causes of Crimes and Ways to Combat them) (Qom, 1353).
1975. *'Adl dar Jahanbini-ye Towhidi* (Justice in the *Towhidi* Worldview) (Qom, 1354).
1977. *Bot-haye Shekasteh* (Broken Idols) (Qom, 1356).
1978. *Mardi az Kavir* (A man from the desert) (Qom 1357).
1985. *Naqdi az 'Shahid Motahhari: Efshagar-e Towte'eh'* (Critique of 'Martyr Motahhari: Divulger of Conspiracy').
1990. (transl. from Arabic) *Imam al-Sadiq wa al-Madhahib al-'Arba'a* (Imam al-Sadiq and the four Mazhabs), by Asad Heydar (Tehran: Enteshar, 1369).
1991. (transl. from Arabic) *Ibn Baris wa al-Jazira* (Ibn Baris and Algeria), by Muhammad Al-Meyli (Tehran: Yadavaran, 1370).
1993. (transl. from Arabic) *Zu'ama al-Islah fi'l-Asr as-Hadith* (Pioneers of Renewal in the Modern Era), by Ahmad Amin (Tehran, 1372).
1994. 'Paradoks-e eslam va demokrasi?' (The paradox of Islam and democracy?), *Kiyan* 21 (Shahrivar/Mehr 1373), pp. 24-29.
1997a, 2000a. *Dar Takapu-ye Azadi: Seyri dar Zendegani, Asar va Afkar-e Mohandes Mehdi Bazargan* (In Search of Freedom: The Life and Thought of Engineer Mehdi Bazargan), 2 vols (Tehran: Bazargan Cultural Foundation, Qalam Press, 1376, 1379).
1997b. *Dara-ye Qafeleh* (The Caravan Bell: Seven Articles on the Work and Thought of Sayyid Jamaloddin Asadabadi) (Tehran: Chapakhsh, 1376).
1998a. *Baz-khuni-ye Qesseh-ye Khelqat (Bahs-e Ensan-Shenasi)* (Re-reading the Story of Creation; Issues in Anthropology).
1998b. *Shari'ati: Ide'uluzhi va Estratezhi* (Shariati, Ideology and Strategy) (Tehran, Chapakhsh, 1377).
1998c. *Nowgara-ye Dini* (Religious Modernism) (collection of interviews with Bazargan, Yazdi, Sorush, Ja'fari, Shabestari, Tavassoli, Peyman, Sahabi, Hojjati Kermani, Musavi Bojnurdi) (Tehran: Qasideh, 1377).
1999. 'Nazariyeh Ayatollah Na'ini dar bab-e hokumat-e eslami' (Ayatollah Na'ini's theory about Islamic government), in Anjoman (1999).
2000a. See 1997a.
2000b. *Shari'ati va Naqd-e Sonnat* (Shariati and the Critique of Tradition) (Tehran: Yadavaran, 1379).
2000c. *Kherad dar Ziyafat-e Din* (Reason at the Feast of Religion) (Tehran: Qasideh, 1379).
2000d. *Yad-e Ayyam* (Remembering the Days) (Tehran: Gam-e Now, 1379).
2003a. 'Akharin nazar-e Bazargan: bim-ha va hoshdar-ha' (Bazargan's last views: fears and warnings, *Nameh* 20 (Bahman, 1381), pp. 68-80.

2003b. *Ta'amolat-e Tanha'i: Dibache'i bar Hermenutik* (Solitary Reflections: A
    Prelude to Hermeneutics) (Tehran: Sara'i, 1382).
2004a. *Name-ha'i az Zendan be Dokhtaram: Moruri bar Tarikh-e Du Qarn-e Avval-e
    Iran va Eslam* (Letters to my Daughter from Prison: An Overview of the
    History of the First Two Centuries of Iran and Islam) (Tehran:
    Ghasidehsara, 1383).
2004b. (transl. from the Arabic) *Naqd-e Goftoman-e Dini* (A Critique of Religious
    Discourse), by Nasr Hamid Abu Zeyd.
2004c. 'Yek qarn-e mashruteh-khahi' (A century of constitutionalism), *Sharq*
    256 (14 Mordad 1383).

Secondary sources

'Abd al-Raziq, 'Ali, 1925. *Al-Islam wa-Usul al-Hukm* (Islam and the Principles of
    Rule) (Cairo).
Abdo, Geneive, 2001. 'Rethinking the Islamic Republic: a conversation with
    Ayatollah Hossein 'Ali Montazeri,' *Middle East Journal* 55/1 (accessed
    20.5.03 at *http://www.mideasti.org/html/full551.html*).
Abou El Fadl, Khaled, 1997. *The Authoritative and the Authoritarian in Islamic
    Discourses: a Contemporary Case Study* (2nd edition, Austin, Texas: Dar
    Taiba).
Abou El Fadl, Khaled (et al.), 2004. *Islam and the Challenge of Democracy*
    (Princeton: Princeton University Press).
Abrahamian, Ervand, 1983. *Iran Between Two Revolutions* (Princeton: Princeton
    University Press).
Abrahamian, Ervand, 1989. *Radical Islam: The Iranian Mojahedin* (London: I. B.
    Tauris).
Abrahamian, Ervand, 2001. Review of Kadivar (1998), *Islamic Law and Society*
    8/2, pp. 295-8.
Ahmed, Leila, 1992. *Women and Gender in Islam, Historical Roots of a Modern Debate*
    (New Haven & London: Yale University Press).
Akhavi, Shahrokh, 1980. *Religion and Politics in Contemporary Iran: Clergy-State
    Relations in the Pahlavi Period* (Albany: SUNY Press).
Akhavi, Shahrokh, 1996. 'Contending Discourses in Shi'a law on the Doctrine
    of *Wilayat al-Faqih*,' *Iranian Studies* 29/3-4, pp. 229-68.
Algar, Hamid, 1969. *Religion and State in Iran 1785-1906: the Role of the Ulama in
    the Qajar Period* (Berkeley & Los Angeles: University of California Press).
Anjoman-e Eslami-ye Mohandesin, 1962. *Bahsi dar bare-ye Marja'iyat va
    Rowhaniyat* (A Discussion about *Marja'iyat* and Clergy) (Tehran, 1341).
Anjoman-e Eslami-ye Mohandesin, 1999. *Din va Hokumat: Majmu'eh-ye Maqalat
    va Sokhanraniha dar Seminar-e Din va Hokumat dar Anjoman-e Eslami-ye
    Mohandesin* (Religion and Government: Collected Papers and Lectures in
    the Religion and Government Seminar of the Islamic Association of
    Engineers) (Tehran: Reza Cultural Services Company, 1378).
An-Na'im, Abdullahi Ahmed, 2000. 'Islamic foundation for women's human
    rights', in Zainah Anwar & Rashidah Abdullah (eds), *Islam, Reproductive
    Health and Women's Rights* (Kuala Lumpur: Sisters in Islam).

Ansari, Ali, 2000. *Iran, Islam and Democracy: The Politics of Managing Change* (London: Royal Institute of International Affairs).

Arjomand, Said Amir, 1988. *The Turban for the Crown: The Islamic Revolution in Iran* (Oxford: Oxford University Press).

Arjomand, Said Amir, 1992. 'The constitution of the Islamic Republic,' *Encyclopaedia Iranica* 6, pp. 151-8.

Arjomand, Said Amir, 2000. 'Civil society and the rule of law in the constitutional politics of Iran under Khatami,' *Social Research* 67/2, pp. 283-301

Arjomand, Said Amir, 2002. 'The reform movement and the debate on modernity and tradition in contemporary Iran,' *Int. J. Middle East Stud.* 34, pp. 719-31.

Ashraf, Ahmad, and Ali Banuazizi (eds), 2001a. 'Intellectuals in post-revolutionary Iran,' special issue of *International Journal of Politics, Culture and Society* 15/2.

Ashraf, Ahmad, and Ali Banuazizi, 2001b. 'Iran's tortuous path toward "Islamic liberalism",' *International Journal of Politics, Culture and Society* 15/2, pp. 237-56.

Aslan, Reza, 2005. *No God but God: The Origins, Evolution, and Future of Islam* (New York: Random House).

Bakhash, Shaul, 1984. *The Reign of the Ayatollahs: Iran and the Islamic Revolution* (New York: Basic Books).

Baktiari, Bahman, 1996. *Parliamentary Politics in Revolutionary Iran. The Institutionalization of Factional Politics* (Gainsville etc.: University Press of Florida).

Baktiari, Bahman, 2005. 'Dilemmas of reform and democracy in the Islamic Republic of Iran', in Robert W. Hefner (ed.) *Remaking Muslim Politics: Pluralism, Contestation, Democratization* (Princeton: Princeton University Press).

Baqi [Baghi], 'Emadoddin, 2001. 'Dadgah-e vizheh-ye rowhaniyat, didgah-e mo'afeqan va mokhalefan' (The Special Clergy Court: perspective of supporters and opponents), *Aftab*, 10 Azar 1380, pp. 40-47.

Bayat, Mangol, 1991. *Iran's First Revolution: Shi'ism and the Constitutional Revolution of 1905-1909* (New York & Oxford: Oxford University Press).

Bazargan, Mehdi, 1966. *Be'sat va Ide'uluzhi* (Appointment and Ideology) (Mashhad: Tulu', 1355).

Bazargan, Mehdi, 1984. *Enqelab-e Iran dar Do Harekat* (Iranian Revolution in Two Movements) (3rd edn, privately publicashed, 1363).

Bazargan, Mehdi, 1993. 'Seyr-e andishe-ye dini-ye mo'aser: goftegu'i ba mohandes Mehdi Bazargan' (A Conversation with Barzargan), *Kiyan* 11 (Farvardin-Ordibehest 1372), pp. 2-11.

Bazargan, Mehdi, 1998. *Akherat va Khoda: Hadaf-e Be'sat-e Anbia* (The Afterlife and God: the Purpose of the Appointment of Prophets) (Tehran: Resa, 1377).

Boroujerdi, Mehrzad, 1996. *Iranian Intellectuals and the West. The Tormented Triumph of Nativism* (Syracuse: Syracuse University Press).

Buchta, Wilfried, 2000. *Who Rules Iran? The Structure of Power in the Islamic Republic* (Washington Institute for Near East Policy & Konrad Adenauer Stiftung).

Burns, John F. 1999. 'Reformers vs. clerics – Nouri trial', *New York Times*, 31 Oct.

Chehabi, Houchang, 1990. *Iranian Politics and Religious Modernism: The Liberation Movement of Iran under the Shah and Khomeini* (London: I. B. Tauris).

Cooper, John, 1998. 'The limits of the sacred: the epistemology of 'Abd al-Karim Soroush', in John Cooper, Ron Nettler and Muhammed Mahmoud (eds) *Islam and Modernity: Muslim Intellectuals Respond* (London, New York: I. B. Tauris).

Dabashi, Hamid, 1993. *Theology of Discontent: The Ideological Foundation of the Islamic Revolution in Iran* (New York: New York University Press).

Dahlén, Ashk P., 2003. *Islamic Law, Epistemology and Modernity: Legal Philosophy in Contemporary Iran* (London, New York: Routledge).

Ehteshami, Anoushirvan, 1995. *After Khomeini: The Iranian Second Republic* (London: Routledge).

Enayat, Hamid, 1982. *Modern Islamic Political Thought* (Austin: University of Texas Press).

Esposito, John L., and John O. Voll, 1996. *Islam and Democracy* (Oxford: Oxford University Press).

Farhadpur, Lili, 2000. *Zanan-e Berlin* (Women of Berlin) (Tehran: Jame'eh Iranian, 1379).

Fischer, Michael, 1980. *Iran: From Religious Protest to Revolution* (Cambridge, Mass: Harvard University Press).

Ganji, Akbar, 1999a. 'Negahi be prozheh-ye reha'i-ye jaryan-e rowshanfekri-ye dini' (A look at the liberation project of religious intellectualism), *Khordad* 25.12.1377 [15 March].

Ganji, Akbar, 1999b. *Tarik-khaneh-ye Ashbah: Asib-shenasi-ye Gozar be Dowlat-e Demokratik-e Towse'eh-gera* (Darkhouse of Ghosts; The Pathology of Transition to the Developmental Democratic State) (Tehran: Tarh-e Now, 1378).

Ganji, Akbar, 2002. *Manifest-e Jomhuri-khahi: Jomhuri-khahi dar barabar-e Mashruteh-khahi* (The Manifesto of Republicanism: Republicanism versus Constitutionalism) (1381) accessed at *http://www.iranian.com/Opinion/2002/December/Sadri/*

Ghamari-Tabrizi, Behrooz, 2004. 'Contentious public religion. Two conceptions of Islam in revolutionary Iran. Ali Shari'ati and Abdolkarim Soroush.' *International Sociology* 19/4, pp. 504-23.

Gheissari, Ali, 1998. *Iranian intellectuals in the 20th century* (Austin: University of Texas Press).

Gheissari, Ali, and Vali Nasr, 2004. 'Iran's democracy debate,' *Middle East Policy* 11/2, pp. 94-106.

Gieling, Saskia, 1997. 'The *marja'iya* in Iran and the nomination of Khamenei in December 1994,' *Middle Eastern Studies* 33/4, pp. 777-87.

Haddad, Yvonne Yazbeck, 1994. 'Muhammad Abduh: pioneer of Islamic reform,' in Ali Rahnema (ed.) *Pioneers of Islamic Revival* (London: Zed Books).

Hefner, Robert W. (ed.), 2005. *Remaking Muslim Politics: Pluralism, Contestation, Democratization* (Princeton: Princeton University Press)

Hourani, Albert, 1962. *Arabic Thought in a Liberal Age, 1798-1973* (London: Oxford University Press).

HRW 2003. *Human Rights Watch World Report 2003: Iran.* (accessed 20.9.04 at *http://www.hrw.org/wr2k3/mideast3.html*).

ICG (International Crisis Group) 2002. *Iran: The Struggle for the Revolution's Soul* (ICG Middle East Report No.5) (Amman/Brussels).

ICG (International Crisis Group) 2003. 'Iran: discontent and disarray,' *ICG Middle East Briefing* (Amman/Brussels 15 October).

Ja'fari, Mohammad Taqi, 1960. *Manabeh-e Fiqh* (Sources of Islamic Jurisprudence) (Tehran, 1349).

Jahanbakhsh, Forough, 2001. *Islam, Democracy and Religious Modernism (1953-2000), from Bazargan to Sorush* (Leiden: Brill).

Jalaiepour, Hamidreza, 2003. 'Religious intellectuals and political action in the reform movement,' in Negin Nabavi (ed.) *Intellectual Trends in Twentieth Century Iran: A Critical Survey* (Gainesville, etc.: University of Florida Press) – also available at *http://www.drsoroush.com.*

Kadivar, Mohsen, 1998. Andisheh-e Siyasi dar Eslam; Vol 1 Nazariyeh-ha-ye Dowlat dar Feqh-e Shi'eh (Theories of the State in Shia Jurisprudence); Vol 2 Hokumat-e Vela'i (Government by Mandate) (Tehran: Nashr-e Ney).

Kadivar, Mohsen, 1999a. 'Negahi beh karnameh-ye bist-saleh-ye jomhuri-ye eslami' (A look at the twenty-year balance sheet of the Islamic Republic), *Khordad*, 25-27 Bahman 1377/13-15 February.

Kadivar, Mohsen, 1999b. *Baha-ye Azadi: Defa'iyat-e Mohsen Kadivar dar Dadgah-e Vizheh-e Rouhaniyat* (The Price of Freedom: Mohsen Kadivar's Defence in the Special Clergy Court), ed. Zahra Rudi-Kadivar (Tehran: Nashr-e Ney, 1378).

Kadivar, Mohsen, 2002. *'Velayat-e faqih* and democracy,' paper delivered at meeting of Middle East Studies Association, November (accessed at *http://www.kadivar.com* on 18.9.04).

Kadivar, Mohsen, 2002. Andisheh-ye Siyasi dar Eslam, Vol 3 *Hokumat-e Entesabi* (Government by Appointment) (Tehran: Nashr-e Ney).

Kamali, Muhammad Hashim, 1989. 'Sources, nature and objectives of Shari'ah,' *Islamic Quarterly* 33, pp. 215-35.

Katira'i, Mostafa, 1999. 'Hokumat az didgah-e Din' (Government from the perspective of religion), in Anjoman (1999).

Keddie, Nikki, 1983 (ed.). *Religion and Politics in Iran: Shi'ism from Quietism to Revolution* (New Haven: Yale University Press).

Keddie, Nikki, 1994. 'Jamal al-Din Afghani,' in Ali Rahnema (ed.) *Pioneers of Islamic Revival* (London: Zed Books).

Kermani, Navid, 2005. 'Religious reformist thinkers in Iran: intellectually victorious, but politically defeated' (transl. by Michael Lawton from German original in *Neue Zürcher Zeitung*), *Al-Qantara* (accessed on 2.2.05 at *http://www.qantara.de/webcom/show_article.php/_c-476/_nr-317/i.html*).

Khiabani, Gholam, and Annabelle Sreberny, 2001. 'The Iranian press and the continuing struggle over civil society 1998-2000,' *Gazette: International Journal for Communication Studies* 63, pp. 203-23.

Khomeini, Ruhollah, 1983-90. *Sahifeh Nur: Majmu'ehi Rahnamudha-ye Emam Khomeini* (The Book of Light: A Collection of the Guidance of Imam Khomeini), 21 v (Tehran: Sazman-e Madarek-e Farhangi-ye Enqelab-e Eslami).

Koran, 1999. *The Meaning of the Holy Qur'an*, New edition with revised translation, commentary and newly compiled comprehensive index by 'Abdullah Yusuf 'Ali (Beltsville, Maryland: Amana).

Kurzman, Charles (ed.) 1998. *Liberal Islam: a Sourcebook* (New York: Oxford University Press).

Kurzman, Charles, 2001. 'Critics within: Islamic scholars protest against the Islamic state in Iran.' *International J. of Politics, Culture and Society* 15, pp. 341-59.

Lambton, Ann K. S., 1964. 'A reconsideration of the position of the marja' al-taqlid and the religious institution,' *Studia Islamica* 20, pp. 115-35.

Mallat, Chibli, 1993. *The Renewal of Islamic Law. Muhammad Bader as-Sadr, Najaf and the Shi'i International* (Cambridge: Cambridge University Press).

Mallat, Chibli, 1994. 'Muhammad Baqer as-Sadr', in Ali Rahnema (ed.) *Pioneers of Islamic Revival* (London: Zed Books).

Martin, Vanessa, 2000. *Creating an Islamic State: Khomeini and the Making of a New Iran* (London: I. B. Tauris).

Masud, Muhammad Khalid, 2003. *Iqbal's Reconstruction of Ijtihad* (2nd edn, Lahore: Iqbal Academy Pakistan).

Matin-Asgari. Matin, 1997. 'Abdolkarim Sorush and the secularization of Islamic thought in Iran,' *Iranian Studies* 30, pp. 95-116.

Menashri, David, 1992. 'The domestic power struggle and the fourth Iranian majles elections,' *Orient* 33/3, pp. 387-408.

Mir-Hosseini, Ziba, 1996. 'Divorce, veiling and feminism in post-Khomeini Iran,' in Haleh Afshar (ed.), *Women and Politics in the Third World* (London: Routledge).

Mir-Hosseini, Ziba, 1999. *Islam and Gender: The Religious Debate in Contemporary Iran* (Princeton: Princeton University Press/London: I. B. Tauris).

Mir-Hosseini, Ziba, 2001. 'Emerging feminist voices,' in Lynn Walter (ed.), *Women's Rights: a Global View* (Westport, Conn.: Greenwood Press).

Mir-Hosseini, Ziba, 2002a. 'Debating women: gender and the public sphere in post-revolutionary Iran', in Amyn Sajoo (ed.) *Civil Society in Comparative Muslim Contexts* (London: I. B. Tauris & Institute of Ismaili Studies).

Mir-Hosseini, Ziba, 2002b. 'The conservative and reformist conflict over women's rights in Iran,' *International J. of Politics, Culture and Society* 16/1, pp. 37-53.

Mir-Hosseini, Ziba, 2005. 'Islamic law, secularism and feminism: a new relationship,' in Qudsia Mirza (ed.) *Islamic Feminism and Law* (London: Cavendish House).

Mirsepassi, Ali, 2000. *Intellectual Discourse and the Politics of Modernization: Negotiating Modernity in Iran* (Cambridge: Cambridge University Press).

Mohammadi, Mohammad Majid, 1999 'Akhlaq, shadi, sabk-e zendegi' (Morality, gaiety and life-style), *Khordad* 20.3.1377 [9 June].

Mohaqqeq-Damad, Sayyid Mostafa, 1996. *Mabahesi az Osul-e Feqh: Daftar-e Dovvom, Manabe'-e Feqh* (Jurisprudential Discussions, Book 2: Sources of Jurisprudence) (Tehran: Markaz-e Nashr-e 'Olum-e Ensani, 1375).

Mohaqqeq-Damad, Sayyid Mostafa, 2003. *Qava'ed-e Feqh: Bakhsh-e Madani* (The Rules of Islamic Jurisprudence: Civil Section) (Tehran: Markaz-e Nashr-e 'Olum-e Ensani, 1382).

Mojtahed-Shabestari, Mohammad, 2000. *Naqdi bar Qara'at-e Rasmi az Din* (A Critique of the Official Reading of Religion) (Tehran: Tarh-e Now, 1379).

Momen, Moojan, 1985. *An Introduction to Shi'i Islam: the History and Doctrines of Twelver Shi'ism* (New Haven; Yale University Press).

Montazeri, Hoseyn 'Ali, 1988-90. *Dirasat fi Wilayat al-Faqih wa-Fiqh al-Dawlat al-Islamiyah* 4 vols (Qom: Dar al-Fikr, 1367-69); Persian edition, *Mabani-ye Feqhi-e Hokumat-e Eslami* (Jurisprudential Bases of Islamic Government), 3 vols (Tehran: Keyhan, 1368-70).

Montazeri, Hoseyn 'Ali, 2000. *Bakhshi az khaterat-e Ayatollah Montazeri* (Part of the memoirs of Ayatollah Montazeri) (accessed at *www.iranvision.com/pdf/khaterat* on 18.4.04).

Motahhari, Morteza, 1960. *Khadamat-e Moteqabel-e Eslam va Iran* (The Mutual Services of Islam and Iran) (Tehran, 1349).

Motahhari, Morteza, 1962. 'Velayat va ze'amat' (Guardianship and leadership), in Anjoman (1962).

Motahhari, Morteza, 1974. *Nezam-e Hoquq-e Zan dar Eslam* (The System of Woman's Rights in Islam) (Tehran: 1353).

Motahhari, Morteza, 1980. *Majmu'eh Yaddashtha, Sokhanraniha va Mosahebehha-ye Ostad-e Shahid Morteza Motahhari Piramun-e Enqelab-e Eslami* (Collection of the Notes, Speeches and Interviews of Martyr Ostad Morteza Motahhari about the Islamic Revolution) (Tehran: Sadra).

Motahhari, Morteza, 1981. *The Rights of Women in Islam* (Tehran: World Organization for Islamic Service). Translation of Motahhari (1974).

Motahhari, Morteza, 1985. *A Discourse on the Islamic Republic* (Tehran: Islamic Propagation Organization). Translation of Motahhari (1980).

Motahhari, Morteza, 1985. *Emamat va Rahbari* (Imamate and Leadership) (Qom: 1364).

Mottahedeh, Roy, 1985. *The Mantle of the Prophet*: Religion and Politics in Iran (London: Chatto & Windus).

Moussavi, Ahmad Kazemi, 1992. 'A new interpretation of the theory of velayat-i faqih,' *Middle Eastern Studies* 28/1, 101-7.

Na'ini, Mirza Mohammad Hoseyn, 1955. *Tanbih al Ummah wa Tanzih al-Millah* (The Admonition and Refinement of the People) (3rd edn. ed. By S. Mahmud Taleqani, Tehran: 1334).

Nazem ol-Eslam Kermani, 1967, 1970. *Tarikh-e Bidari-ye Iranian* (History of the Awakening of Iranians), ed. 'Ali Akbar Sa'idi Sirjani, 2 vols (Tehran: Bonyad-e Farhang-e Iran, 1346, 1349).

Nuri, Abdollah, 1999. *Showkaran-e Eslah: Defa'iyat-e 'Abdollah Nuri* (Hemlock of Reform: the Defence of Abdollah Nuri, including the Judgment of the Special Clergy Court) (Tehran: Tarh-e Now, 6th edition).

Paydar, Omid, 1994. 'Naqdi bar nazariyeh hokumat-e demokratik-e dini: paradoks-e eslam va demokrasi' (A critique of the theory of religious democratic government: the paradox of Islam and democracy), *Kiyan* 19 (Khordad 1373), pp. 20-27.

Quchani, Mohammad (ed.), 2000. *Dowlat-e Dini, Din-e Dowlati* (Religious Government, Government Religion) (Tehran: Nashr-e Sarabi, 1379).

Rahnema, Ali (ed.), 1994. *Pioneers of Islamic Revival* (London: Zed Books).

Rahnema, Ali, 1998. *An Islamic Utopian: A Political Biography of Ali Shari'ati* (London: I. B. Tauris).

Rida, Sayyid [Rashid], 1923. *Al-Khilafah aw al-Imamah al-'Uzma* (The Caliphate or the Supreme Imamate) (Cairo).

Riyahi, Sahar et al. (comp.), 2000. Hoviyat, Cheragh va Konferans-e Berlin: Negareshi-ye Tahlili be Pruzheh-ye Bohransazi (Hoviyat, Cheragh and the Berlin Conference: An Analytical View of the Project of Crisis-Creating) (Tehran: Vazhegan, 1379).

Ruthven, Malise, 2000. *Islam in the World* (2nd edn, Oxford: Oxford University Press).

Sa'idzadeh, Sayyid Mohsen, 2002. '*Fiqh va fiqahat*', translated by Kambiz GhaneaBassiri, *UCLA Journal of Islamic and Near Eastern Law* 1/2, pp. 239-68.

Sachedina, Abdulaziz, 1988. *The Just Ruler in Shi'ite Islam: The Comprehensive Authority of the Jurist in Imamite Jurisprudence* (Oxford: Oxford University Press).

Sadri, Mahmood, 2002. 'Attack from within: dissident political theology in contemporary Iran,' *The Iranian*, Feb 13 (accessed on 20.9.04 at *http://www.iranian.com/opinion/2002/february/theology/index.html*)

Sadri, Mahmoud, 2001. 'Sacral defense of secularism: the political theologies of Soroush, Shabestari, and Kadivar,' *International Journal of Politics, Culture and Society* 15/2, pp. 257-70.

Schirazi, Asghar, 1998. *The Constitution of the Islamic Republic: Politics and the State in the Islamic Republic* (London: I. B. Tauris).

Shadid, Anthony, 2001. *Legacy of the Prophet: Despots, Democrats, and the New Politics of Islam* (Boulder: Westview).

Shari'ati, 'Ali, 1969. *Eslam-shenasi* (Islam-ology) (Mashhad: 1347).

Shari'ati, 'Ali, 1979. *On the Sociology of Islam*, translated by Hamid Algar (Berkeley: Mizan Press).

Soroush, Abdolkarim, 1993. 'Farbehtar az ide'uluzhi' (Richer than ideology), *Kiyan* 14 (Shahrivar 1372), pp. 2-20.

Soroush, Abdolkarim, 1994a. *Farbehtar az Ide'uluzhi* (Richer than Ideology) (Tehran: Sarat, 1373).

Soroush, Abdolkarim, 1994b. *Hekmat va Ma'ishat* (Philosophy and Living) (Tehran: Sarat Press, 1373).

Soroush, Abdolkarim, 1995. 'An-ke benam bazargan bud' (He who was a trader [only] by name), *Kiyan* 23 (Bahman-Esfand 1373), pp. 12-21.

Soroush, Abdolkarim, 2000a. *Reason, Freedom and Democracy in Islam: Essential Writings of 'Abdolkarim Soroush*, translated and edited by Mahmoud Sadri and Ahmad Sadri (Oxford: Oxford University Press).

Soroush, Abdolkarim, 2000b. 'The idea of democratic religious government', in his *Reason, Freedom & Democracy in Islam*.

Tajbakhsh, Kian, 2000. 'Political decentralization and the creation of local government in Iran: consolidation or transformation of the theocratic state?' *Social Research* 67/2, pp. 377-404.

Taleqani, S. Mahmud, 1962. 'Taqlid-e a'lam ya towlid-e fatva' (Following the most learned and the production of fatwas), in Anjoman (1962).

Tavassoli, Gholam 'Abbas, 1995. 'Din va siyasat az didgah-e Mohandes Bazargan' (Religion and politics from the perspective of Engineer Bazargan), *Kiyan* 23 (Bahman-Esfand 1373), pp. 22-26.

Vahdat, Farzin, 2000. 'Post-revolutionary discourses of Mohammad Mojtahed Shabestari and Mohsen Kadivar: reconciling the terms of mediated subjectivity,' *Critique, Journal for Critical Studies of the Middle East* 16, pp. 31-54 and 17, pp. 135-57.

Vahdat, Farzin, 2002. *God and Juggernaut: Iran's Intellectual Encounter with Modernity* (Syracuse: Syracuse University Press).

Vakili, Valla, 1996. *Debating Religion and Politics in Iran: the Political Thought of Abdol-Karim Soroush* (Council of Foreign Relations, Occasional Papers, no.2).

Wells, Matthew C., 1999. 'Thermidor in the Islamic Republic of Iran: the rise of Muhammad Khatami,' *British Journal of Middle Eastern Studies* 26/1, pp. 27-39.

Zakariya'i, Mohammad 'Ali, 2000. *Konferans-e Berlin: Khedmat ya Khiyanat* (The Berlin Conference: Service or Treason) (Tehran: Tarh-e Now, 1379).

Zubaida, Sami, 1993. 'The ideological preconditions for Khomeini's doctrine of government,' in his *Islam, the People and the State: Political Ideas and Movements in the Middle East* (London: I. B. Tauris).

Index